BLACK TO THE FRONT

A CORK SUBURB
AND IRELAND'S GREAT WAR 1914-1918

MARK CRONIN was born and reared on Dublin Hill in Blackpool. He gained a great love of history at the North Monastery School. A member of the Blackpool Historical Society and the Western Front Association, his other interests include literature, theatre, cinema and music. His grandfather, Gus Birmingham, was one of the Blackpool men who survived the First World War. (The author is donating his royalties to Cork Foyer).

CORK FOYER in Blackpool provides safe and affordable accommodation, support and training under one roof for up to eighteen young adults aged 18–25, who are homeless or at risk of becoming homeless.

To the soldiers and sailors from Blackpool who participated in the First World War

BLACKPOOL TO THE FRONT

A CORK SUBURB
AND IRELAND'S GREAT WAR 1914–1918

MARK CRONIN

The Collins Press

First published in 2014 by
The Collins Press
West Link Park
Doughcloyne
Wilton
Cork

© Mark Cronin 2014

Mark Cronin has asserted his moral right to be identified as the author of this work in accordance with the Copyright and Related Rights Act 2000.

Ordnance Survey Ireland Permit No. 8926 © Ordnance Survey Ireland/ Government of Ireland

A CIP record for this book is available from the British Library.

Paperback ISBN: 9781848891951
PDF eBook ISBN: 9781848898356
EPUB eBook ISBN: 9781848898363
Kindle ISBN: 9781848898370

Typesetting by Carrigboy Typesetting Services
Typeset in Garamond
Printed in Malta by Gutenberg Press Limited

Contents

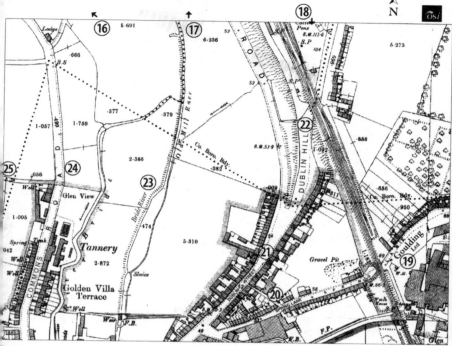

Scale: 1:2,500

North Blackpool

Blackpool

1. Walshe's Avenue
2. Thomas Davis Avenue
3. Bullen's Alley
4. Slattery's Lane
5. Blackpool Bridge
6. St Nicholas Church
7. Madden's Buildings
8. Murphy's Brewery
9. North Infirmary
10. Quarry Lanes
11. North Monastery & St Vincent's Convent
12. Seminary Road
13. Narrow Lane
14. Farranferris College entrance
15. Hatton's Alley

North Blackpool

16. Shandon Chemical Works (Harrington's)
17. Flax Factory and Millfield Cottages
18. Kilbarry Train Depot
19. Goulding Ltd
20. Spring Lane
21. Dublin Street
22. Dublin Hill
23. Bride River
24. Commons Road
25. Spangle Hill

The Western Front Lines

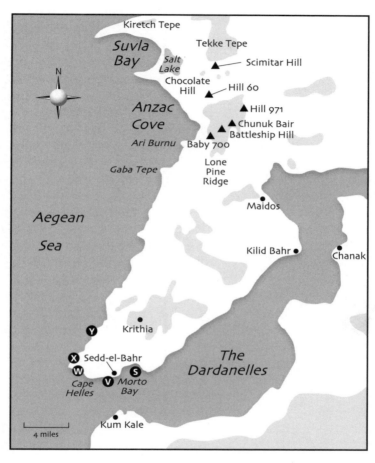

Gallipoli

Gallipoli (Y, X, W, V, S are the five beaches assigned for the Helles attack on 25 April 1915, conducted mainly by the 29th Division of the British army, which included battalions of the Royal Munster and Dublin Fusiliers).

Blackpool Soldiers and Sailors who died in the First World War

Dublin Hill

TIMOTHY O'LEARY Private
No. 8059, 2nd Battalion Royal Irish Regiment
Son of Timothy and Kate O'Leary of 16 Upper Dublin Hill
Killed in action on the Western Front, 19 October 1914, aged 32
Commemorated on the Le Touret Memorial, Pas-de-Calais, France

THOMAS WILLIAMS Company Sergeant Major
No. 553, 15th Battalion Australian Infantry, Australian Imperial Force
Husband of Ellen Williams of 12 Lower Dublin Hill
Died of wounds en route to Egypt received during the Gallipoli Campaign, 12
    August 1915, aged 37
Buried in Chatby Military and War Memorial Cemetery, Alexandria, Egypt

Millfield Cottages and Kilbarry

JOHN DOUGLAS BANKS Private
No. 10225, 2nd Battalion Royal Munster Fusiliers
Son of Mary Banks of Millfield Cottages, brother of Patrick who died at Aubers.
Killed in action on the Western Front, 4 October 1918, aged 23
Buried at Templeux-Le-Guerard British Cemetery, France

PATRICK BANKS Private
No. 6781, 2nd Battalion Royal Munster Fusiliers
Son of Mary Banks of Millfield Cottages, brother of John, who died at the Western
    Front.
Killed in action at the Battle of Aubers, 9 May 1915, aged 22
Commemorated on Le Touret Memorial, Pas-de-Calais, France

JAMES GLEESON Private
No. 7321, 2nd Battalion Royal Munster Fusiliers
Son of James and Margaret Gleeson of 1 Millfield Cottages
Killed in action at the Battle of Aubers, 9 May 1915, aged 24
Commemorated on Le Touret Memorial, Pas de Calais, France

WILLIAM HIGGINS Sergeant
No. 2445, 2nd Battalion Irish Guards
Son of John and Kate Higgins of Kilbarry
Killed in action during a raid on enemy trenches, 21 October 1915, aged 27
Buried in Vermelles British Cemetery, Pas-de-Calais, France

DENIS JONES Private
No. 7633, 2nd Battalion Royal Munster Fusiliers
Son of Henry and Annie Jones of Millfield Cottages and brother to James Jones,
    Royal Munster Fusilier, who was killed in Gallipoli.
Killed in action on the Western Front, 4 November 1918, aged 24
Buried in Fontaine-au-Bois Communal Cemetery, France

JAMES JONES Private
No. 1953, 7th Battalion Royal Munster Fusiliers
Son of Henry and Annie Jones of Millfield Cottages and brother to Denis Jones,
    Royal Munster Fusilier, killed on the Western Front.
Killed in action at Gallipoli, 9 August 1915, aged 21/22
Commemorated on Helles Memorial, Gallipoli, Turkey

MICHAEL MCAULIFFE Private
No. 9918, 1st Battalion Royal Munster Fusiliers
Son of Jeremiah and Kate McAuliffe of 4 Millfield Cottages
Killed in action at Gallipoli, 25 April 1915
Buried in V Beach Cemetery, Gallipoli, Turkey

Spring Lane and Ballyvolane Road

MICHAEL HEGARTY Stoker 1st Class
No. 299877, HMS *Recruit,* Royal Navy
Husband of Mary, of 16 Ballyvolane Road and son of John and Margaret Hegarty
    of Glenville, County Cork
Died at sea after his ship struck a mine, 9 August 1917, aged 36
Commemorated on Plymouth Naval Memorial, Plymouth, England

PATRICK MURPHY Private

No. 3075, 5th Battalion Connaught Rangers
Son of Ellen Murphy and resided at 45 Spring Lane
Died of wounds at Gallipoli, 23 August 1915, aged 39
Commemorated on Helles Memorial, Gallipoli, Turkey

DENIS O'CONNELL Private

No. 9318, Depot, Royal Munster Fusiliers, formerly, 1st Battalion Royal Munster
    Fusiliers
Son of Michael O'Connell of Spring Lane and brother to Michael O'Connell who
    died on the Western Front.
Died of illness in Ireland on 1 November 1916 after being wounded at Gallipoli
Buried in Rathcooney Cemetery, County Cork.

MICHAEL O'CONNELL Corporal

No. 2962, 2nd Battalion Leinster Regiment
Son of Michael O'Connell of Spring Lane and brother to Denis O'Connell who
    died in Ireland after being wounded in Gallipoli
Killed by sniper fire while aiding fellow soldier to First Aid Station, 2 August 1915
Buried in New Irish Farm Cemetery, Ieper (Ypres), Belgium

ROBERT SPILLANE Private

No. 1335, 2nd Battalion Royal Marines, Royal Naval Division
Son of John and Minnie Spillane of 85 Spring Lane
Killed in action at the Third Battle of Ypres, 26 October 1917, aged 22
Commemorated on Tyne Cot Memorial, Zonnebeke, Belgium

Dublin Street

JEREMIAH PATRICK BALDWIN Private

No. TF292878, 3rd/10th Battalion Middlesex Regiment
Husband of Mary Anne and son of Edward Baldwin of 26 Dublin Street
Died at the Battle of Broodesinde, Third Battle of Ypres, 4 October 1917, aged 31
Commemorated on Tyne Cot Memorial, Zonnebeke, Belgium

PATRICK BARRY

Trimmer, SS *Ardmore*
Son of Thomas (Merchant Sailor) and Mary Barry of 23 Dublin Street
Died at sea after ship sunk by torpedo, 13 November 1917, aged 39
Commemorated at Tower Hill, Mercantile Marine Memorial, London

JOHN HYLAND Private
No. 9619, 1st Battalion Irish Guards
Son of Patrick Hyland of 30 Dublin Street
Died of wounds at the Battle of the Somme, 24 September 1916, aged 24
Buried at Dartmoor Cemetery, Somme, France

Commons Road and Spangle Hill

JOSEPH CORRIGAN Guardsman
No. 1039, 5th Battalion Guards Machine Gun Regiment
Son of Mary A. Corrigan of 6 'Spring View' Commons Road
Died in Great Britain, 6 August 1918
Buried at St. Finbarr's Cemetery, Cork.

DANIEL DONOVAN Private
No. 811337, 50th Battalion Alberta Regiment Canadian Infantry
Fourth son of Jeremiah Donovan of 35 Commons Road and brother to James
    Donovan, Leinster Regiment, who died in the Palestine Campaign
Died during an advance on Lens, 3 June 1917, aged 30/31
Buried in Villers Station Cemetery, Villers-au-Bois, France

JAMES DONOVAN Private
No. 6/12, 6th Battalion Leinster Regiment
Fifth son of Jeremiah Donovan of 35 Commons Road and brother to Daniel
    Donovan, Canadian Infantry, who died on the Western Front
Died of pneumonia in Egypt after involvement in the Palestine Campaign, 15
    November 1917
Buried in Kantara War Memorial Cemetery, Egypt

PATRICK HOURIGAN Private
No. 6194, 2nd Battalion Royal Munster Fusiliers
Son of Patrick and Catherine Hourigan of 12 Commons Road
Killed in action at the First Battle of Ypres, 12 November 1914, aged 21
Commemorated on the Menin Gate Memorial, Ieper (Ypres), Belgium

TIMOTHY F. KELLY Sapper
No. 236015, 171st Tunnelling Company Royal Engineers
Son of Timothy and Kate Kelly of Rathmore Buildings, near Victoria Barracks,
    and husband of Bridget Kelly of 8 Spangle Hill. Brother to William Kelly,
    who also died on the Western Front.
Killed in action during the German Offensive, 23 March 1918, aged 31
Buried in Nine Elms British Cemetery, Poperinge, Belgium

JAMES LEE Lance Corporal

No. 38967, 3rd Battalion Canterbury Regiment, New Zealand Expeditionary Force
Son of George and Annie Lee of 9 Commons Road
Died in Christchurch, New Zealand, on 3 July 1919, aged 32, from wounds
  received during the war
Buried at Ashburton Cemetery, Ashburton, New Zealand

JEREMIAH McCARTHY Private

No 7825, 2nd Battalion Royal Munster Fusiliers
Resided at 62 Commons Road
Died on the Western Front, 26 June 1918
Buried at Glageon Communal Cemetery, Nord, France

FRANCIS MOONEY 2nd Lieutenant

1st Battalion Royal Dublin Fusiliers
Son of Patrick Mooney (a former member of the Royal Irish Constabulary at
  Bandon) of 8 'Spring View', Commons Road
Killed in action, 28 February 1917
Commemorated on Thiepval Memorial, Somme, France

JOSEPH O'SULLIVAN Stoker 2nd Class

No. K/21989, HMS *Monmouth,* Royal Navy
Son of William and Margaret O'Sullivan of 52 Commons Road
Died at the Battle of Coronel, South America, 1 November 1914, aged 20
Commemorated on Plymouth Naval Memorial, Plymouth, England

JEREMIAH MURPHY Pioneer

No. 463129, 3rd Battalion Canadian Pioneers
Eldest son of John and Hannah Murphy of 9 Spangle Hill
Killed in action during the Battle of the Somme, 17 September 1916, aged 39
Commemorated on Vimy Memorial, Vimy, France

Thomas Davis St (formerly York St)

JEREMIAH DWYER Private

No. 8233, 1st Battalion Royal Munster Fusiliers
Resided at 15 Thomas Davis Street and survived by his wife
Killed in action during the Battle of the Somme, 9 September 1916
Commemorated on the Thiepval Memorial, Somme, France

PATRICK KIELEY Private
No. 1371, 11th Battalion Australian Infantry, Australian Imperial Force
Son of Elizabeth Kieley of 29 Thomas Davis Street
Killed in action at Gallipoli, 25 April 1915, aged 28
Commemorated at Lone Pine Memorial, Gallipoli, Turkey

FREDERICK WILLIAM OAKLEY Private
No. 25692, 7th Battalion Royal Irish Regiment
Son of William and Anne Oakley of Distillery House, 31 Thomas Davis Street
Killed in action during the German offensive, 21 March 1918, aged 19
Commemorated on the Pozieres Memorial, Somme, France

Walshe's Avenue

TIMOTHY CROWLEY Stoker 1st Class
No. K/3529, HMS *Indefatigible,* Royal Navy
Only son of Joseph and Hannah Crowley, of Blackpool and cousin to the Mason
    family of Walshe's Avenue.
Killed in action at the Battle of Jutland, 31 May 1916, aged 28
Commemorated on Plymouth Naval Memorial, Plymouth, England.

PATRICK DOYLE Private
No. 9398, 1st Battalion Royal Munster Fusiliers
Son of Patrick and Bridget Doyle of 21 Walshe's Avenue
Killed in action during the Battle of the Somme, 4 September 1916, aged 22
Buried in Bernafay Wood British Cemetery, Montauban, France

JAMES DWYER Stoker 1st Class
No. K/22241, HM Submarine *E22,* Royal Navy
Son of Patrick and Margaret Dwyer, of 13 Walshe's Avenue
Died at Sea after submarine sunk by enemy action, 25 April 1916, aged 22
Commemorated on Plymouth Naval Memorial, Plymouth, England

WILLIAM HENRY Private
No. 4115, 6th Battalion Connaught Rangers
Brother of Kate Henry of Walshe's Avenue
Killed in action during the Third Battle of Ypres, 4 August 1917, aged 43
Commemorated on Menin Gate Memorial, Ieper (Ypres), Belgium

JOHN MASON Private
No. 15217, 5th Battalion Connaught Rangers
Son of John and Mary of 19 Walshe's Avenue. Cousin of Stoker Timothy Crowley
    from Blackpool who died at the Battle of Jutland.
Died of bronchial influenza in Belgium, 16 February 1919, aged 26
Buried at Huy Communal Cemetery, La Sarte, Belgium

WILLIAM O'SULLIVAN
Cattleman, SS *Bandon*
Son of Mary O'Sullivan of 16 Walshe's Avenue
Died at sea after ship was sunk by torpedo, 13 April 1917, aged 45
Commemorated at Mercantile Marine Memorial, Tower Hill, London

Thomas Davis Avenue and Slattery's Avenue

DENIS COLLINS
Able Seaman, SS *Ardmore*
Husband of Mary Collins of 12 Thomas Davis Avenue
Died at sea after ship was sunk by torpedo, 13 November 1917, aged 49
Commemorated at Mercantile Marine Memorial, Tower Hill, London

PATRICK McNAMARA Gunner
No. 61210, 'A' Battery Royal Field Artillery
Husband of Margaret McNamara of 1 Slattery's Avenue
Killed in action on the Western Front, 30 November 1917, aged 34
Buried in Duhallow Advanced Dressing Station Cemetery, West-Vlaanderen,
    Belgium

JOHN O'DRISCOLL Lance Corporal
No. 148442, Royal Engineers
Son of John O'Driscoll of 3 Thomas Davis Avenue
Died of wounds received during the Palestinian Campaign, in Egypt, 11 March
    1918
Buried in Cairo War Memorial Cemetery, Egypt

MICHAEL O'KEEFE
Fireman, SS *Castlebar*
Husband of Catherine O'Keefe of 17 Thomas Davis Avenue and son of Michael
    and Margaret O'Keefe.
Died at sea, 13 March 1918, aged 20
Commemorated at Mercantile Marine Memorial, Tower Hill, London

EUGENE O'LEARY
Fireman and Trimmer, SS *Bellucia*
Husband of Hannah, of 11 Thomas Davis Avenue, and son of John and Margaret
    O'Leary
Died at sea after ship was hit by a torpedo, 7 July 1917, aged 31
Commemorated at Mercantile Marine Memorial, Tower Hill, London

Watercourse Road

DENIS O'CALLAGHAN Gunner
No. 40842, 65th Siege Battery Royal Garrison Artillery
Son of Patrick and Nora O'Callaghan of Watercourse Road and brother to Thomas
    O'Callaghan, Royal Munster Fusilier, who also died in the war
Died of gas poisoning on the Western Front, 13 September 1918, aged 24
Buried in Mont Huon Military Cemetery, Le Treport, France

THOMAS O'CALLAGHAN Private
No. 7381, 2nd Battalion Royal Munster Fusiliers
Son of Patrick and Nora O'Callaghan of Watercourse Road and brother to Denis
    O'Callaghan Royal Garrison Artillery who also died in the war
Killed in action on the Western Front, 11 March 1915
Buried in Brown's Road Military Cemetery, Festubert, France

MAURICE RIORDAN Stoker 1st Class
No. K/28573, HMS *Defence,* Royal Navy
Son of John and Ellen Riordan of 21 Watercourse Road
Killed in action at the Battle of Jutland, 31 May 1916, aged 19
Commemorated on Plymouth Naval Memorial, Plymouth, England

PATRICK SULLIVAN Shipwright 1st Class
No. 127183, HMS *Victory II,* Royal Navy
Husband of Elizabeth Sullivan of 23 Watercourse Road
Died in Ireland, 5 March 1917, aged 55
Buried in St Joseph's Cemetery, Cork

Great William O'Brien St (formerly Great Britain St)

MICHAEL COLEMAN
Fireman, SS *Kenmare*
Son of Michael and Mary Coleman, husband of Mary and father of four children,
    of 98.1 Great William O'Brien Street.
Died at sea after ship was sunk by torpedo, 2 March 1918, aged 41
Commemorated on Mercantile Marine Memorial, Tower Hill, London

BATT COLLINS
Trimmer, SS *Bandon*
Husband of Mary and father of four children, of 98.3 Great William O'Brien
    Street
Died at sea after ship was sunk by torpedo, 13 April 1917, aged 35
Commemorated on Mercantile Marine Memorial, Tower Hill, London

H. James Gunner
No. 76891, 56th Reserve Battery Royal Field Artillery
Husband of Catherine of 79 Great William O'Brien Street and son of Thomas and
Margaret James. Born in England.
Died in service, 1 December 1915
Buried in Greenwich Cemetery, London, England

Cornelius (Con) O'Callaghan DCM Sergeant
No. 6403, 2nd Battalion Royal Munster Fusiliers
Husband of Ellen, father to one daughter, of 7 Broad Lane and later Great William
O'Brien Street
Killed in action at the Battle of Passchendaele, 10 November 1917, aged 40/1
Commemorated on Tyne Cot Memorial, Zonnebeke, Belgium

Joseph O'Donnell Private
No. 9/4565, 9th Battalion Royal Munster Fusiliers
Son of M. (formerly RIC Sergeant) and Mary O'Donnell of 84 Great William
O'Brien Street
Died of wounds on the Western Front, 3 June 1916, aged 20
Buried in Southern Cemetery, Calais, France

Denis O'Shea
Fireman, SS *Inniscarra*
Son of Edward and Elsie O'Shea of 76 Great William O'Brien Street
Died at sea after ship was sunk by torpedo, 12 May 1918, aged 30
Commemorated on Mercantile Marine Memorial, Tower Hill, London

Michael Twomey Sergeant
No. 5052, Regimental Depot Royal Munster Fusiliers
Husband of Mary Twomey and father of five children, of 72 Great William
O'Brien Street
Died in service in Ireland, 5 March 1918, aged 50
Buried in Tralee Military Cemetery, County Kerry

John Walsh
Fireman, SS *Bandon*
Husband of Nora of 48 Great William O'Brien Street
Died at sea after ship sunk by torpedo, 13 April 1917, aged 42
Commemorated on Mercantile Marine Memorial, Tower Hill, London

Hatton's Alley and Narrow Lane

MICHAEL ALLEN Private
No. 3937, 2nd Battalion Royal Munster Fusiliers
Son of Ellen Allen of 12 Narrow Lane. Probable brother-in-law to Private Michael
    Donovan also of 12 Narrow Lane.
Died on the Western Front, 8 October 1915, aged 38
Buried in Étaples Military Cemetery, Pas-de-Calais, France

MICHAEL DONOVAN Private
No. 4544, 2nd Battalion Royal Munster Fusiliers
Son of Patrick and Mary Donovan. Husband of Sarah (probable sister of Michael
    Allen above) and father of Patrick, aged six, of No. 2 Narrow Lane.
Killed in action at the Battle of Aubers, 9 May 1915, aged 39
Commemorated on Le Touret Memorial, Pas de Calais, France

JOHN DUNLEA Gunner
No. 43308, 13th Heavy Battery Royal Garrison Artillery
Husband of Margaret of 12 Hatton's Alley
Died at Salonika, 29 July 1918, aged 37
Buried in Lembet Road Military Cemetery, Thessalonika, Greece

Madden's Buildings

DENIS DONOVAN Private
No. 4593, 1st Battalion Royal Munster Fusiliers
Brother of John Donovan of 18 Madden's Buildings
Killed in action at Gallipoli, 21 August 1915
Commemorated on Helles Memorial, Helles, Turkey

JOHN LEE Driver
No. 76576, 79th Brigade Royal Field Artillery
Son of Bridget Lee of 15 Madden's Buildings
Killed in action on the Western Front, 5 July 1917, aged 19
Commemorated on Arras Memorial, Pas-de-Calais, France

CORNELIUS LENIHAN Private
No. 9044, 1st Battalion Leinster Regiment
Son of Jeremiah and Mary Lenihan of 32 Madden's Buildings
Died on the Western Front, 10 February 1915, aged 30
Commemorated on Menin Gate Memorial, Ieper (Ypres), Belgium

SIMON LOURO
Able Seaman, SS *Bandon*
Husband of Margaret and father of four children, of 49 Madden's Buildings
Died at sea after ship was sunk by torpedo, 13 April 1917, aged 48
Commemorated on Mercantile Marine Memorial, Tower Hill, London

PATRICK WALSH Bombardier
No. 62275, 45th Brigade Royal Field Artillery
Son of John Walsh of 66 Madden's Buildings
Died of wounds on the Western Front, 23 November 1918, aged 26
Buried at St Roch Communal Cemetery, Valenciennes, France

Seminary Road

DAVID MULCAHY Private
No. 5614, 8th Battalion Royal Munster Fusiliers
Son of Edward and Margaret Mulcahy and resided at 11 Seminary Road
Died of wounds (received in the trenches at Hulluch) in Great Britain, 29 July
1916, aged 21
Buried in Tottenham and Wood Green Cemetery, London

CORNELIUS O'BRIEN Private
No. 7773, 2nd Battalion Royal Munster Fusiliers
Son of Michael and Julia O'Brien of 7 Seminary Road
Died of wounds on the Western Front, 10 October 1915, aged 24
Buried in Lillers Communal Cemetery, France

THOMAS TYSON Acting Sergeant
No. 9648, 2nd Battalion Royal Munster Fusiliers
Resided with his three brothers at 18 Seminary Road and later at Great Britain St/
Great William O'Brien St
Died of wounds from shellfire on the Western Front, 7 March 1916, aged 23
Buried in Chocques Military Cemetery, Pas de Calais, France

Sunday School Lane, St John's Square and Upper, Middle and Lower Quarry Lane

HENRY CLARKE Private
No. 8439, 2nd Battalion Leinster Regiment
Husband of Bridget of 9 St John's Square
Died during the Battle of the Somme, 1 September 1916, aged 26
Buried in Caterpillar Valley Cemetery, Longueval, France

JOSEPH JONES Lance Sergeant
No. 9016, 3rd Battalion Connaught Rangers
Son of Mrs B. Jones and resided at 11 Quarry Lane
Died while travelling on the SS *Leinster* (which was sunk by torpedo), 10 October
    1918, aged 35
Buried in Whitechurch Cemetery, County Cork

THOMAS MURPHY Private
No. 10286, 5th Battalion Connaught Rangers
Son of Patrick and Bridget Murphy and resided at 9 St John's Square
Died at Salonika, 16 November 1915, aged 24
Buried in East Mudros Military Cemetery, Lemnos, Greece

TIMOTHY O'BRIEN Private
No. 12886, 8th Battalion Loyal North Lancashire Regiment
Son of Patrick and Mary O'Brien of 7 Sunday School Lane
Killed in action on the Western Front, 23 April 1916, aged 29/30
Buried at Ecoivres Military Cemetery, Pas de Calais, France

JAMES SHEEHY Private
No. 10097 2nd Battalion Royal Munster Fusiliers
Son of Mary Sheehy of 2 Upper Quarry Lane
Killed in action at the First Battle of Ypres, 10 November 1914, aged 17
Commemorated on Menin Gate Memorial, Ieper (Ypres), Belgium

Introduction

THIS PUBLICATION IS A commemoration of the men from Blackpool who died as a result of the Great War, 1914–1918. Fifty-three were soldiers, six were with the Royal Navy and ten were merchant seamen. There may be more Blackpool men who died in the war but my subject matter involves only those who had a known connection to the area. While my hope is to commemorate these sixty-nine men who gave the greatest sacrifice in one of the most defining events in modern history, my aim is also to set out that history and explain the participation of these men. As such, it has been a journey of discovery.

The history of Blackpool that modern generations have learned is deeply wedded to a republican rebelliousness that was embodied in Tomás MacCurtain and the Delaney brothers, Jer and Con, and their roles in the War of Independence. Their murders by branches of the British forces were perceived as the ultimate sacrifice made in the centuries-old struggle to rid Ireland of British rule and were the most notable political events in Blackpool's history. It was therefore disturbing to discover that on nearly every street in Blackpool not only had numerous men fought in the British army in the First World War, but many had died. Growing up in Blackpool I had no idea that men in significant numbers had left these very streets to fight and die in foreign fields and seas. I was vaguely aware of my grandfather's own participation in the Great War but it held no ritual place in my family upbringing which was largely ahistorical in its engagement with the world. My awareness of the First World War, through school and cultural references, was very limited and fragmented, and certainly bore no relation to the streets of

Blackpool. As a community, Blackpool had forgotten these men, an amnesia that was replicated all over southern Ireland and most particularly in urban areas.

I asked myself how a community could forget such a grievous wound. I had picked up on some of the answers already: men had joined the British army out of financial necessity and become mercenaries. They were deluded and duped into joining the colonising army of the British. The war was a war among empires and was not Ireland's war. These particular reasons for forgetting were also entwined with a broader international understanding of the First World War as a colossal and futile waste of human life. The 10 million military deaths coupled with the hundreds of thousands of civilian casualties gave a profoundly tragic perspective that made the outbreak of the war itself appear the result of the hubris of empires. This pacificist rejection of the war gained a kind of cultural orthodoxy even in Britain as early as the late 1920s and in this context it would help explain how southern Irish amnesia in relation to the war could have more easily developed. This was given even greater credence when the Second World War broke out as the 'war to end all wars' failed to prevent the outbreak of another war of even greater brutality and inhumanity.[1] Importantly, the First World War lacked the clear-cut moral dimension that a war against Nazi fascism had and whose impact dominated Europe for decades thereafter. But of course the fundamental reason behind this Irish amnesia was that those who led Ireland to independence and now goverened the new Irish state had rejected totally Irish involvement in aid of Britain in the Great War and, in fact, had been broadly sympathetic to Germany and others, 'their gallant allies in Europe'.

'England's difficulty is Ireland's opportunity' was the dictum that led a significant minority of extreme Irish nationalists, which included aspects of the Labour movement under Connolly, to launch the Easter Rising of 1916 which would eventually shatter the political binds of Edwardian Irish politics. Their 'Great War' was not in Europe but the 750 hundred years of the Saxon yoke of which they were the latest representatives in the struggle for Irish liberty. Their pro-German rhetoric was tactical, propagandistic in trying to discredit Britain, and subservient to the goal of complete Irish independence. This pro-Germanism was easily discarded and de-emphasised once victory for the Allies had been achieved and especially as the United States under President Wilson was one of the victors. In biographies of Tomás MacCurtain and Terence MacSwiney the Great War is a moral blank, a distant event whose reasons belong to other realms, while the only references to the British soldiers of the Great War were in the form of atrocities committed by them in the guise of the Black and Tans during the War of Independence.[2]

In this context it is easy to understand how the sacrifice of those men from Blackpool, and from all over Ireland, could have been forgotten. They were on the wrong side of history, it has been written; perhaps they were on the wrong side of Irish history but in the context of world history they were not. They were part of the victorious armies of Britain, France and America who tried to forge new democratic states and witnessed the deposing of a number of monarchs and emperors. The Irish soldiers themselves saw the war in terms of a historic clash between civilisations where freedom and liberty for all were at stake. The war was interpreted in this manner and they, by and large, agreed that this was so. The inscription on the war memorial in Cork is a testament to that perception as it declares that they fought for 'the Freedom of Small Nations'. Whether Irish soldiers joined up because of financial necessity or not is a discussion largely borne out of the contested interpretation of the war within Irish society. In other countries where a national consensus is held on the war this question is confined to academia but in Ireland it is used to dismiss the contradictions in not only Irishmen but Irish nationalists joining the British army. For it was nationalist leaders like John Redmond and William O'Brien from Cork who at the start of the war declared that it was a war to free and liberate Belgium and it was the soldiers at the end who declared that they had fought for the freedom of small nations. This of course included the small nation of Ireland.

The failure of John Redmond to achieve Home Rule and institute Ireland as an independent political entity obviously seriously undermined the possibility that participation in the war could have had a vibrant and real meaning in Irish society. The Home Rule movement was, unsurprisingly, nationalistic in tone and rhetoric. Its usurpation by Sinn Féin after 1918 hides their shared political lineage. In fact the Civil War was fought, in part, over whether the treaty was in reality just an enhanced Home Rule Bill or not. The nationalistic credentials of the Irish Party might have been purposely obscured as a means of justifying and vindicating the death and destruction that the War of Independence and Civil War entailed. Can it not be argued that, had Redmond and the Irish Party been firmly in control of Ireland politically and socially in December 1918, a Home Rule parliament would have been set up? And would not a Home Rule parliament have been, as Michael Collins said for the Treaty, a stepping stone to a Republic? Of course they could not foresee the future but subsequent history has taught us that it could have been if Irish people had persisted in that desire. Ireland could have declared itself a republic in 1948 after thirty years of a Home Rule parliament, just as India did at that time. What price the War of Independence and the Civil War? The issue of partition was an emotive one but here again it is forgotten that for Redmond and the Irish Party a unified Ireland was a fundamental part of their politics. Redmond recognised that the establishment of some sort of separate northern Irish political entity was necessary to achieve a peaceful solution to the Irish Question. It was a compromise that all nationalists, north and south, had to make to create the current peace process.

These are important questions and considerations because they are directly related to why those Irish soldiers in the British army are not seen as heroes as undoubtedly they would have been if a Home Rule parliament had been set up. We would resemble France and Britain, I imagine, with our local memorials dotted here and there in honour and remembrance of the contribution and sacrifice they made in the Great War. Instead we have those dedicated to the

War of Independence either between 1919 and 1921 or the 1798 Rebellion. Ironically, a Home Rule Ireland would have venerated 1798 as well, as their 'heroics' could be lauded a hundred years on as a violent reaction to injustice in a pre-democratic age but in the contemporary age of Home Rule and the advance of Parliamentary democracy, Parnellism would lead the way to freedom. To understand those men from Blackpool who joined the army and fought in the war we have to understand the post-Parnellite Ireland that emphasised all the historical wrongs done to Ireland by Britain, as did Irish national separatists, yet sought Home Rule as its salvation. There were powerful centrifugal forces at work in Edwardian Ireland that kept Ireland within the British Empire and only a war of the magnitude of the Great War and importantly its wearying duration weakened these forces and allowed the separatists Sinn Féin to emerge and dominate.

It was probably urban Ireland that was most receptive to the draw of the Empire and moderated any extremism regarding separatism or republicanism. Daniel Corkery alludes to this in a preface to Florrie O'Donoghue's biography of Tomás MacCurtain. He writes of the 'rootless' aspect of Irish urban life in contrast to rural culture that cherished and cultivated an awareness of Irish traditions in music, song and stories.[3] Tomás MacCurtain came from Mourne Abbey, County Cork. Cities are by their nature more 'rootless' or, less disparagingly, more cosmopolitan than life in the countryside. Interestingly it was the use of the word 'cosmopolitan' to describe the distant concern of the war in Europe to Irish people and in particular Irish country people from Connemara in October 1915 by Bishop Delaney of Limerick that marked the first tear in the fabric of official Ireland's support for the war effort and emboldened further public opposition.[4] Irish cities, Cork included, were receptive to the cosmopolitan influences that came with the British Empire and globalisation in general. The culture of Vaudevillian-type entertainment, song and dance, and the growth of cinema were clearly established in Cork and popularly enjoyed. The British Empire as a dynamic trading and commercial system that spanned the globe had, of course, a financial appeal. Cork being a port city relayed the goods of the empire in and exported Irish produce out: it built its trading links and established commercial ties with various British people and places.

A powerful symbol and presence of the British Empire was the British army and no more so than in a large town like Cork with Victoria Barracks. The sight and sound of English, Welsh and Scottish soldiers around the streets of Cork not only brought benefits to the local service industry, it was also a direct reminder of the interconnectedness of the Empire and the union with Britain. Some of these soldiers settled down within the communities of Cork and socialised; probably telling stories in the pubs of Cork of death-defying feats in India and Africa. My own great-grandfather and grandmother were such a soldier family from England who eventually settled in Cork and had a house in Dillons Cross. These military and commercial connections to the Empire coupled with the peaceful democratic (partial but expanding with the years) political system which governed through the rule of law created powerful forces of inertia within Irish society for a moderate nationalist stance in relation to the Imperial Question. It was harder to create the dichotomy of nationalism between 'us' and 'them' in urban areas than in the more isolated (and romantic) rural Ireland where the Irish soil got under one's nails. But there was also the question of practicality. The British Empire was considered, though dented by the Boer War, to be a very formidable foe. Physical-force nationalism in Ireland pre-1916 was lauded from afar but dismissed in the present as foolish, dangerous, anarchical and ineffectual. The Great War would change this.

In the light of these considerations I hope to explore Blackpool, this historic suburb of Cork city, in relation to the Great War and in particular to relate the story of the First World War through the participation of its soldiers, sailors, seamen, clergy, and its industrial input to the war effort. Blackpool is probably emblematic of other urban areas in southern Ireland, which were predominantly Catholic and Nationalist, in so far as one can relate the whole history of the Great War – from the great battles of the Western Front, to the Gallipoli, Balkans and Palestine fronts, to the great naval battles of the war as well as the war against merchant shipping – through its sons that fell. Every major decision made by British High Command, and in a lot of cases German High Command, had a direct effect on communities like Blackpool. Every painful twist of the war brought more tragedy to the locality. The only significant area of the war in which Blackpool men did not die was in Mesopotamia (modern-day Iraq, then part of the Turkish Empire) and in the air. I have no doubt that there were Blackpool men who fought with Tom Barry in Mesopotamia as there were pilots for the Royal Flying Corps (RAF in 1918) but their identities have escaped my search.

This book aims to give a local perspective on the Irish contribution to the Great War and will hopefully add to the growing body of historical work that has, finally, shone a light on a shaded part of our past. A reason for this has undoubtedly been the peace process in Northern Ireland which has opened up a willingness to look at our respective pasts in a more empathic manner. But it is also a result of our more individualistic, consumerist and globalised society, which has diluted our sense of the past and its meaning to us. One indicator of this has been the sight of the insignias of British football teams being inscribed on the gravestones of Irish people. These people might not be any less Irish but seem to have a more layered, sophisticated array of identities in this fast-paced, information-loaded, 21st-century world. In that respect they might have shared something in common with those Irishmen who joined the British army and fought in the Great War, when Irish identity or identities were more fluid and plural and joining the British army was not incompatible with Irish nationalism. Maybe the post-Cold War modern world is more akin to the Edwardian world than at any other time in the last hundred years and our membership of the EU might have resembled, at least faintly, membership of the British Empire then.

This, however, is primarily a memorial to the men from Blackpool who died in the war: for the ten merchant seamen who went to work with no belligerence in mind and lost their lives on the seas; for the fifty-three soldiers and six navy men who went to war to protect Europe from a military domination that had trampled on the rights of small nations. They formed part of the biggest army of Irishmen that ever was or ever will be, the majority of whom were Irish nationalists who fought not only to protect Ireland but also to contribute to the establishment of an independent Ireland. They died on foreign fields and on the seas and were remembered in foreign lands. This book aims to rectify the neglect which the memory of these men has suffered. It is my hope that the complexity of Irish history is more fully appreciated and the sacrifice made in our name is acknowledged.

1

The story of Blackpool and the Lead-up to the Great War

BLACKPOOL IS AN old suburb of Cork city. In the years prior to 1914 it was a vibrant village with distinct rural aspects despite being one of Cork city's poor working-class districts. Its centre was St Nicholas Catholic Church and the National School nearby on Brocklesby St. Its origin, however, was not as a place of monastic learning but as an industrial, or proto-industrial, hub, powered by the two rivers that flow through the valley. These two rivers, the Bride and the Glen, are tributaries to Cork's principal river, the Lee. They brought the tanneries of the eighteenth century to the Blackpool area and some ascribe the name 'Blackpool' literally to the black pools of wastewater that resulted from the tanning of hides. (It might be a coincidence or not, but as Blackpool formed part of the old route to Dublin from Cork, it could have derived its name from the Irish version of Dublin, *Dubh Linn*, or black pool.) As the tanneries declined during the nineteenth century they were replaced by other industries, from distilleries to various mills, a brewery, chemical works which included a large fertiliser factory (or as it was called a century ago, 'Manure Works'). With industry came workers and with workers came housing, and a bustling village was created with shops of various descriptions: hairdressers, public houses, a pawn shop, post office, carriage makers, undertakers and more, all catering for the passing trade from the countryside but mostly for the inhabitants of Blackpool, many of them crammed into the laneways that branched off the main thoroughfare of York St (now called Thomas Davis St). Tenement housing was common in Blackpool but not as prevalent as the Shandon St area.[1]

Slattery's Lane, one of the
many laneways in Blackpool.
(Blackpool Historical Society)

Blackpool was an urban spur that jutted out from the city into the
rural hinterland. Yet it retained aspects of the rural world it colonised
with widespread holdings of small piggeries and fowl hatches in the
backyards of houses. The roads were not surfaced until 1912. The
train station at Kilbarry (off Dublin Hill) was a loading depot for
the cattle and pig export trade and the sight of herds of cattle being
guided through Blackpool to the port was common. Toll houses
existed at the end of Dublin St and midway up the Commons Road
to exact the levies charged on the incoming animals as they passed
through. Some of them might have been diverted to Denny and
Son's on the Watercourse Road where Dunn Brothers Tannery also
existed. This tannery dealt in hides from as far away as Argentina.
In 1915 there were three 'Carriers (Forwarding Agents)', nine
businesses involved in cattle exporting and five registered pig buyers.
One such person who helped drive the cattle through Blackpool

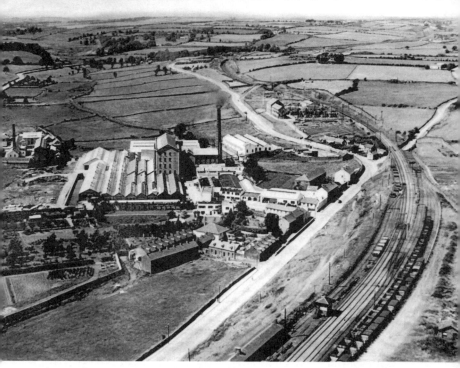

Cork Spinning and Weaving Company and Millfield Cottages, with Harrington's Paint Factory (*left*) and the Kilbarry Railway Depot (*right*). (Blackpool Historical Society)

was Thomas Lee of 55 Madden's Buildings. His son, Thomas junior, followed him into the job. He (Thomas senior) and his wife Bridget were born in County Cork, which was typical of Blackpool and wider urban Ireland at the time as more and more people left the countryside to live in the towns and cities. All the family were bilingual, speaking both English and Irish, which in 1911 included their youngest Norah, aged 9, followed by John, aged sixteen, both schoolgoers. John would join the Royal Field Artillery of the British army during the First World War. His three elder sisters, Margaret, Ellen and Kate, worked in the Flax Factory, or 'the Mill', in the Kilnap townland which was situated a few minutes' walk from the end of Dublin St and known locally as Millfields. This introduces another vital aspect of Blackpool: its industries.[2]

Patrick Beirne, a National School teacher in Blackpool, left behind brief descriptions of the place around 1912. The sense of

Blackpool as a vibrant hive of activity is evident: 'Coal carts with bells, milk carts with rattling churns, hooting of factory horns, shouting of school children – these were the pleasant sounds of life and industry.' He could have also mentioned the sight of telegram messenger boys, probably on bicycle, which was a prominent occupation amongst the teens of Blackpool, just like Joseph O'Donnell of 84 Great Britain St (now called Great William O'Brien St) who would join the Royal Munster Fusiliers during the war. Beirne does, however, recall women and grown-up girls, who wore shawls and were barefooted, going to the Flax Factory.[3] Those factory horns might have been not only for the Flax Factory but also for Harrington's Paint Works on the Commons Road or Goulding's fertiliser factory on Spring Lane. Undoubtedly, however, the biggest employer in Blackpool was the Flax Factory, the Cork Spinning and Weaving Company.

Set up in 1867 by a man named Shaw, it employed 630 workers, mainly women, but included 70 men from Belfast whose experience and tradition were vital in what was still, in the south of Ireland, the embryonic industry of linen production. The factory was trying to exploit a gap in the market caused by the American Civil War but it closed in 1885. It soon reopened under the control of James Ogilvie, Thomas Lenihan and Francis Henry Thompson, who were prominent personages in Cork commercial life in the early twentieth century. They were involved, most notably, in Thompson's Bakery, amongst other various business ventures. The Flax Factory employed 650 around 1900 but this would increase to 1,000 by 1919, an increase aided by military contracts during the war. By 1915 the only other flax mill in County Cork was at Dunmanway. The success, however, of the Blackpool factory 'indicate[s] that mechanised flax-spinning and weaving could perhaps have been carried out on a more extensive scale in the Cork area', and that this success centered around its ability to withstand the changing demands of the market which was due to the Belfast tradition it had imported.[4]

This Belfast tradition involved the enticement of a number of Protestant linen workers from Ulster, and Belfast in particular, to Blackpool which augmented the tiny Protestant population of the locality, a population which in 1911 consisted of a total of seventy-six men, women and children out of a total of 4,730. (The population of Cork city at the time was 76,600.) One of these Protestants was Mary Banks (a widow aged sixty at the time of the 1911 Census) who lived next to the factory in purpose-built housing called Millfield Cottages. It seems likely that her husband had been coaxed from Belfast to impart his weaving skills to the workforce at Blackpool. There they had a family and of the six children mentioned in 1911 three worked in the factory:

Flax factory worker Robert Spillane, later of the Royal Marines. (*Cork Examiner*)

Lena as a winder and her two brothers, Patrick and John, as general labourers. Patrick (born in 1892/93) and John (born in 1895/6) were the youngest and both would join the 2nd Battalion of the Munster Fusiliers in the Great War. From the small collection of cottages at Millfield many sons would join Patrick and John Banks in the war, including Michael McAuliffe (whose mother Kate worked as a spinner in the factory), the four Jones brothers – James, Denis, Joseph and Patrick (whose sister Margaret worked as a reeler) – and James Gleeson who also worked in the factory as a yarn dryer.

Even though the Mills predominantly employed women, a male presence in the workforce was needed for the more physically demanding roles that might have involved rippling, steeping or retting, breeching, scrunching and hackling of the flax in the process of producing linen. Of course those employed lived beyond the environs of Millfield Cottages themselves and populated all of Blackpool. Robert Spillane, aged fifteen at the time of the 1911 Census, from Spring Lane was a machine boy, as was David Mulcahy (aged sixteen) from Seminary Road. Thomas Murphy (aged eighteen) from St John's Square was a 'hackler'. A visitor to the factory noted:

> In the hackling room machines are attended by young boys who do their work with rapidity and in a style to which we are so little accustomed in the south of Ireland. Looking at them working as they do we could not help thinking that training such as they get there must have a wonderful effect in sharpening them up for the rest of their lives.[5]

Robert, David and Thomas would all join the British army and participate in the war just three and half years later.

Though the Flax Factory was the biggest employer in the area, Blackpool was also noted for its other industries. Adjacent to and west of the Flax Factory was a chemical works on the Commons Road which was set up in the 1880s. It became known as Harrington's Ltd or Shandon Chemical Works, and later Harrington's and Goodloss Wills. During this period it was the only manufacturer of fire-red paint colour in Britain and Ireland and it was the only firm in Ireland making distempers (powder-based colours painted onto plaster and chalk) and varnishes.[6] It also produced a potato blight preventative. A much older established industry of Blackpool and linked directly to the rivers Bride and Glen was distilling. However, as the nineteenth century progressed distilling in Blackpool became increasingly unviable and both Greene's Distillery, off York St/ Thomas Davis St, and the Watercourse Road Distillery closed in 1868 when they were amalgamated to form the Cork Distilleries Company. There was still the Glen Distillery Company at Kilnap, just outside Blackpool, and in 1915 it had offices on Carroll's Quay in the city centre. The distillery on the Watercourse Road became a store house from 1880s onwards and during the war it was converted to manufacture yeast and industrial spirit. At 31 York St/ Thomas Davis St was the Cork Distilleries Company Stores, which consisted of a large yard to the rear of the house, run by William Robert Oakley, originally from King's County (Offaly), and his wife Anne from Tipperary. They lived there with their three daughters and three sons all of whom were under fifteen in 1911. They were

W. & H. M. Goulding Ltd on Spring Lane, with a view of Spangle Hill (*right*) and Farranferris College (*left*) overlooking Blackpool. (Blackpool Historical Society)

a Church of Ireland family. The eldest son, Frederick William, only twelve at the time of the 1911 Census, would join the South Irish Horse (later amalgamated into the Royal Irish Regiment) during the war.

One of the major financial stakeholders in the Cork Distilleries Company at this time was James T. Murphy who also owned and ran Murphy's Brewery. Its brewery stack was a noted landmark at the time and cast a shadow over Blackpool for many years. It was a significant employer of Blackpool men and during this period they numbered sixty-five in total. No doubt Murphy's Brewery supplied all the ale and stout to the public houses in Blackpool at this time, which amounted to over thirty establishments of various sizes in 1915. Some of these public houses are still trading, such as Geaneys on Dublin St which was owned by Martha Geaney in 1911, and The Groves was run by a Mrs Burns. Con Coughlan had a pub at 41 York St/Thomas Davis St, near the focal point of Blackpool Bridge, which also acted as the Public Telephone Call Office. Con also ran Blackpool's only undertakers at 51/52 York St/Thomas Davis St.

A tram line serviced Blackpool, with a terminus at Blackpool Bridge and ran along the Watercourse Road to the city centre and on to Douglas. Richard Fitzgerald from Seminary Road was a tram driver and he lived with his wife, Margaret, and her nephew David Mulcahy, who, as mentioned earlier, worked in the Flax Factory and would later become a Royal Munster Fusilier in the war.

The main means of transportation at the time was horse and cart, and so blacksmiths were quite common. Jeremiah Lenihan from Madden's Buildings was one such blacksmith, and his son Patrick was a blacksmith helper. Another son, Cornelius, had in the years before the war become a soldier and had been to India. He worked subsequently with the *Cork Examiner* and when the war came he had already rejoined the army. Another blacksmith helper was Joseph O'Sullivan from the Commons Road. The allure of the sea and the Royal Navy might have enticed him to join up, which he did in February 1914.

Some of the carts filled with barrels that passed through Blackpool contained pyrite for the fertiliser plant at Spring Lane, W. & H. M. Goulding Ltd. Its location in Blackpool had a coincidental family connection: William and Humphrey Manders Goulding were the sons of Joshua Goulding and Sarah Manders and it was Sarah who hailed from Blackpool originally. The family moved from King's County to Cork in 1826 after Joshua died. His son William started a business in the city centre which his brother, Humphrey, joined in 1846. They slowly developed an interest in fertiliser production and by 1854 their super-phosphate product was so successful they were able to purchase the Glen Distillery at Spring Lane in Blackpool in 1856 and expand production. The Blackpool factory contained mills, kilns, stoves, chimneys, spacious yards and various classes of machinery which again proved so successful that Goulding Ltd set up six further plants in Ireland. They became one of the largest fertiliser producers in the British Isles and the Blackpool plant was the foundation of their success. This achievement was recognised by King Edward VI when William J. Goulding (the son of William) was knighted in 1904.[7]

ployed 300 people, one of whom was James Dwyer
venue, which was one of the many laneways off York
St. James was eighteen in 1911 but he did not stay
anure factory' for at some time he became a merchant
the Cork Steam Packet. He eventually enlisted in the
in March 1914. His fellow worker, Patrick (Paddy)
Dublin St, joined the Irish Guards in the British army
war. William Mehigan from Spring Lane would remain
in Gouldings until the war began and enlisted then.
Blackpool had its fair share of merchant seamen with the majority
working for the reputable and long-standing shipping companies,
the Cork Steam Packet and the Cork Steam Company, both run
by the Pike family from Penrose Quay, Cork city. From Blackpool
Bridge to the docks of Cork it is only a half an hour's walk and there
the seamen would man the 'Packet' ships that sailed to Britain or
the 'Company' ships that sailed the world bringing materials and
goods to and from the busy port of Cork.

Many a Blackpool labourer would have hauled these goods and
materials that came through the port, for 'labourer' was the most
common description of those employed in Blackpool at the time.
Some of these goods made their way to grocers and tea merchants,
like James Simcox which had branches at Patrick St, Barrack St,
North Main St, Shandon St and 68 York St/Thomas Davis St in
Blackpool. There were many other retail shops in the area, including
Joseph Kieley's Flour and Meal Stores, also on York St/Thomas
Davis St, at No. 29. Among his large family was his son Patrick who
in 1911 worked as an 'Ingen Fitter' at the 'Works' (which probably
meant Gouldings as it was commonly referred to as the 'Manure
Works' but could have been Harrington's Chemical Works). He
followed his brother Robert to Australia but while Robert ended up
in Melbourne, Patrick found work near Perth in Western Australia.
They would both join the Austalian army when their adopted
country entered the war.

Another emigrant was Thomas Williams who followed his
brother to Brisbane in Australia. Thomas was educated at the

Thomas Williams from Dublin Hill, who served with the Australian Army.
(Margaret McGrath)

Christian Brothers North Monastery, one of the most prominent schools on the north side of Cork city and only five minutes' walk from Great Britain St/Great William O'Brien St and the Quarry Lanes. He had been in the army before the Great War and experienced war in South Africa and was later stationed in India. He left the army in 1907 and joined the Great Southern and Western Railway in Cork. The railway was a significant employer in Cork in those days with an estimated 515 employed at the turn of the century.[8] He may have been employed at the Kilbarry Station dealing with the freight trains shuttling in and out. If so, he would have been only a few minutes' walk from his house on lower Dublin Hill. He left his job in 1913 and emigrated to Australia, leaving his wife, Ellen, and one-year-old daughter Hannah behind with the expectation that they would join him when he had established himself.

Emigration had been a feature of Irish life for a long time. Prior to the Great Famine (1845–52), emigration was more noted among Irish Protestants than Catholics but after the devastation of that seminal event, Irish Catholics would swamp cities in Britain, Australia, Canada and the United States. It is estimated that within sixty-five years of the Famine the population of Ireland declined from 8 million to 3½ million, creating a network of Irish communities stretching the globe, facilitated in part by the British Empire. However, the Irish Party under John Redmond, the dominant nationalist political movement in Ireland prior to the war, claimed that emigration had been halted and the population decline stabilised, for which they claimed the credit. The evidence from Blackpool in 1911 was that unemployment was not significant though emigration, probably, had been a contributing factor to that appearance. Low wages were also a major spur to emigration and undoubtedly Blackpool had a lot of low-wage employment and attendant poverty.

Timothy O'Brien from Sunday School Lane emigrated to Lancashire in England and found work as a labourer. James Lee left his parents, George and Annie Lee, at 9 Commons Road in 1911 and travelled to his aunt, Mollie Lee, in Ashburton, New Zealand, a town on the Canterbury Plains 60 miles from Christchurch. James found employment as a truck driver for L. McGinness and lived at Tinwald, a village on the outskirts of Ashburton. The Prime Minister of New Zealand during the war, William Ferguson Massey, was from Tinwald but originally was from Limavady in County Derry/Londonderry. Daniel Donovan, also from the Commons Road, went to Alberta, Canada, and became a fireman. Around the corner from Daniel lived Jeremiah Murphy of Spangle Hill. Like Thomas Williams, he had been in the army and saw service in South Africa and India but he moved to the province of British Columbia in Canada and became a miner. He maintained links to his army life by enlisting in the Canadian militia. All these men would participate in the war.

One fairly steady source of employment for Blackpool men, and central to this study, was, of course, the British army and navy. Irishmen had a long and distinguished record in the British military forces. They were numerous too, especially after Catholics were allowed to join in the 1770s. In the early part of the nineteenth century it is believed that up to one third of the British army were Irish but this had declined to one ninth, or 30,000 soldiers, in 1914 (which matched the proportion of the Irish population in the United Kingdom). There were also 30,000 reservists in Ireland of differing degrees of training and battle readiness.[9] The more training they had the more money they received and reservists' supplement pay could be vital to homesteads in places like Blackpool. At least half the soldiers from Blackpool who died in the war had been either professional soldiers from the start or reservists. The Royal Navy was also a career choice amongst some Blackpool men. Patrick Sullivan from the Watercourse Road joined in 1884 while Michael Hegarty from Ballyvolane Road and Timothy Crowley became 'tars' in 1902 and 1907 respectively. All six Royal Navy sailors from Blackpool, bar one, who died in the war, were career sailors.

Prior to the war there were no great cultural or political pull factors within Irish society to join any branch of the British military forces. The Catholic Church did not encourage enlistment as it might expose recruits to licentious ways that the Good Lord might deem improper.[10] The Irish Party was equally reluctant to endorse a major arm of the British state while Home Rule was being denied. They had opposed the Boer War.[11] Other nationalist minority groups, like Sinn Féin, actively discouraged enlistment but importantly their voices remained weak. Sinn Féin was actually not only in decline in Cork city prior to August 1914 but moribund, a state which continued up to 1917.

As in other relatively poor areas in Ireland and Britain, soldiering provided a steady income but other factors were involved in inducing men to enlist. Military training might have been viewed by some as a means of acquiring new skills which would be beneficial in gaining employment in civilian life at some future date. The sense of adventure was another attraction. The drudgery of daily toil could certainly be relieved by doing such chores in more exotic climes like India, the West Indies or Africa, or sailing the high seas. Tradition was an important factor: many soldiering fathers guided their sons towards the military life. A brother or friend joining up could have

Patrick Condon (*below*) of the Connaught Rangers and his two sons, Patrick (*left*) and James (*right*) from Bullen's Alley, Blackpool, all of whom would participate in the war. (*Cork Examiner*)

The four O'Leary brothers from Dublin Hill (*clockwise from top left*): Timothy (Irish Regiment), Micheal (Irish Guards), Bryan (Connaught Rangers) and Jeremiah (Irish Guards). (*Cork Examiner*)

acted in the same way, opening up a new way of life and cajoling his siblings to follow suit. Though the Irish Party and the Catholic Church in Ireland stood aloof from any endorsement of the British army, it certainly was not deemed traitorous by a broad swathe of Irish society for Irishmen and in particular for Irish Catholics to join. This stemmed from a complex relationship between Irish nationalism of the nineteenth and early twentieth centuries and the British Empire. Before examining this in more detail and the dynamics of national politics in the lead-up to the war that affected Blackpool as much as elsewhere, it is appropriate to finish this portrait of Blackpool by recounting what Blackpool people did in their spare time, what little of it that they had.

For many, spare time from work was a scarce commodity. Work at the Flax Factory, for example consisted of a twelve-hour day, for five days and a half day on Saturday. A lot can be done, however, when there is no television or radio. St Nicholas Church stands at the centre of the Blackpool community and epitomised how religion was central to most people's lives Less pious pursuits were of course the order of the day. Public houses were numerous in Blackpool and no doubt many a song and story told, maybe by soldiers who had seen strange sights from as far away as the northern frontier of India. There were stage shows and song concerts in the city centre at the Palace Theatre and the Opera House, which were relatively expensive but maybe on a special occasion. Cinemas were established in Cork before the war and the Opera House also showed moving pictures during the war. Walking was popular and the Mardyke promenade was a famous Cork haunt for a Sunday stroll. No doubt walks into the countryside were also carried out where the Blackpool harriers roamed the country fields with their dogs. Drag hunts were festive occasions where harrier clubs would run their dogs against each other. Further forays into the country were done by bicycle, a particularly popular pastime nearly everywhere both before and after the war. The Mulcahy brothers from Blackpool were the all-Ireland cycling champions at one time.

Probably more famous than the Mulcahy brothers was Pakey Mahoney, a boxer from Blackpool. He established Blackpool as a

St Nicholas Church, Blackpool, viewed from Great Britain St/Great William O'Brien Street. (*Cork Examiner*)

hotspot for boxing when he won the Irish heavyweight title on St Patrick's Day 1913. He was trained by fellow Blackpool man Ned Regan, who would later become a sergeant with the Connaught Rangers during the war. Both were members of the Blackpool Boxing Club situated at Spring Lane, as was Robert Spillane (mentioned previously), nicknamed the 'Kid'. Pakey remained one of the most famous boxers in Cork, if not nationally, during the next few years. However, Blackpool would be primarily associated in sporting terms with the Glen Rovers Hurling and Football Club and specifically with hurling, although the Glen Rovers were not established until April 1916 – a fateful time in Irish history – and hurling remained weak in the area for a number of years after the club was established. In the *Cork Almanac* of 1915 there is only one reference to a football club in Blackpool and that was O'Brien's, which was probably a reference to William O'Brien. St Nicholas's football team had also been active in the area since 1901 and would be incorporated into the Glen Rovers Club when it was established. As the GAA was only thirty years old at the outbreak of the war it was still expanding nationally and had to compete with other sporting pursuits that were very popular at the time including, of course, soccer and rugby and also, surprisingly, cricket. There is no evidence that any of these sports had a club presence in Blackpool but there is no doubt that Blackpool men played them.

The GAA was set up in 1884 specifically to promote the sporting expression of Gaelic culture and to counter the growing threat of the more regulated and organised 'foreign' sports. It thus formed part of a wider Gaelic cultural movement embodied in the organisation the Gaelic League. This organisation was set up by Douglas Hyde to save and even spread the Irish language and to create an interest in Irish poetry, song and music. It might have been seen as the 'spiritual' corollary of the GAA in its efforts to preserve and recreate the Gaelic past that modern life threatened with extinction. Craobh na Linn Dubh was a Gaelic League branch of Blackpool, which strangely had its meeting room on Pine St, off Coburg St, which was closer to the centre of Cork city than to Blackpool itself. One of its presidents was Sean McMahon and in 1901 he accepted a sixteen-year-old Tomás MacCurtain, living in Blackpool with his sister but recently arrived from Mourne Abbey, County Cork, as a member. Tomás MacCurtain would become a very dynamic leader within this Gaelic League branch over the next five years and establish himself within the wider movement in Cork. He was an able fiddle player with the 'Blackpool Orchestra', of which he was a founding member, which probably provided the music for many a ceilí.[12]

Music was very important to people in a pre-visual media age and this was expressed in the plethora of local bands that existed in Cork city and throughout the country. The only band that remains on the north side of the city from that period is the Butter Exchange Band from Shandon which used to play in Fitzgerald Park, attracting strollers along the Mardyke. Music bands were a great attraction for the working classes as they provided both a creative outlet for their members and added pageantry and even prestige to localities. They would often parade down their local streets adding excitement and festivity to the area and were rewarded by a faithful following. This

Blackpool Band, 1908. (Blackpool Historical Society)

local pride in Blackpool a century ago would have been evident in at least three bands: the Quarry Band (near upper and lower Quarry Lane), the Blackpool Band, which had their practice room at the beginning of the Watercourse Road, and the Spring Lane Band, obviously situated in Spring Lane. The Spring Lane Band probably shared their premises with the Blackpool Boxing Club as Pakey Mahoney's trainer, Ned Regan, was also a member of the Spring Lane Band and such practices were common at the time. When Pakey Mahoney went to London in June 1913 to fight for the British Heavyweight title, one of the most prestigious in the world at the time, the Spring Lane Band provided the entertainment to the crowds outside the *Cork Examiner* office on the night of the fight in anticipation of the news of the outcome. He lost but at least the band helped to cheer somewhat the disappointed crowd.[13]

This very emotional identification of a band with its locality made it very territorial and sometimes that could spill out into violence when another band was deemed to have infringed on 'home' streets. This band rivalry also developed a political hue as bands increasingly identified with certain political personages. This

Blackpool Boxing Club: Pakey Mahoney, Irish Heavyweight champion (*second row sitting, third from right*) and his trainer, Ned Regan (*on right of Pakey*), who was a sergeant in the Connaught Rangers in the war. Robert 'Kid' Spillane sits far right, front row, a future Royal Marine. (Blackpool Historical Society)

political association had developed during the Parnellite era and it became more fractured just as constitutional nationalism did after the fall of Parnell. In Cork these divisions were sharpest with rivalry between John Redmond's Irish Parliamentary Party and William O'Brien's All for Ireland League. William O'Brien's political movement had a strong presence in Blackpool with a prominent office of the 'All For Ireland League' at Blackpool Bridge. The Spring Lane Band took the name of the 'Roche's Guards Band' in honour of Augustine Roche, a Cork Redmondite politician, who had donated some instruments to them in 1911 during an election.[14] The rivalry can be gauged by, in this case, a pro-William O'Brienite chant being heard on a Saturday night in Blackpool in the pre-war era:

> Up the Antis, Hurrah! Hurrah!
> Up the Antis, Hurrah!
> We don't care about old Fair Lane [another band on Fair Lane]
> All we want is our own Quarry Lane.
> Up the Antis, Hurrah! Hurrah!
> Up the Antis, Hurrah!

The thirty-seven members of the Spring Lane Band (Roche's Guards Band) who went to war. (*Cork Examiner*)

Row 1 (*l–r*): Frank Searles (Royal Munster Fusiliers), Denis Burns (Ordinance Corps), Denis Mulcahy (Royal Engineers), Patrick Condon (Royal Munster Fusiliers), James Condon (Royal Munster Fusiliers); **Row 2** (*l–r*): John Connors (Royal Munster Fusiliers), John Joyce (Royal Munster Fusiliers), William Quinlan (Royal Engineers), Con Buckley (South Wales Borderers), Patrick O'Connor (Royal Munster Fusiliers); **Row 3** (*l–r*): John Driscoll (Royal Engineers), Matt Daly (Royal Marines), Eugene O'Connell (Royal Munster Fusiliers), Patrick Doyle (Royal Munster Fusiliers), Dan Murphy (Leinster Regiment), Paddy Jones (Royal Munster Fusiliers), James Murphy (Royal Munster Fusiliers), Ned Regan (Connaught Rangers, trainer to Pakey Mahoney), William Joyce (Irish Guards); **Row 4** (*l–r*): Michael Barry (Royal Field Artillery), James Fenton (Royal Field Artillery), John Mason (Leinster Regiment, later Connaught Rangers), William O'Connell (Irish Guards), Patrick Murphy (Connaught Rangers), James Wallace (Leinster Regiment), Patrick Kelleher (Royal Warwicks), Ned Foley (Royal Garrison Artillery), Thomas Bagnell (Royal Royal Garrison Artillery); **Row 5** (*l–r*): Patrick Barry (Royal Navy), Corporal Higgins (London Irish Rifles), John Murphy (Connaught Rangers), Denis Leahy (Royal Garrison Artillery), Denis Driscoll (Royal Engineers), John Cronin (Royal Navy), Patrick Joyce (Royal Munster Fusiliers), Morty Kelleher (Royal Munster Fusiliers), Thomas Fenton (Royal Field Artillery).

Despite such intense rivalry, these bands were evidence of a working-class endorsement of moderate nationalism as embodied by John Redmond and William O'Brien, who both agreed that Ireland, all thirty-two counties, should be self-governed by Irishmen within a Home Rule parliament that was part of a wider political and constitutional fabric called the British Empire. The same British army and navy would be protector of all. When the war came and Redmond and O'Brien asked Irishmen to join the war effort, thirty-seven members of the Roche's Guards Band from Spring Lane Blackpool would do so.

* * *

Joining the British army or navy in the years leading up to 1914 might not have been actually endorsed by the Irish Party or the Catholic Church, but this does not mean that significant sections of southern Irish Catholic society did not support the defence forces and, for that matter, the whole British Empire itself. Outright rejection of the Empire, and its most physical presence in Ireland, the army, was decidedly a minority opinion, with Sinn Féin founded in 1905 being its most public advocate. But even here in recognition of such a consensual endorsement of the imperial framework for a future Home Rule Parliament, Sinn Féin's founder and leader, Arthur Griffith, had advocated a dual monarchical system akin to that of the Austrian-Hungarian Empire. Sinn Féin would abandon that proposal for outright anti-imperialism but its presence in Cork disappeared in 1911 due to internal policy splits and did not resurface as a political force (literally on the streets of Cork) until 1917 after three long years of Ireland being at war.[15]

The problem for Irish nationalists was threefold: they recognised that Ireland could be a major security threat to Britain if it allied itself with Britain's enemies like Spain in the fifteenth and sixteenth centuries, or France in the eighteenth and nineteenth centuries. Faced with implacable British opposition to complete independence on security grounds, Irish constitutional nationalism believed it futile and even dangerous to the fabric of Irish society to oppose a world superpower with physical force.[16] Secondly, and related to the third point, Irish Catholic nationalists realised the contribution Irish Protestants had made to the development of the modern functioning state and by accepting the imperial framework to Home Rule, it was a historical compromise to the undoubted justness of their long-standing cause. Irish Unionists' outright rejection of Home Rule, personified in the leadership of Edward Carson, only filled nationalists with indignation and even outrage at such a rebuff to a reasonable offer. Thirdly, the British Empire had some appealing aspects which were highlighted and embodied in the sense of self-achievement which enveloped the late Victorian and Edwardian British imperial project that had seen the empire expand to become the biggest in world history, spreading the virtues of 'Liberty', 'Christianity' and 'Commerce' through the ever widening use of the English language. The British army and navy were seen by Britons as the protectors of individual liberties from the whims of arbitrary government, a perception that was often justified by reference to a tradition that stemmed from the thirteenth century and Magna Carta. It was a tradition that had fostered a parliamentary governance which would eventually evolve into a modern democracy. The steamships in Cork harbour and the steam engine trains with their vast network of railway lines were evidence to Cork people of such beneficial progress. The Empire also helped bring Catholic and Protestant missionaries to the heathens of the world and often in doing so opened up the way to increased trade and commerce.[17] In rejecting such a tradition, would Ireland be in danger of being seduced by vagaries of the modern world such as syndicalism or communism?

This was the heritage of constitutional nationalism embodied in the Irish Parliamentary Party and led by John Redmond. It was the legacy of Daniel O'Connell, Isaac Butt and Charles Stewart Parnell. Parnell, the uncrowned King of Ireland, was still in the memory of Irish and Cork people (whom he represented in Parliament) before the war and Parnellism represented in one respect the subsuming, even appropriation, of the physical-force tradition of the Fenians within the broad church of constitutional agitation. Thomas Davis'

'A Nation Once Again' could be sung with gusto at Irish Party meetings as John Redmond called for a 'repeal' of the Union as Daniel O'Connell once did. The distant heroics of Fenian men, like the Manchester Martyrs who were commemorated in the years leading up to the war, could be celebrated but their methods were deemed impractical and, amongst some, even foolish in the present. Why resort to arms when reform could be, and was, achieved by other methods? Michael Davitt was a great hero of the Irish Party for he had helped solve the land question in Ireland. The 1903 Wyndham Act passed by Parliament had given the land back to the Irish. Michael MacDonagh wrote in the 1920s that what makes men mad with injustice and provokes revolution seemed to have been remedied with that Act.[18] The Conservative government that introduced it wanted to kill Home Rule with kindness and make the Irish unionist – it did not: the Irish Party under Redmond retained its strength and support.[19]

The vigorous campaign for Home Rule conducted by the Irish Party and William O'Brien's 'All For Ireland League' used the language of nationhood for Ireland but they also retained an imperial context. It is important to emphasise how the trappings of empire could have been more seductive in urban Ireland, in places like Blackpool, than in rural heartlands where the land itself was a reminder of the power struggles of the past. The merchant seamen, of which there were many in Blackpool, dealt weekly with many a nationality but primarily with those from Britain. Their trade was a constant reminder of the benefits of Empire and helped import products that might have epitomised the exciting dynamism of commercial Britain while in turn exporting the agricultural produce that Ireland was famous for. Blackpool partook in this reciprocal trade. British culture also made headway in Ireland with the latest catchy tunes and songs from the West End in London being sung at gatherings in Cork and elsewhere. The advent of the picture house or cinema represented the irrevocable advance of what could be called 'Anglo-American' culture into the daily lives of Irish people. It has been argued that the failure of the Gaelic Revival to stem such anglicisation turned people like Terence MacSwiney in violent national revolutionaries.[20] But it was the evidence of the British Empire on the ground in urban areas, the Royal Irish Constabulary, the legal courts, and of course the army, and the respect they were shown, that made the imperial aspect of Irish constitutional nationalism such an accepted position.

When the new king, Edward VII, visited Cork in 1903, people lined the streets to give him a hearty welcome. Union Jacks were everywhere. Protest was very low-key with a few arrests – including Terence MacSwiney.[21] The King came and went but the bastion of the British army, Victoria Barracks, remained overlooking the city. It was less than twenty minutes' walk from Blackpool Bridge. Patrick Beirne, a Blackpool National School teacher, fondly remembered passing the barracks and hearing the soldiers marching and being able to recognise where they came from by the tunes they belted out: 'Men of Harlech' for the Welsh, 'Bonnie Prince Charlie' (a Jacobite song, by the way) and many a Harry Lawder favourite, for the Scots.[22] Seemingly, visiting the barracks to see the soldiers parading was a popular pastime for some Cork families, including the writer Sean O'Faolain's. His father was a Royal Irish Constabulary man and he learned from him to embrace all aspects of the British Empire. He described Cork before the war as thoroughly 'Imperial' in its outlook. He was particularly impressed by the sight of a judge arriving at the courthouse on Great George's St (now Washington St), surrounded by well-attired soldiers, the prestige of ordered imperial government in action.[23]

Imperial governance was sensitive to Irish needs and desires. The Catholic Church concerns about education were conceded to. The development of Gaelic culture could be pursued freely, admittedly with little help from the state, but even here the Irish language became a matriculation subject for the civil service in 1909. Anyway, a Home Rule Parliament would enlarge on that whole project, it was hoped by those who promoted it.

In poor areas, like Blackpool, it was not unreasonable to think that radicalism would gain a foothold or the socialism of labour leaders

Augustine Roche, MP.
(*Cork Examiner*)

like Jim Larkin or James Connolly, which had an anti-imperialist agenda. However, even though Blackpool was poor, the Society of St Vincent de Paul was active in the community at the time and there existed a pawnshop on Great Britain St/Great William O'Brien St, called Jones Brothers (they owned a number of other pawn shops in Cork), radicalism seems not to have gained a strong foothold. The cultural hegemony of the Catholic Church was a powerful force against any revolutionary experiments. A lot of Blackpool people at this time were first-generation city dwellers and were still imbued with what could be called a traditional peasant conservatism in these matters. The Irish Party claimed to understand the demands of labour and the plight of the poor. Statistically, Ireland was a relatively well-off country in Europe but whether it was seen as such in localities like Blackpool is doubtful.[24] However, in general, things seemed to be improving. The Irish Party would claim credit for this and promise more, especially with a Home Rule Parliament.

The change of name of the Spring Lane Band to the Roche's Guards Band sheds some light on the relationship between the Irish Party and working-class districts like Blackpool. The band changed its name to honour the well-known Cork nationalist politician Augustine Roche after he donated instruments to the band during the 1911 elections. Most men in Blackpool, including those in the band, could not vote due the restrictive franchise still in operation at the time yet a politician like Roche could claim to represent the interests of all classes of society when he stood in the chamber of the local council in Cork or in the House Commons in London. It was in this sense a paternalistic type of representative democracy where the gulf between the people from places like Blackpool, both economically and educationally, from those elected politicians who had to self-finance their elected position in Parliament up to 1911, was often quite wide. It could be inferred that the paternalism that seemed to characterise Irish constitutional politics at the time was reciprocated by a deferential mentality amongst swathes of working-class people to people in high social standing like the members of the Church and to the often well-to-do politicians. Bands in Cork, which represented certain localities, supported certain political candidates and probably acted as a lever of influence on that politician and on the body politic as a whole. Deference had its limits; a band could support other candidates.

If paternalism was a characteristic of the relationship between local politician and localities like Blackpool then none epitomised it more than Augustine Roche. He was born at Douglas St, Cork, in 1849 and eventually took over and then expanded his father's business in the vintner trade 'to every part of Munster'. Even though Protestant, he was a nationalist and became involved in the land agitation in the 1880s in support of Parnell. He entered the Cork Corporation in 1883 and was Mayor in 1893 and 1894 and Lord Mayor in 1904. He supported Parnell during the split and John Redmond when the Irish Parliamentary Party reunified in 1900. When he was elected MP for Cork City in 1905 he had gained a wide reputation for his philanthropic work. In his obituary of December 1915, the *Cork Examiner* wrote:

> By the time [of being elected Mayor in 1893] he was clearly connected
> with the work of practically every charitable organisation in Cork, and
> there is no estimating how much he did, both directly and indirectly, in
> the cause of the poor. It was during his term of office in the Mayoralty,
> and on his suggestion that the excursion to the seaside for the Poor
> Children of the city was initiated ... Since then it has been a normal
> event eagerly looked forward to by the little ones of our lanes and alleys.
> Thousands upon thousands of them have been during the last twenty-
> three years given one day in the year by the seaside, [Youghal was the
> destination] and as a rule Mr. Roche was always a prominent helper
> at the excursions. The children always know who their friend was and
> they in their own way displayed their love for him. Their handclaps and
> cheers were to him a more grateful pleasure than any honour that could
> be bestowed upon him.

The *Examiner* also recorded that 'one of his last acts of his life was
to sign a cheque for a handsome subscription to the Coal Fund'
(a charitable fund set up to aid poor families to buy coal for the
winter). Undoubtedly many a child from Blackpool would have
partaken in those excursions to the seaside organised by Augustine
Roche, including members of the Roche's Guards Band. Such
politicians were a great balm to class friction and helped create a
unified nationalist movement behind the Irish Party. Such harmoni-
ousness was captured by Sean O'Faolain's description of Cork just
before the outbreak of the Great War in August 1914 as 'sleepy' and
peaceful and the whole age as one of 'blissful somnambulism'.[25]

In his youthful thrall to all things 'Imperial', O'Faolain might
have missed out on the Irish Volunteers who were parading
military style around Cork city and county in the first half of 1914.
After reform of the House of Lords in 1912, Home Rule seemed
inevitable for Ireland. John Redmond would hail it as the triumph
of British democracy and Home Rule as the bond of friendship
between the two peoples. The prospect of Home Rule, however,
produced a massive response from, primarily, the Ulster Protestants
in opposition to it and were supported by a significant body of
conservative opinion in Britain. Opposition was so vehement in
Ulster that the Ulster Volunteer Force (UVF) was set up to resist

Home Rule by force if necessary. The gun was being brought centre stage in Irish politics for the first time since 1798. Irish nationalists, especially those of a more extremist persuasion, led the response through the formation of the Irish Volunteers. The first meeting of the Irish Volunteers in Cork was held on 14 December 1913 at City Hall where the head of the national committee, Eoin MacNeill, spoke. It was also attended by Sir Roger Casement. The Irish Volunteers were not separatists but vowed to resist any attempt to impede Ireland's march towards nationhood. This was the language of Parnell, of Redmond and of Home Rule, and separatists could support such nebulous nationalistic language (as Fenians did in Parnell's time). Five hundred Volunteers signed up after the first meeting in Cork, including three from Blackpool.[26]

The first military instructors of the Volunteers in Cork were two former British army members: Bill Godwin (Royal Field Artillery) and then John Donovan, a former sergeant of the Dublin Fusiliers. By the end of April 1914 twenty-eight Blackpool men had joined. Negotiations between Eoin MacNeill and John Redmond were initiated in May with the prospect of Irish Party involvement. Though these talks broke down, the threat of a Redmond-led rival organisation forced the hand of the leadership of the Volunteers to cede control effectively to Redmondite supporters and they took over from June onwards. On the eve of war in August there were fifty-eight Blackpool Volunteers taking part in drills and marches with over 1,000 other Volunteers from the city. It must be noted in the context of this study that when efforts to raise money for the Volunteers were made on 31 July 1914, conducted through the offices of the Lord Mayor of Cork, Henry O'Shea, among the many donations received was a sum from a group calling themselves 'The Sympathisers' with an address as care of 'The British Army, Cork Barracks'.[27]

Civil War was a possibility. The Curragh Mutiny had occurred in March 1914 when a large body of the army officers in Ireland signalled that they would not act coercively against the Ulster Protestants in their opposition to Home Rule. Such defiance and contradiction of government policy was noted by nationalists at the time and coloured their thinking for years. The staunchly Redmondite *Cork Examiner* would consistently mention this 'mutiny' over the next four years as a possible sign of 'perfidious Albion's' real intentions towards a divided Ireland. The successful landing of guns and ammunition at Larne, County Antrim, in April by the UVF signalled an escalation which in turn prompted the Irish Volunteers to match such deeds. Unlike the UVF, the Irish Volunteers received some harassment and attempted confiscation by the authorities when they brought ashore their cache of military goods at Howth, County Dublin, in June and even though most of arms got through, the different responses of the government were noted. This disparity was accentuated by the actions of the soldiers returning from Howth when they encountered a hostile crowd at Bachelor's Quay and reacted violently, killing four people. By the end of July 1914, after the Home Rule talks in London had stalled over the question of exclusion of the northern counties, a sense of foreboding over the fate of Ireland must have been palpable. Suddenly, however, attention was drawn away as on 28 July Austria declared war on Serbia, prompting Russia to mobilise its army as a retaliatory gesture. Germany declared such an action as threatening and when the Austrian shells started to land on Belgrade on 29 July, the slide into war was inevitable. The prospect of civil war in Ireland would have to wait.

Why the assassination of Archduke Ferdinand, heir presumptive to the Austro-Hungarian throne, in Sarajevo on 28 June 1914 should have led Europe to a cataclysmic abyss a month later has complex origins but a good historical case can be made against the German Reich under the leadership of Kaiser Wilhelm II as the main cause of the war.[28] Kaiser Wilhelm's accession to the throne in Germany in 1888 heralded the end of Bismarckian diplomacy and the assertion of a more aggressive nationalistic German imperialism. This assertion of a greater role for the German Empire in world affairs, their 'place in the sun', to rival their neighbours France, Russia and Britain created greater instability in international relations. The massive development of their navy was a signal of such intentions and in turn provoked Britain to increase investment in its navy, heightening tension.

It could be argued that German imperialism was the response of a conservative aristocratic ruling elite, headed by the Kaiser, to a rapidly changing Germany, both economically and socially, which produced democratic forces that threatened the political nature of that society. When its ally, the Austro-Hungarian Empire, decided to deal harshly with Serbia over their links with the assassination of Archduke Ferdinand, Germany backed them, believing they were right to assert control over Serbia in that region, to not only stamp out internal nationalism within its multi-ethnic empire but also as a rightful assertion of imperial hegemony. Such a power play was a gamble as Serbia had close ties to Russia but again there is evidence that elements within the German Reich wanted a war at that time as they feared the ongoing military development of the Russian and French armies.[29]

Germany knew that in confronting Russia at the end of July 1914 it was declaring war on France as both countries had been bound together precisely to contain a more assertive Germany. Germany's pre-war Schlieffen Plan came immediately into operation, which entailed a swift war in the west against France before defeating the slower-mobilising Russians. Great Britain was a consideration but an unknown one. It was not obliged to defend France and certainly not Tsarist Russia but the prospect of a victorious Imperial Germany under Kaiser Wilhelm II dominating Europe was profoundly disturbing. What relieved the British government, under the Liberal Herbert Asquith, of this dilemma was the German army's invasion of Belgium as part of their military plan for a quick knockout blow against France. Britain was treaty-bound to defend Belgium but the German invasion was also a strategic security threat to British interests in that area. When the Germans did not respond to a British ultimatum to withdraw from Belgium, the British government declared war on Germany on 4 August 1914. Ireland was at war and the rallying cry of Catholic Belgium would echo throughout the land for years to come.

In August 1914 there were 30,000 Irishmen in the British army, just over 9 per cent of the force and roughly equivalent to the proportion of the Irish population in the British Isles.[30] There were a further 30,000 Irish reservists who were immediately called to active service. Over half the soldiers commemorated in this study from Blackpool were either professional soldiers or reservists at this time. Liam Russell, who could be described as an extreme nationalist in the context of the time, later described the mood in Ireland when war was declared:

> a tremendous wave of imperialism swept the country. Red, white and blue badges were worn everywhere, and were it not for a hard core of Gaelic League and Volunteer people, Irish-Ireland would have been swamped. Recruiting meetings, processions with bands, were regular features [used for] recruiting for the British Army.[31]

This imperialistic enthusiasm was emboldened by reports from Belgium of the devastation wrought by the Germany army during the first few weeks of the war. Not only was there a mass of refugees fleeing the invasion but there were stories of atrocities against men, women and children. Old centres of Catholic learning like Louvain were reported as being wantonly burned and priests and nuns killed. This shocked opinion in Ireland and Britain as Europe plunged into the abyss leaving the seemingly near serene gentility and quiet optimism of the Edwardian era shattered forever. Tom Kettle, a former Irish Party MP who was in Belgium at the time trying to locate guns for the Irish Volunteers, was morally outraged by what he witnessed. He supported the British effort in the war and joined an Irish regiment of the army.

These first few weeks defined what the war was about. It was seen as a German war, in particular born out of Prussian militarism, that applied by its actions the principle that 'Might is Right', which not only threatened the liberty of peoples everywhere but posed a threat to civilisation itself. It was the new barbaric 'Hun' army with the Kaiser as Attila. Letters from Cork soldiers published in the *Cork Examiner* throughout the course of the war would reiterate these charges against Germany continually. Interestingly, the letters rarely, if ever, condemned the German people: it was the Kaiser and the Prussian Junker class that were to blame, which chimed with a growing faith in democracy that was echoed in Ireland through the struggle of the land wars of previous years and the final defeat of the Irish landlord and ascendancy class. The Irish Parliamentary Party had hailed the coming of Home Rule for Ireland in the same vein, as the triumph of 'British Democracy' over British aristocracy and this too would be one of perspectives through which they viewed the war against Germany: Democracy against German Aristocracy.[32]

Irish and Cork support for the British war effort not only reflected concerns for the fate of Europe, but also a response to a clear and present danger of invasion by the German army. This was echoed by William O'Brien MP at one of the first recruiting meetings for the British army in Cork City Hall on 2 September when he warned:

> If they [the Irish people] remained with their hands folded much longer they might bring to their own beloved land the scenes of massacre and spoliation and nameless horrors which were devastating the heroic little nation of Belgium as though the very legions of hell had been let loose upon their fields and possessions.[33]

The main focus of O'Brien's speech, however, was an attempt to reposition Irish nationalism and nationalists behind the war effort conducted by the old foe, England. The struggle for Irish freedom, he pleaded, was no longer against the British authorities but amongst the 'marching millions of soldiers of the three mightiest Empires in the world [Britain, France and Russia]: for wherever the flags of these mighty armies of this war waved there also would wave the flag of the hopes of Ireland.' O'Brien went as far as likening the present war to a sacred cause, 'as holy, as that of say 1867 [Fenian uprising in Ireland], the cause of a united Ireland, happy, great and free' as 'in restoring the territorial integrity of a martyred nation [Belgium], but would also have the privilege of restoring the territorial integrity of Ireland as a nation ...' but an Irish nation that by their participation in the war would be created 'undivided and indivisible' and 'Ulster and Munster as strong as the waves in the sea'. To O'Brien in September 1914, the war was Ireland's war, a war for the freedom of small nations including that of Ireland and by engaging in it, forging unbreakable bonds with their fellow Irish Protestants.[34]

Such emphatic encouragement of Irishmen to join the British army was not matched by John Redmond and the Irish Party who were initially more circumspect. Redmond gave his support to the British declaration of war against Germany but limited the commitment of the Irish Volunteers to home defence only, thus freeing the British army in Ireland to active duty in France. However, once Home Rule was put onto the statute books with the official signing by King George V on 18 September to be implemented when the war was over or after one year, its prospect became seemingly undeniable and Redmond fully endorsed Irish nationalist recruitment to the British army on 20 September at a speech at Woodenbridge, County Wicklow. This was the fulfilment of the promise of Irish constitutionalism, from O'Connell to Parnell, that the restoration of 'Grattan's Parliament' to Ireland would make Britain more secure, not less.[35]

In December at Limerick, Redmond would claim 'that Ireland had at long last won a free Constitution, and a better and freer Constitution than that which Grattan won in 1782' and thanked the Volunteers, at whose meeting he was speaking, for their part in the 'machinery' that was witnessing 'the rebirth of Ireland'. Now like William O'Brien in Cork in September, Redmond fully supported the British war effort in the fight against Prussian militarism which had brought devastation to Europe and threatened the independence 'of Belgium, Holland, Denmark and Switzerland, and probably of every small nation in Europe'. Again echoing O'Brien, Redmond sought to shift Irish nationalist anti-British thinking to a European paradigm in which Germany had taken up the role of the 'Sassanach' in their invasion of Belgium while the Home Rule Bill was a 'peace treaty' between the peoples of Ireland

and Britain and was 'an honest and generous attempt to settle the long and disastrous quarrel between Ireland and Britain'. Within the context of his Home Rule thinking, Redmond also had a hard-nosed pragmatic 'policy' task in urging Irishmen, implicitly Irish Catholic men, to enlist in the British army and that was the whole issue of northern Protestant claims for exclusion from the Irish Home Rule Parliament.

An Amending Clause had been added to the Home Rule Bill which would allow the British government to exclude a portion of Northern Ireland, either temporarily or permanently, if sufficient agreement was not reached between the differing parties in Ireland. Redmond argued that if Irish Home Rulers did not support Britain in its hour of need, as the Ulster unionists under Carson were doing, then the Irish Party would lose political leverage in determining the nature of the proposed amendments of the new Irish state or states. Without a strong Irish Catholic presence in the war, British fears of the Irish as instinctively treacherous would be stoked and their sympathy to the Ulster Protestants increased. Redmond also hoped, though he did not mention it explicitly in this speech to Irish Volunteers, that the war would break down the sectarian distrust and barriers by creating unity between Irish Catholics and Protestants through the shared experience of one of the most momentous events in history. Redmond plainly warned in his Limerick speech of a 'stab in the back' by more extreme Irish nationalists.[36] Little did he know that already a plan of intention for a rebellion had been initiated by what the *Cork Examiner* had called in August 'a minuscule' portion of the Irish people.

They certainly appeared to be minuscule amongst the widespread support within Irish society for the British war effort. The main political parties, the Catholic Church and the business community were largely united in their support for what they believed was a just war. This was, of course, predicated on the expectation that the war would last, if not until Christmas, then at most a year. The extreme Nationalists' rejection of cooperation with the British war effort was based on the belief that only an Irish Parliament could send Irish soldiers to war. Their whole world view, it could be argued, was based on a romantic spiritualism that envisioned a Gaelic Ireland reborn from the 750 years of subjugation under colonial rule.[37] The militarised world of the Volunteers, both north and south, and the violence of the Great War itself, helped give the old adage that 'England's difficulty is Ireland's opportunity' new possibilities. It would mean that not only would these Irish nationalists seek to strike a blow militarily against Britain and its empire in Ireland, they would also seek the aid in doing so from their new allies, the Germans. There was a bit more to their alliance with Germany than just military opportunism. They also shared a nationalist criticism of the British as a decadent, modernising force whose great attachment to the grubby materialism of trade spiritually debased the world. The Germans considered themselves the spiritual guardians of high 'Kultur', while some Irish nationalists saw spiritual resurrection solely through Gaelic culture.[38]

James Connolly, a prominent leader in the Labour movement, was to a certain extent blinded by a violent anti-British imperialism which enabled him to view Germany as one of the most progressive countries in Europe and a leader in the quest for a socialist world. He might have been able to vindicate his argument at the time with the strength of the socialist movement in Germany but he seriously underestimated the force of pan-German nationalism within a society that was still adjusting to the rapid industrialisation it had undergone over the last fifty to seventy years. His antagonism to Britain was increased by the failure of the 1913 Lockout in Dublin where he felt that fellow union members in Britain had abandoned him and the Dublin workers.[39]

The most visible political representation of the extreme nationalist perspective were the Irish Volunteers. Connolly produced a newspaper expressing his views but circulation was not large. Terence MacSwiney also printed a newspaper called *Fianna Fáil*, expressing support for Germany but it had closed down by December 1914. The Irish Volunteers survived the split caused by Redmond's endorsement of the war effort and his call for Irishmen to join the British army: to them only an Irish Parliament had that authority.

The split in Cork actually prefigured the national separation between the Irish Volunteers, who kept the name, and the new National Volunteers under Redmond. It was precipitated by the pro-British attitude of the leader of the Irish Volunteers in Cork, Major Talbot Crosbie, who pre-emptively forced the Volunteers in Cork to choose between Redmond's endorsement of the war effort and the possibility of enlistment and those like Tomás MacCurtain and Terence MacSwiney who rejected any contemplation of such a move. On 31 August 1914, on Cornmarket St where 1,000 Volunteers had assembled, the vast majority chose to follow Redmond into what would become the National Volunteers. Nationally, the split saw 170,000 Volunteers siding with Redmond while 12,000 remained with the Irish Volunteers.[40]

If this percentage was replicated in Blackpool, and there is no reason to suggest it was not, then of the fifty-eight Irish Volunteers from Blackpool, fifty-two would have become National Volunteers and five would have remained with the Irish Volunteers. (Tomás MacCurtain was not living in Blackpool at the time of the split.) It has been subsequently estimated that of the 170,000 National Volunteers some 27,000 enlisted in the British army, most at the behest of John Redmond.[41] If this ratio was applied to Blackpool then between eight and eleven Volunteers enlisted but as Blackpool was an urban area and enlistment was significantly higher in such areas then it would be reasonable to suggest that this figure would have been higher, maybe even double to near twenty. One such Irish Volunteer from Blackpool who enlisted was Denis O'Riordan from 12 Commons Road who had joined the Volunteers soon after their formation in Cork in December 1913. He had been working in the cellar at Murphy's Brewery since 1909 and enlisted in the British army on 26 September 1914, six days after Redmond's Woodenbridge speech.[42]

If employers like James Murphy of Murphy's Brewery and William Goulding of W. & H. M. Goulding Ltd are a gauge to the attitude of industrialists and business in Blackpool (and the wider country, for that matter) then they were very supportive of the war effort. Both Gouldings and Murphy's assured their employees who wanted to enlist that their jobs would be retained for them. Gouldings even went as far as to offer a financial supplement to enlisted employees' wives and children. They both made direct financial contributions to the war effort. In all, eighteen workers from Murphy's would enlist, including Jerh. Mullins from 16 Commons Road (who could have been as young as fifteen when he enlisted in May 1915), John Murphy from Sunday School Lane and Matt Martin from the Watercourse Road who was one of the first to enlist in August 1914.[43] Between thirty and forty could have enlisted from Goulding's Chemical Factory in Spring Lane as over 200 Gouldings employees had enlisted from its six Irish plants by August 1915. In the mainly female-dominated Cork Spinning and Weaving Company at Millfield, six past employees would die in the war which suggests that even among its male employees there was a significant number who enlisted.[44]

In all, if a ratio of six to one is used to calculate the number of Irish soldiers who enlisted to those who died in the war, then it can be estimated that around 350 Blackpool men participated in the war through the British army or the Royal Navy. This was almost 17 per cent of the total male population of the Blackpool area of this study if the census figures of 1911 are applied. This could rise to 30 per cent of the eligible male population for enlistment of the Blackpool area, which was a very significant contribution.

2

'Blackpool to the Front!' The Beginning of the War on the Western Front

THE BRITISH EXPEDITIONARY FORCE (BEF) that arrived in France in August 1914 consisted of four infantry divisions and a cavalry division, totalling 80,000 soldiers. It was deemed 'contemptible' by Kaiser Wilhelm in comparison to the millions of men both the German and French armies were able to put into the field due to their policies of pre-war conscription. The British army remained a voluntary force up to January 1916 in Britain and was always a voluntary force in Ireland. The BEF in France would receive two more infantry divisions soon after August as these units were being recalled from the further reaches of the Empire. Plans to raise many new military divisions in Britain and Ireland were already afoot. There were nine Irish regiments in the 'Old Contemptibles' (a nickname the British soldiers took themselves after the Kaiser's comment) army which represented 15,000 soldiers and service personnel. By December this had risen to 40,000. The first Irish regiment to land in France was the 1st Battalion Irish Guards on 13 August at Le Havre. Private Paddy Foley from Dublin St was among them and could claim to be the first soldier from Blackpool in France. Later on the same day and place many more Cork soldiers, including men from Blackpool, would arrive with the landing of the 2nd Battalion Royal Munster Fusiliers. The 2nd Battalion Royal Irish Regiment would land at Boulogne on 14 August.[1]

The BEF task was to stem the northern and most dynamic prong of the German invasion of France which was proceeding through

Sergeant William Foley (*left*) with unknown fellow prisoner of war in Giessen prison camp, Germany. (Adrian Foley)

Private John Connors (Spring Lane Band member). (*Cork Examiner*)

Private J. Donnelly of Blackpool. (*Cork Examiner*)

Belgium in an attempt to envelop the whole French army, and even Paris itself, in a crushing manoeuvre as the main French army was being engaged in the centre. When the BEF arrived at the border of Belgium they joined the Belgian army and the French Fifth Army which amounted to 254,000 men in the field against three German armies amounting to 750,000 soldiers.[2] The German army was considered one of the best in the world for the quality of military material they had and their military preparedness. The first battle in which the BEF were engaged was at Mons in Belgium on 23 August, in which the Royal Irish Regiment were involved. After heavy fighting in which British soldiers demonstrated a furious ability to fire fifteen shots per minute from their Lee-Enfield rifles, they were overcome by larger German forces and retreated. The Irish Regiment suffered 300 casualties as at one point they were nearly totally surrounded but owing to covering fire from the Royal Irish Rifles, amongst whom were the Lucy brothers, John and Denis, from Montenotte in Cork city, a channel was created though which they escaped.[3]

Thus began an eight-day retreat by the BEF towards Paris in which most of the men would have to march 140 miles. To prevent the British army being engulfed by the advancing German forces rearguard actions by sections of the BEF were executed to impede and delay the Germans. The 2nd Connaught Rangers were caught by surprise and fought at Grand-Fayt while the Irish Guards faced an attack at Landrecies on 26 August. The stand taken at Le Cateau on 26 August, which involved the Irish Rifles and the 2nd Battalion Irish Regiment to a lesser extent, enabled General Smith-Dorrien's II Corps to proceed in an orderly retreat. Haig's I Corps needed the heroic help of the 2nd Munster Fusiliers at Étreux on 27 August.

The fame gained by the Munsters at Étreux was due to the tenacity of their fighting which enabled them to halt for eighteen hours (six hours of which after they had been totally surrounded) a whole German Army Corps and thus allow the BEF to get a 12-mile advance on their pursuers and escape. Two years later the *Cork Examiner* stated in a piece on the Roche's Guards Band from Blackpool that:

> At Mons [in fact, Étreux, as the Munsters were not really involved at Mons] when absolute destruction threatened the Munsters it is said, that the Germans often heard the rallying cry 'Blackpool to the Front!' and it meant a call to desperate men to dash to the support of those who were even harder pressed and it was the last call that many a Prussian heard.[4]

The Munsters fought till they ran out of ammunition and, when they did, they continued with the ammunition taken from the dead. At dusk in an orchard 240 men, including many wounded, staggered to their feet with four wounded officers and surrendered. Included in this group from Blackpool were Sergeant William Foley, Private J. Donnelly, Private James O'Connell, Private Cornelius Murphy and Private John Connors, a Roche's Guards Band member. My own grand-uncle, Corporal Mick Birmingham from Dillons Cross, was also taken prisoner. Sergeant William Foley would earn a Military Medal for his actions that day. Next day they witnessed what was claimed to be at least 1,500 German wounded on the streets of Étreux. Nine officers of the Munsters and 118 of ordinary rank were killed or died of wounds. For most of those captured the next four years would be spent in prison camps in Germany.[5]

The retreat of the BEF finally ended around 4 September at Melen, southeast of Paris. The Irish Guards lost 9 officers and 115 men at Villers-Cotterêts on 1 September. The German army were suffering from the effects of over-extending their line of advance from their supply base while experiencing losses in men from actions taken by the British and French armies, which still retained an ability for offensive manoeuvres. The German command began to lose confidence. Their army did not envelop Paris as planned but pursued the French southwards and east of Paris, thus exposing their right flank. The French attacked and started a general Allied offensive that pushed, firstly, the German army back over the River Marne, and then on to the River Aisne, a distance of 40 miles.[6] At the Marne, the 2nd Battalion Royal Irish Regiment were involved in taking Orly on 8 September where they also took some prisoners. By 12 September the German defences had begun to solidify with a line of entrenched positions behind the Aisne. The 2nd Connaught Rangers had captured the village of Cour de Supir on 14 September but then needed the help of the Irish Guards to repulse a series of German counter-attacks. The Guards succeeded in clearing a road to the left of the Rangers in the process but suffered significant casualties, including an episode where the ruse of a 'treacherous white flag' was used.[7]

By the end of September a line of makeshift trenches covered the front line, stretching from Switzerland to the River Aisne. This necessitated enveloping manoeuvres ever further northwards by all armies towards Flanders and the Channel ports in order to gain military advantage and defeat the enemy. For the BEF the Channel ports were vital for the naval protection of Britain itself and the urgency of defending them was made more important when the German army took Antwerp on 9 October, relieving more soldiers for their northbound offensive. Antwerp had been defended by the Belgian army but it managed to escape, or large parts of it, westwards aided by the presence of a hastily formed corps under Sir Henry Rawlinson, which had landed at Ostend and Zeebrugge. This Corps consisted of 3rd Cavalry Division and 7th Infantry Division and they made contact with the Germans at Ghent, which allowed the Belgians to retreat.[8] The Belgians fortified their position at Nieuwpoort by flooding the plains after opening the sluice gates on the River Yser. Fighting then began to concentrate inland on what would become the famous salient, or bulged front line, around the town of Ypres.

H. Moore who was a bombardier with the 35th Brigade Royal Field Artillery, which was part of the 7th Division, wrote home to his wife at 10 Spangle Hill, Blackpool, telling of his experiences in Belgium during that time and it was printed in the *Cork Examiner* on 4 January 1915.

> My Dearest Wife, – I am now going to give you a little detail of my experiences during the time I am out here. I will give you no dates as I am lost in some of them. Those which I am stating are true incidents of my experience since the time I landed in Belgium. My battery landed

in Zeebrugge and marched to Bruges, from where we made our way towards Ostend. The reason for this was, we were leading the Germans a dance. We kept on marching round then got back to Rouliers, then to Bruges again. We left Bruges one day; the Germans marched in on the next. We were playing hide and seek, but eventually our little lot beat them at their own game; so we marched to Kruizeke and came into action. Nothing very serious happened on the first day, but on the second day one of our gunners was shot through the neck. That was first blood. From that until we got to Ypres we seemed to lose our men. We were in this first position for six or seven days, fighting day and night. Of course we belong to the good old fighting 7th Division. The Germans outnumbered us 4 to 1, but they did not know it, thank God. The next little item was where we put a German battery out of action. On the following day the Germans cut us up rough. They blew our observation station to pieces; a few of our men were seriously wounded ... for the remainder of the day we all had hard fighting. But what topped the lot was, when night came on everything seemed to be very calm, but suddenly a rifle shot was heard ... Then all of a sudden bullets came raining on the pits in thousands; but we were up and at the guns while you would wink, and we got the order to fire. First our range was 1,400 yards, then it dropped to about 1,000 yards; then the order was one round gun fire then two rounds gun fire, and then we were ordered three rounds gun fire. Well, we kept that up for about one hour and a half. All our detachments were very cool, and they did their work splendidly. During this time the enemy's bullets were pouring in, but it was marvellous we did not have a casualty. The 1st Grenadier Guards were in our front, and they did some very good work, and at the end of an hour and a half we made the Germans retire ... On the following morning some of the Grenadier Guards were passing our position, and they asked if it was our battery that responded to the night attack. Of course we said 'yes'. Then they told us the story of what havoc we played with the enemy. They said when 'cease fire' went they were going to give us a cheer, for we saved their lives by the way we shelled the enemy, and these are the words they said – If ever they met us at home we should have whatever we wanted (I mean the best drink), and then they departed. On the following day we had it very rough ... we had our Q.M.S. killed, also several others. We lost several horses. Here again our major showed himself very brave, also one of our drivers, whose name was Driver Holford, and who fetched ammunition to the guns under heavy fire. He also fetched the guns out of action under heavy fire, and was recommended for the D.C.M. One of our officers, a very brave fellow, was killed in this position. He was sent to reconnoitre the enemy's trenches, but he did not return, poor fellow. We retired from that position with several wounded. We came into action in several places, but there was nothing to speak of happened, but in one position where we were there was an aeroplane brought down; it was in flames when it reached the ground. Our next position was in the woods. We were in action there for several days, but on the very day that we were going to shift, we were told that we were going to be attacked, so were ready. Our left section guns opened fire on the German infantry about 700 yards away. They were running from house to house on the crest of the hill. We were doing some very good work, when all of a sudden a German howitzer battery opened fire on us and got our range very quickly. We were in action just about 20 yards in front of the wood. Well, their shells absolutely mowed the trees down and wounded one of our men, for a start, who was replenishing ammunition. After that they shortened their range and got us nicely. Of course, we could do nothing but get away, while we were alive to our first line. Of course our wounded were got away, but the dead remained. At all events, we got to the first line, and we met our captain. We explained the matter to him, so he said to have us remain quiet, and that we would go back for the guns, or what remained of them, by night. We did so, and it was a sad sight that met our eyes. One of our guns was properly smashed up and turned upside down, and the others were damaged almost as badly. Then we went to view the pits, and found our poor comrades who got killed. Some of them were unrecognisable. They were removed. Then the guns were removed, but one, and it took 16 horses to pull them to safety. There were no wheels on the gun carriage – they were blown off – so we had to skid it. We got safe away and saved the guns, and that was the end of our troubles and casualties. We retired to Ypres, where we stopped for some days, and while we were camped there the Germans were bombarding that lovely town ... as I am writing this, one of my comrades got such a great big parcel from home. I also got one from Mr. Stone of the British Legal Co. I am sure, with God's help, we will have a happy Christmas, and hoping you all had the same. – H. MOORE

In another letter, to his mother, Bombardier Moore wrote:

I have seen some awful sights in Belgium – towns and churches battered and destroyed, and the poor people driven from their homes, and poor children with babies in their arms, or following them hunted and homeless. I have seen the priests and nuns flying from their churches and their Convents ... May God help these poor priests and nuns and put an end to their misery.[9]

Military narratives can sometimes ignore the trail of devastation on places and civilians that war leaves in its wake. Glimpses of such scenes can obviously be detected in Bombardier Moore's letter but the effects were evidenced in Cork itself when Belgian refugees arrived on 29 September 1914. Some of their children would come under the educational care of the nuns at St Vincent's Convent on Gerald Griffin Avenue (Old Peacock Lane) near Blackpool.

The 'race to the sea' by parts of the French army and the BEF from the static front on the Aisne proceeded throughout October. It was a series of engagements between the opposing armies that tried to envelop each other's right flank thus driving both sides ever further northwards, leaving entrenched positions in their wake. The 2nd Royal Irish Regiment, part of 3rd Division, received orders on 5 October that they were aiming for Calais. They became involved in fighting in the Bassée region where they stormed the enemy trenches and drove them back through the village of St Vaast at bayonet-point.[10] The 3rd Division soon captured a village called Aubers and on 15 October the 2nd Irish Regiment received 6 new officers and 353 men from Ireland which brought them up to regulation numbers. A company of the Irish Regiment supported an attack on 18 October which captured Fromelles and that company later that day reached La Riez where they beat off a heavy German attack. On the morning of 19 October, with all the 2nd Irish Regiment at Le Riez, they were ordered to take the village of Le Pilly at 2.30 p.m. in conjunction with a French attack at Fournes.

Divisional artillery shelled Le Pilly from 2 p.m. to 3 p.m. but it was claimed most of this fire ended up to the left of the village. At 3 p.m. A and B Company (which included Private Timothy O'Leary of Dublin Hill who had landed with the regiment in August) moved forward, supported by C Company, with D Company in reserve. According to the battalion's war diary, 'The advance was carried forward under a heavy rifle fire + without falter – the heaviest fire apparently came through gap in woods N.E. of Le Pilly. The enemy's artillery had by this time got an accurate gauge.' B Company had reached the main road through Le Pilly but was heavily 'infiladed by Artillery fire from the left' while A Company

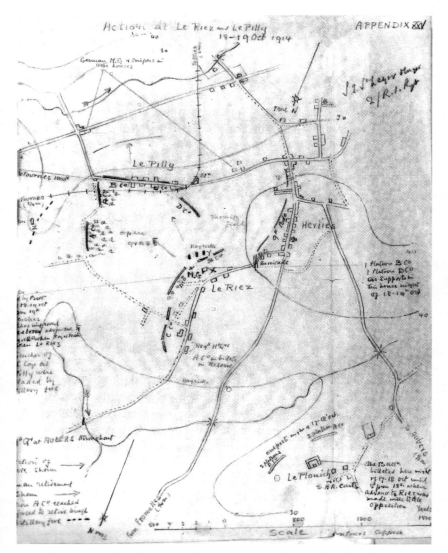

Irish Regiment War Diary map of the attack at Le Riez and Le Pilly. (National Archives, Kew, England)

were forced back to a line of woods just southeast of the village at about 4 p.m. A new draft of 63 men with the reserve company then came forward to help establish a front line through the village but flanked back on either side. The Germans were still firing heavily from three sides and their artillery shelling was 'very accurate' and

coming from the direction of Fournes to the left. When it was dark
the 'Batt. Dug themselves in ... The R.E. [Royal Engineers] put up
some barbed wire about 20* [yards] in front of A Coy trenches'
and German fire 'practically ceased' while their artillery fired only
occasionally though 'the enemy brought into play two search lights
in the distance'. By this stage 163 men were reported as wounded
with an unknown number killed. It was subsequently established
that among those who fell in the attack was Timothy O'Leary from
Dublin Hill, the first soldier from Blackpool to die in the war.[11]

The decision to entrench at Le Pilly was based on the assumption
that the French were succeeding at Fournes to the northeast, but
this would prove to be false. The Irish Regiment had called upon
the 4th Battalion Middlesex, who had recently arrived at Le Riez,
to shore up their left flank but they were judged too depleted to
help. The surrounding BEF forces were pulled back after the French
defeat at Fournes, leaving the Irish Regiment dangerously exposed.
The Germans realised this and diverted entire troop units to bolster
a concentrated attack which started at daybreak, 6.45 a.m., on 20
October. 'The Irish began to realise their isolation but refused to
retire without orders. They fought on hourly expecting a British
counter attack to restore the situation'.[12] By the end the Germans
were attacking in 'converging directions' and took Le Pilly at 4 p.m.
Casualties of the 2nd Battalion Irish Regiment on that day amounted
to 7 officers and 170 NCOs and men killed, 302 taken prisoner,
and a large number wounded. Testimony to the bravery of the Irish
at Le Pilly was given by a German prisoner later in the war.[13]

Le Pilly demonstrated the dangers for a battalion in fluid warfare
especially when communication with the wider front was difficult.
How many times would a battalion gain advantageous ground,
hold it tenaciously and receive the expected reinforcements to
win plaudits for their steadfastness? The 2nd Battalion Royal Irish
Regiment had to rebuild with fresh troops from Ireland just as
the 2nd Battalion Royal Munster Fusiliers had done since Étreux
in August. Many a Blackpool man joined the Munsters during
this period, all of them probably reservists and some only hastily
retrained. They included James Sheehy from Quarry Lane and

Thomas Tyson (a butcher) from Seminary Road who arrived in France on 28 August. Michael Donovan and Michael Allen were brothers-in-law from Narrow Lane and landed in early September and November respectively. Patrick Hourigan from the Commons Road joined up with the Munsters on 9 October. On 2 December Patrick Banks and James Gleeson, one a Protestant and the other a Catholic, both from Millfield Cottages and both worked in the Flax Factory, entered the fray together. The 2nd Battalion Royal Munster Fusiliers were being rebuilt and Lieutenant Colonel A. M. Bent took command of them on 4 October.[14] They were needed urgently.

After the fighting at La Bassée finished a line mostly of trenches had formed from Switzerland to the Channel coast. The British held a precarious section that bulged around the town of Ypres in Belgium (Ypres Salient) which Bombardier Moore alluded to in the letter above. It was his 7th Division that were facing the brunt of ferocious German attacks. This was the beginning of the First Battle of Ypres. On 21 October the Irish Guards were sent to the front line at Ypres to help the battered 7th Division. They helped clear Polygon Wood on 23 October and held the line against incessant attacks. A week later the Guards were holding part of the line between Klein Zillebeke and Zandvoorde road when their trenches were taken in an attack but they retook them after a counter-attack. They then faced a renewed bombardment by the German artillery on 1 November and during very heavy fighting in the following days managed to repulse a major German attack. When the Irish Guards were relieved on 9 November their losses totalled 16 officers and 597 ordinary rank either killed or wounded.[15] By then the 2nd Munsters were preparing to enter the line.

The Germans were adding even greater number of soldiers and artillery to their already superior force at Ypres. Among them were the fresh German Guards Division and the 3rd Prussian Division. On 10 November the 2nd Munsters moved from Zillebeke to the woods near Klein Zillebeke where they relieved the Grenadier Guards. En route they were shelled and suffered casualties which was probably when Private James Sheehy from Quarry Lane was killed.[16] The front line itself had no trench system as yet and consisted of a series of holes with two men every five yards. Despite sniping from the Germans, they were in line by 2 a.m. on 11 November. The first German attack came an hour later with one of the heaviest bombardments by artillery experienced in the war so far. Soon after, loud whistles were heard, heralding the sight of German soldiers, a number of them newly enlisted students, who were singing 'Die Wacht an Rhein'. Facing such masses of infantry and knowing that there were no reinforcements behind, it was a case of do or die for the Munsters and a hail of fire cut down swathes of the advancing enemy. For forty-five minutes 'the enemy pressed the attack, but were defeated by the dogged pluck of rain-sodden, scattered groups of Fusiliers trying in vain to keep the mud from clogging their rifles, and then taking those of their wounded comrades when all else failed.'[17] To the Germans the line appeared impregnable and they began to dig in a couple of hundred yards away. However, the Germans were more successful in another part of the line but after heavy losses and the danger of a serious setback, the BEF regained the line with the help of the 2nd Battalion Royal Irish Rifles.

On 12 November, the Munsters tried to improve their shelter pits by further entrenchment which proved difficult and were only able to reach down 4 feet. At 6.30 a.m. a bombardment started which lasted two hours and which was followed by a strong attack. Again the Munsters hung on tenaciously. Quartermaster Sergeant Fitzmaurice was killed and his role was taken over by John Ring, a position he held for the rest of the war. Twenty-one-year-old Patrick Hourigan from the Commons Road was also killed on that day. The following days witnessed renewed German attacks and periods of shelling. On 13 November the Germans managed to capture a portion of the line but a counter-attack led by Lieutenant Colonel Bent regained them for the Munsters. They withstood another strong attack on 14 November and were relieved the next day when they were brought back to Brigade Reserve for the first real meal they had had in ninety-six hours.[18]

The First Battle of Ypres soon ended after these attacks due primarily to the depletion of artillery shells within the German army.[19] The casualties suffered on all sides matched those of the more famous Third Battle of Ypres (also known as the Battle of Passchendaele) with the total for the BEF being 58,000. The true sense of the carnage that occurred could not be conveyed back at home but it was recorded later that little boys of Cork (which of course included Blackpool) could be heard singing about the Munsters:

> Oh the Kaiser Bill tried very hard
> When he lined our front with Prussian Guard
> But the brave old Munsters still fought hard
> And held them back at Ypres.[20]

The *Cork Examiner* was resiliently upbeat in the face of reporting Cork casualties of the war and the descriptions were not gruesomely graphic as yet. On 14 December they published the following extract from a letter of Private Charles McCarthy of the 1st Battalion Irish Guards (the same battalion as Paddy Foley of Dublin St) to his mother in Cork:

> Just a few lines hoping you are quite well also my father and all the lads. I am grand myself, thank God. I got all the papers, but I only got one box of cigarettes. The weather here is awful cold. The country is covered with snow. We are relieved out of the trenches this past 14 days, and are having to rest in a village about fifteen miles away from the fighting. We lost a lot of men. Out of those who left with me from London there are only forty-three left. We were then eleven hundred strong. I saw by the 'Examiner' that a chap named Donovan [Private Michael Donovan, 1st Batt. Irish Guards, killed in action 27th October 1914. Son of Stephen and Mary Donovan of Upper Dominick St] was killed I knew him well. There is also a boy from Blackpool. He was wounded, but I think he was not picked up and is missing. I have no idea when this war will finish. I wish it would finish soon. The wounded suffer very much on account of the cold but they are well looked after. We get plenty of clothes: more than we can carry. We are also very well fed.[21]

The letter clearly indicates that by December the trench system was well established. It was a military system that seemed for some time to make defensive warfare almost invincible. Private McCarthy's wish for the war to end soon would prove to be a vain one.

Irish Guardsmen attending a wounded German soldier, 31 July 1917, at the Third
Battle of Ypres. (Imperial War Museum)

By the end of 1914 the trench system had developed across the
whole Western Front, stretching in total for 475 miles from
Nieuwpoort in Belgium to the Swiss border. Mobile warfare of the
first four months produced shockingly high casualty rates: for the
small British force it resulted in 17,000 deaths while the French
suffered a horrendous 450,000 casualties.[22] No doubt casualty rates
for the Germans were high too. It was they who initiated the trench
system as a means of halting the allied advance. The system enabled
troops to be switched from sector to sector, or, importantly for
the Germans at this stage, to the eastern front as trenches can be

successfully defended using much fewer soldiers. What resulted was a subterranean engineering feat that mirrored that of the Great Wall of China, cleaving Europe in half. The Belgians held 15 miles of the front, the BEF held 25 miles at the start, rising to at most 123 miles but reduced to 65 miles by 1918, while the French commanded 300 miles and never fewer than 202. It was a front that would only move at most 5 miles in either direction between late 1914 and March 1918 (excluding the voluntary withdrawal of the Germans to the Hindenburg Line in 1917).[23]

The trench system was a brilliant defensive mechanism that was able to withstand the most prolonged military bombardment and attack that an opposing army could muster using all the technological know-how available to them at the time. It would take the BEF years to build up the military resources and learn the tactics to overcome such a formidable obstacle but at a cost of hundreds of thousands of lives. The Germans were in the initial years of the war better prepared for attritional warfare with the use of trench mortars and grenades and their trench system was purposefully more developed and extensive than the British and French. They chose trench lines that were usually on higher ground and hence drier and easier to maintain and, importantly, forcing the Allies to attack uphill. It also enabled better means of bombardment by its artillery as it had greater visual range. They were able to produce greater amounts of barbed wire which lined the front portion of the trench and had a higher proportion of machine guns than the French and British. They not only developed a front line of trenches, but second and third lines. The first was more thinly manned but heavily armed with machine guns while more troops could be easily transferred forward from the second and third. An attacking force would have to overcome not only the barbed wire of the first line but subsequent lines as well.[24]

The BEF would also develop a three-lined trench system. The first line, like the Germans, was zigzagged to limit the damage range of artillery shells and was more easily defensible if one section was taken over by the enemy. The Allies would never create a trench system to match that of the Germans because of the nature of the war they were fighting. The Germans were an invading army on French and Belgian soil and thus had to be repulsed continually. This was 'war to the hilt' and well-developed trenches might make the Allied soldiers too defensively orientated. Their trenches were adequate for defence but the spirit of the French army's offensive mentality pervaded the BEF lines. Like so much in the war, it would be a learning curve for the British army in adapting to this new warfare involving millions of men and new military technology and tactics.[25]

The BEF trenches were at their worst during the winter of 1914/15 when they were hastily constructed in the light of what was called a 'valour of ignorance'.[26] There were little amounts of entrenching tools and virtually no sandbags, making them prone to collapse. The Royal Engineers were too busy building a whole network of railways and roads to connect the new buildings like hospitals, headquarters of various kinds, ammunition dumps, etc., to keep a massed army supplied and fit for purpose. There were initially no proper latrines, sleeping dugouts or bathing facilities. The trenches were claustrophobically smelly and dirty, not only because of the detritus of feeding an army but primarily because of the mud. The BEF trench lines were generally on low land and prone to flooding.

The first winter of the war in Flanders was particularly cold and wet as just eighteen days were dry between 25 October 1914 and 10 March 1915.[27] Private John Browne, 1st Battalion Irish Guards, wrote in a letter to his family near Macroom, County Cork, dated 22 March 1915:

> During the wet weather, and we had lots of itching the past winter here, we had some rough times in the trenches. In a few of them the water was up almost to our waists. The frost and cold too, at some places, were almost unbearable.[28]

The conditions of mud and waterlogging led to rheumatism and other ailments but most particularly, 'trench foot'.[29] This was a painful swelling of the foot which was eventually controlled by better use of footwear and the spreading of grease on the foot itself.

As the war went on the BEF trenches did improve and even by the spring of 1915 John Browne was noting the improvement with the sunny weather.

Trenches were still very dangerous places, no matter how well built or improved, due to artillery or mortar shelling. Analysis by the Royal Army Medical Corps indicated that over 2 per cent of wounds received by soldiers were due to grenades, 39 per cent due to bullets (either rifle or machine gun) and over 58 per cent (a source suggests 70 per cent) by artillery or trench mortars.[30] One of the factors that would win the war for the Allies was their eventual numerical superiority of artillery over the Germans as the war progressed.

PRIVATE'S ESCAPE FROM DEATH

> Private Patrick Tobin, R.A.M.C., who resides at 40 Madden's Buildings, Blackpool, Cork, writing under the date fo the 7th inst. From Heaton Mercy Hospital, Manchester, to the 'Examiner,' says – 'I have been at the front since August 18th 1914, and was in the retreat from Mons. I had a marvellous escape at Zellibek, Ypres, in April. Myself and three more stretcher bearers were bringing in a wounded man from the dug-outs, when the Huns started shelling us. All their shells went wide, except one, which dropped not one yard from us, and thanks to the Sacred Heart Badge and Miraculous Medal my sister sent to me, which I was wearing, the shell did not burst, but sank into the soil.'[31]

In the early months of 1915 there were localised battles being fought over sections of trenches with some of them been taken only to be lost to a counter-attack. Michael O'Leary from County Cork won his Victoria Cross with the Irish Guards retaking some trenches that had been lost in his sector in early February 1915.

There was little respite for the BEF at St Eloi on the Ypres Salient as the Germans realised that both 28th and 27th Division were new to the front line. The 1st Battalion Leinster Regiment was with the 27th Division and one of the soldiers was Private Cornelius Lenihan from Madden's Buildings in Blackpool, who had arrived on the Western Front on 19 December. The Leinsters were at camp at Dickenbusch on 4 February 1915 when they experienced

Private Cornelius Lenihan, Leinster   Private Thomas O'Callaghan, 2nd Battalion
Regiment. (*Cork Examiner*)   Royal Munster Fusiliers. (*Cork Examiner*)

'hostile aeroplane drop bombs close to huts' but luckily there were
no casualties. Aeroplane technology was a mere twelve years in
existence in 1915. The Leinsters then relieved another battalion at
trenches near St Eloi from 4 to 7 February and again from 9 to 11
February and suffered some casualties on both occasions. For the
period of 9 to 11 February the war diary records that 'casualties
during tour 2nd Lt. H.C. Albon: 3 men killed: 10 men wounded.'[32]
One of those men was Cornelius Lenihan and the following
appeared in the *Cork Examiner*:

CORKMAN KILLED AT THE FRONT

The relatives of Private C. Linehan [*sic*], 1st battalion Leinster
Regiment, have received notification of his death in action on the 10th
February. Private Linehan's family originally hailed from Macroom, but
for several years past resided at 32, Madden's Buildings, Cork. He was
formerly employed in the 'Examiner' Office, and on joining the army
was sent to India. After the outbreak of the war he returned with his
regiment to Europe, and had been in France but a few weeks before he
met his end. He was about 27 years of age [in fact, he was aged 30], and
a fine type of young Irishman. His loss will be deeply felt by his many
friends, among whom he was held in high esteem.[33]

The Leinsters subsequently retook the trenches and were heavily attacked on 14 February when their trenches were taken but through a concerted effort they recaptured them.

The 2nd Munsters had also been involved in retaking lost trenches at Festubert on 22 December 1914 which involved some harsh soldiering and fighting. Subsequently they were posted at a sector 2 miles from their old battleground at Givenchy, just north of La Bassée Canal. Like every front-line battalion they had to withstand casualties from sniper bullets and occasional shelling. There were also direct attacks on their positions but they were repulsed. On occasion the BEF also mounted attacks on German trenches. The war diary of the 2nd Munsters records that one such attack on 10 March 1915, after a bombardment of German trenches, 'failed owing to the fact that the artillery bombardment had not succeeded in breaking the German wire' and received shelling in return with two killed and twelve wounded. On 11 March there was 'heavy fire on our left front. Some desultory shelling of the German trenches in front of Givenchy'. During the day a reconnaissance patrol of Munsters was sent out to spy on the enemy line. Thomas O'Callaghan from the Watercourse Road was killed in action on this day. The 2nd Munsters suffered more casualties on 12 and 14 March, on which day they were finally moved to billets at Les Choqueux.[34]

In the spring of 1915 the French, under supreme commander General Joffre, launched large offensives in the belief that they would win the war within a few months. The French put pressure on the British to support them as the British were reluctant to commit troops. There was a fear within the British War Office that if the French were not supported they would collapse but also that a British attack would demonstrate to the French that the BEF 'had to be taken seriously'.[35] General Haig within the British army was nearly as optimistic as Joffre with regard to the prospect of success as he expected an easy overrun of German lines with the much greater quantities of high explosives now available.[36] It must be remembered that the scale of the war was new to all concerned and all plans were expected to succeed. The BEF attacked Neuve

Chapelle on 10 March 1915 with the heaviest concentration of artillery amassed so far by the British army. Despite initial success in breaking through the German lines the offensive failed when German reservists were able to re-establish their line after two days.

Though the Germans had been transferring their troops to the Eastern Front (their main concern in 1915), they decided to launch a pre-emptive strike against the Allies on the Western Front. They had thinned the line on the Western Front but expanded the trenches there and added more machine guns per unit. On 22 April the Germans launched the Second Battle of Ypres with the first use of gas as an integral part of their attack. It was very successful as the Allies were unprepared and the town of Ypres itself appeared to be in danger of being taken. However, the Germans failed to exploit the opportunity as they had started the attack with limited tactical aims and never readjusted.[37] Still, desperate fighting by the French and British was needed to secure Ypres. On 25 April at St Julian, the 1st Battalion Royal Irish Fusiliers and especially the 2nd Battalion Royal Dublin Fusiliers suffered horrendous casualties. The French launched their offensives with the first at Woevre from 5 to 18 April and then a bigger one in May at Artois. It was to support the French for their Artois battle that the BEF launched at attack at Aubers on 9 May which again involved the 2nd Battalion Royal Munster Fusiliers.

The BEF general command on 1 April had given the French an assurance that they would attack within four weeks and set about planning and preparation for the event. British commanders were briefed of the plans on 27 April and 6 May, with the start date of 8 May, and launched in conjunction with the 10th Army of the French under General D'Urbal to the right of the British. The BEF were to use the element of surprise in their attack as the bombardment was going to be only forty minutes, the last ten minutes of which was to be very intense. The French, however, shelled their Germans lines for days in advance. The BEF would attack on two separate sectors at Rue de Bois with the 4th Corps, including the 2nd Munsters and 1st Corps with Indian Corps at Fromelles. The aim was to take the German line, fan out and both sectors would meet at Auber Ridge about 4,000 yards (1½ miles) behind the German line with the vague order then to press on to the Haute Deale Canal another 6 miles beyond.[38]

With the Munsters were 22-year-old Patrick Banks and 24-year-old James Gleeson of Blackpool. They had arrived at the Western Front on the same day, 2 December 1914, and both came from a small collection of red-bricked dwellings called Millfield Cottages and worked in the Flax Factory around the corner from where they lived. James was a yarn dryer while Patrick was a general labourer there. Patrick was a Protestant whose parents had come to the factory from Belfast to impart some of the Ulster linen skills to the locals at Blackpool. His brother, John Banks, was training to be a soldier back in Ireland as Patrick arrived in France. For three weeks prior to the attack Patrick and James, along with all the 2nd Munsters, were 'working strenuously day by day practising the assault'.[39] This consisted of jumping ditches, scaling parapets, creeping past wires, and short sharp rushes, according to 2nd Munster Fusilier Private Patrick Meehan of Aghada, County Cork.

Meehan was wounded at the battle and six months later wrote a series of articles about the events at Aubers for the *Cork Examiner*. They have a certain insightful value but it must be borne in mind that he was writing, as he sympathetically stated, with regard to the 'mothers, fathers, sisters, brothers, sweethearts and wives of the gallant men we lost that day' while also consciously aware of the necessity for more Irishmen to enlist. On 7 May, he related, 'they [were] properly introduced as to the modus operandi of attack, points of _____ action, and ultimate concentration.' According to Meehan the men were far from 'down-hearted' despite knowing that the German guns were still 'spitting death' and that their troops were still in their trenches:

> Were they [the Munsters] down-hearted? If they were they didn't look it to me. What with flags waving [they had received green flags with an Irish harp and 'Munster' written on them] and 'Tipperary' on the wing, mouth organs and melodians creating, which seemed to me, a melodious discord. A song here and a 'jest there, and somewhere else in our ranks an intimation that we'd shake 'em up'. And by jove, sir, we did.

The battle was delayed by a day due to the inability of the French artillery to get adequate sight of the German position, mainly due to the haze caused by the sunny weather in the region at the time. Meehan's description of the Munsters' return to the attack trenches on 8 May indicates the importance of *esprit de corps* in every fighting formation: 'They little knew the havoc that would make itself felt in our ranks inside of twelve hours. They cared less. You might take them to be a merry crowd going to a hurling match either at Limerick or Tralee, and proceeding by orderly cohesion to the railway terminus. Such was their attitude.'

This *esprit de corps* was greatly aided by one particular figure, Fr Gleeson, the Munsters' chaplain. On 8 May he 'was as busy as ever hearing the men's Confession ... The men of the regiment adored him ... [and even] those of a different denomination trusted him entirely with their personal affairs.' He was with the Munsters right up to the trenches giving the companies general absolution, singing hymns and when general silence had to be observed in preparation for the attack, he was saying to the men that their next Mass would be at La Bassée far beyond Auber Ridge.[40]

Meehan relates the feelings and thoughts of the men before they went over the top:

> On the morning in question our boys from the province of Munster gave no little thought to their wives and families, sisters and brothers, fathers and mothers, and I may as well mention sweethearts also. From this you will glean one obvious fact, that on the morning I am going to describe to you our thoughts were with you all.[41]

The British artillery bombardment started at 5 a.m. on Sunday 9 May. The objective of the Munsters was German positions near the village of Lorgies. The shelling lasted for forty minutes but by the thirty-third minute A and B Companies of the Munsters were climbing up the ladders and over the parapet which was an occurrence that was replicated all along the line. Despite the British shelling the Germans still managed to open up withering machine-gun fire and artillery shelling. 'Even before the start B Company suffered loss, a shell wiping out an entire section.' German machine-gun fire was continually enfilading the Munster's front line, and those of A and B Companies that could dropped down 50 yards in front of the German line as planned. When the artillery barrage lifted after forty minutes the Munsters rose to attack but found the German barbed wire still largely intact and the enemy fire as continuous as before. The attacking forces all along the line were failing to reach the German front line. Somehow, some Munsters managed to breach the barbed wire and take a section.

Private Meehan was part of the supporting C and D Companies of the Munsters who came through. He recalls 'the boys cheering and laughing' and mentions the exhilarating rush of vitality, of 'life ephemeral however disgusting and abhorrent the immediate environment may be. In such circumstances one has not time to reflect. It is well. It would spell disaster.'[42] Watchers from the British line could see, for a few minutes, several of the Munsters standing on the enemy breastwork waving a green flag: then one of them was shot and the rest disappeared.[43] B Company had taken a trench, one of the few to do so that day, and moved on to the next objective. Supporting companies, though much depleted, aided them. They reached a small river but the advance faltered as the expected makeshift bridges never arrived. By then it was clear that the whole offensive was failing. High command ordered a final bombardment which rained down on the few Munsters who had reached the river.

Private Meehan was by this time wounded by a bullet after he became entangled in barbed wire: 'I had no idea how hard a bullet could strike. I was out of it. The curtain had rung on the climax so far as I was concerned.' He was one of only two Munsters of that company to survive. By 10.30 a.m. the order was received to withdraw and when the remaining Munsters lined up at Rue de Bois at 11.00 a.m. it was recorded that they had lost 19 officers and 320 men with only 8 taken prisoner. Among those who fell were three from Blackpool: Michael Donovan from Narrow Lane, and the friends from Millfield Cottages, Patrick Banks and James Gleeson who were probably side by side when the battle commenced. It was the worst military day on the Western Front of the war for Blackpool as it would be for Cork in general. The names of the three Blackpool soldiers who died are inscribed on Le Touret Memorial at Richebourg-l'Avoué, which is dedicated to the servicemen who fell whose graves are unknown. Overall the BEF lost 458 officers and 11,161 men.[44]

The Germans had made significant improvements in their trench system since Neuve Chapelle.

> The front breastwork, revelled with large mesh wire had been doubled or trebled in thickness from 15 to 30 feet. The shells had failed to break the wire due partly to the number of duds while the German soldiers remained relatively safe under large sand bag mounds built at varying distances behind the front for living in. And as at Neuve Chapelle there were a number of machine gun nests situated some distance behind the line to act as rallying centres in the event of a breakthrough which the attacks were unable to deal with.[45]

The BEF would, as planned, launch another attack at Festubert on 15 May, again in support of the French Artois offensive. Even though they used a longer period of bombardment the attack was again a failure. The Irish Guards suffered badly with over 400 casualties out of a force of 1,100. In the May-to-June fighting on the Western Front, the Germans sustained 73,000 casualties, the French 104,000 and the British 37,000. It marked the end of the old and regular British army, the 'Old Contemptibles'.[46]

3

The Blackpool Home Front and Support for the War

BLACKPOOL, AS AN INDUSTRIAL AREA, responded very cohesively to the outbreak of the war. Immediately families were concerned with the fate of as many as fifty to sixty professional soldiers and sailors from Blackpool and, in the few weeks after mobilisation on 4 August, said goodbye to eighty to ninety reservists from the railway station. Enlistment in the army from civilian life occurred straight away and Blackpool probably mirrored national trends of higher rates for the first year and a half, trailing off significantly thereafter. Enlistment as civilians from the Blackpool area could have reached as high as 140 to both the army and navy. A further forty may have enlisted as emigrants who had family in Blackpool. So in every street and laneway of Blackpool multiple families had a direct involvement in the war.

It would be natural then for Blackpool to echo the widespread pro-British and empire sentiment that Liam Russell claimed was sweeping Cork at the time. It must be remembered that for Irish people, and indeed most Europeans, empires were of the past, the present and the future and this was a war between them. From that perspective the British Empire had some very positive aspects that could have been highlighted to forge a patriotic consensus. A hint of such imperial patriotism was given by Augustine Roche MP, the well-respected Irish nationalist politician and patron of the Spring Lane Band, when he gave a farewell speech to Royal Irish Constabulary enlisters to the army as they boarded a train at Lower Glanmire Road, Cork. The 'large and enthusiastic crowd', with the Leinster Regimental Band in the background, heard Roche praise the

> splendid spirit which prompted the fine body of young Irishmen
> he saw before him to go forward and take their place in the fighting
> line. (Applause) The cause for which they would fight was one of the
> worthiest. It was the cause of the Empire, which was as much their
> Empire as that of any Englishman. He felt sure they would give a
> splendid account of themselves, and would, by their valiant action in
> the field, perpetuate the fine tradition of the fighting race. (Applause)[1]

Just before the train left the crowd sang 'It's a Long Way to Tipperary'
and 'Auld Lang Syne'. Though not explicitly stated in the report, but
implicitly understood by the crowd Augustine Roche was speaking
to, was that the cause of the British Empire was the cause of 'liberty'.

John Redmond made this more explicit in other speeches during
the year, most especially at the Free Trade Hall in Manchester (an
emblem of Victorian imperialism) close to St Patrick's Day 1915.
It was a speech he knew would be widely reported in Ireland. He
stated that one of the reasons Kaiser Wilhelm started the war
was the expectation of division within the Empire but Redmond
declared:

> Ten years ago he might have found revolt and dissatisfaction in South
> Africa, in Ireland, Egypt, and India, but he had forgotten the march of
> events and the march of ideas in this country. He forgot that the rule
> of the people had been substituted for the rule of an ascendancy class.
> He forgot that the rule of the English democracy had united the empire
> upon the only firm and secure foundation – that of liberty (cheers).
> Irishmen had entered on terms of equality into the Empire, and they
> would defend it with loyalty and devotion. It was a blessed day when the
> democracy of Britain trusted Ireland. That trust had done what force
> could never do, and what centuries of coercion failed to accomplish.
> It had given them as a watchword for the future that old classic motto:
> Imperium et Libertas – Empire and Liberty (cheers).

It was an imperialism that could be endorsed because the historic
wrongs had been righted by the granting of Home Rule for Ireland
which had been on the statute books since 18 September 1914.[2]
This enhanced greatly the goodwill towards the British Empire
which was seen by elements within Irish society, and Irish Catholic
society at that, as the greatest the world had known. Great not only

Constable Keefe from Kilbarry, who joined the
army early in the war. (*Cork Examiner*)

in its expanse (which seemed to be in
itself a validation) but in its moral worth
as it extended civilisation to the barren
stretches of the earth, bringing in its
wake technology, education, Christianity
and 'liberty' through the rule of law and
representative structures of government.
(No doubt there was a racist pillar to British imperialism but it was
an ingredient of all empires and was an element in the United States'
expansion westwards over Native American lands.) And now this
'liberty' was being threatened in Europe by a militarised Germany
that had illegally invaded Belgium. The justness of the Allied cause
was to most contemporary Irish people self-evident but the threat
to Ireland of a German invasion was also emphasised at recruiting
meetings and public speeches. At such meetings friendship with
Britain was proclaimed while Germany was denounced, not only as
the barbaric 'Hun' who burned towns, churches and libraries, but as
a present-day version of the old colonial English and in one instance
Poland was cited as an example of the new set of 'Penal Laws' the
Germans were imposing there.[3]

Undoubtedly the Catholicism that Ireland shared with countries
like Belgium and Poland added to the wave of pro-war patriotism
that characterised the first year or two of the war. The Irish Catholic
Church, by and large, supported John Redmond and the Irish
Parliamentary Party's position in relation to the war. On 13 October
1914 the Irish Catholic hierarchy authorised a national diocesan
collection in aid of Belgium which by February 1915 had collected
£28,352 which was close to €11 million in today's terms, taking
into consideration inflation and average income increase over the
period. Later on in the war they would organise the same for Poland
after a request by the Polish episcopacy and then collected £11,000,
which is equivalent to over €4 million. A total of 649 Irish Catholic

Belgian refugee children with nuns at St Vincent's Convent, near Blackpool. (*Cork Examiner*)

priests would join the British army as chaplains and minister to the troops.[4] Blackpool's own parish priest at St Nicholas Church, Fr Charles O'Connor, did so with the Dublin Fusiliers, while from Farranferris College which overlooked Blackpool, Fr Duggan and Fr Scannell became army chaplains.

Evidence of the devastating impact of the invasion of Belgium had already arrived in Cork on 29 September 1914 with a boatload of Belgian refugees. Fund-raising efforts immediately commenced in Cork to assist them and soon the Belgian children were being schooled at St Vincent's Convent on St Mary's Road, only a few minutes from Blackpool itself. More reminders of the Belgian plight beyond the newspaper reports and the rhetoric of speeches arrived in Cork in the shape of Fr Vandamme, an emissary of Cardinal Mercier of Belgium, seeking to start a general appeal amongst the

Catholics of Cork for a sum of £2,000 for his native town of Vilvarde near Brussels. It was described by the *Cork Examiner* as 'a poor little town of 15,000 inhabitants, mostly poor workmen', which suffered 'the destruction of its parochial works, such as schools (attended by 1,300 poor children), social institutions, etc., which are mostly supported by charity'. Fr Vandamme stayed with the Christian Brothers at the North Monastery, again only a few minutes' walk from Blackpool, and his mission received the approval of the Bishop of Cork, Rev. T. A. O'Callaghan on 11 August 1915.

The *Examiner*'s report goes on to quote other sources on the historical relationship of reciprocal support between Ireland and Belgium, notably during the penal times, and framed Ireland's aid during the war as repayment of a past debt:

> Irish Catholics are repaying the debt not only of kindness to the Belgian refugees but by shedding their blood for the restoration of Belgian independence. The ties of sympathy between the two nations will be strengthened by suffering.[5]

A week later, on Wednesday 18 August 1915, 'two wounded Belgian soldiers' and others came to a specially organised recruiting meeting at Blackpool Bridge and one of them, Henri Bodart,[6] spoke to the Blackpool people gathered there. The meeting began at 7.30 p.m. when 'a gaily decorated tram car left the depot in Patrick St with the speakers, attended by the fine band of the Dublin Fusiliers and an immense concourse of people, and a halt was called at Blackpool bridge'. The reporter added that 'this district has the honour of sending more men to the front in proportion to its size than any other in the city, and under these circumstances it was not surprising that the various speakers had a deeply sympathetic audience'.

> Mr. F. Lyons said he need not explain to them the object of their meeting. They all heard of the war, and the purpose of the meeting was to appeal for men. They wanted men badly, very badly indeed, and the recruiting officer informed him that Blackpool had done magnificently, but they wanted Blackpool to out-do itself. (Hear, hear). He did not know what questions were before their minds to-day, but all these questions should be over-shadowed by the one great quest before them

now, and that was, were they going to rule themselves, or were they going to let the Germans rule them? ... There was only one way to keep those fellows out, and that was by pouring more men into Flanders. They would be in this country now but for the Munster Fusiliers, Connaught Rangers, Mike O'Leary and people like him, and but for the bluejackets [Navy]. He had no doubt but that many of these men came from Blackpool ...

Mr Joe Devlin [Irish Party M.P. from Belfast], at an historic occasion at the beginning of the war, stated that the frontier of Ireland was the fighting line in Flanders, and he was perfectly right. It was out there they should keep the Germans back. (Cheers)

Mr. J.C. Flynn (a Justice of Peace from York Terrace) said that it had been his fortune on many occasions to address the people of Blackpool, but never had he spoken to them on an occasion as the present of such enormous gravity, of such enormous importance, and one that concerns them – the safety of their beloved country. Though it seemed almost a work of supererogation to address the people of Blackpool, because if Cork had done its work in the great contest, Blackpool and the North Parish had done theirs splendidly. But the need was urgent, the time was fleeing, and never had the world been confronted with so great a struggle. It was no ordinary combat, no ordinary struggle between peoples, between Kings and dynasties: it was a struggle between barbarity, strengthened with all that was latest in science against civilisation and liberty – all that Ireland held dearest. The men who stated that Ireland had no interest in that struggle, and that she ought to remain neutral in that fight, were either cranks, cowards, or lunatics. (Cheers.) ...

Henry Bodart, a wounded Belgian soldier, who was received with ringing cheers, spoke briefly in the Flemish language, and Mr Larmoor, acting as interpreter, said Henri Bodart has just told them in his own tongue that his comrade and himself had seen a good many of the atrocities committed by the Germans in Belgium. His last words, translated into English, were 'For God's sake, come over and help us to drive out our oppressors.' (Cheers.) ...

A number of other speakers then addressed the crowd gathered at Blackpool Bridge including the Reverend A. E. French from Rushbrooke, Queenstown, who warned of the perilous state of the Russian army on the Eastern Front and the prospect of a subsequent onslaught by the German army in the west which necessitated more men. A point to note was that Rev. French was Protestant; Catholic

2nd Lieutenant St John Joseph Vincent
Anthony Giusani, 10th Battalion Royal Dublin
Fusiliers. (*Cork Examiner*)

priests were rarely seen at recruitment meetings. Next to speak was the well-known lawyer Lieutenant Maurice Healy, son of O'Brienite, nationalist MP Maurice Healy senior. William O'Brien's All For Ireland League office would have been in sight from the tram stopped at the heart of the village, indicative of O'Brien's popular standing in the area. Lieutenant Healy asked the young men of the community to join him at the front. As did the next to address the crowd, 2nd Lieutenant John Giusani, of the Dublin Fusiliers (who would be killed on the Western Front on 13 November 1916). He was the only son of Joseph and Nora Giusani from Patrick's Hill, Cork. The rally was ended by Captain Philips who said

> nobody knew better than he did what Blackpool had done because he had the pleasure and honour at recruiting many stalwart men from that district. He wanted them to pay a compliment to him, and try to do even better this week, before he had to return to his larger sphere of labour in Dublin. (Cheers, and a voice – 'We Will.')

'The meeting concluded', according to the *Cork Constitution*, 'with the projection of a series of lantern pictures depicting the march of the Huns through Belgium and France, and the horrible atrocities which they committed.'[7]

Three Corkmen off to the front with the 9th Munsters: (l–r) Florence Cronin (Barrack Street Band), Thomas Sheehan (Blackpool) and Joseph Cronin (Redmond Hurling Club). (*Cork Examiner*)

Such rallies were to a certain extent successful in recruiting troops especially from industrial, urban areas like Blackpool. It has been estimated that 75,000 enlisted in the first year of the war in Ireland and a further 20,000 between August 1915 and February 1916.[8] Those that enlisted chose their regiment and supplemented the existing Irish regiments fighting in France while others joined the newly formed 10th Division, which was predominantly Irish in composition, and the 16th (Irish) Division which was most closely associated with John Redmond and the National Volunteers.

An example of one of over 170 Blackpool men who enlisted during the war was William Mehigan from 76 Spring Lane. In 1911 he was married to Anne and had three children, the eldest of whom was eight. He was working in Goulding's Chemical Factory across the road in Spring Lane. He enlisted some time after the war started and was in his mid-thirties. He ended up with the newly formed 8th

Battalion of the Royal Munster Fusiliers with the 16th Irish Division which arrived in France, after over a year's training, in December 1915. An interesting reference was made by Justice of the Peace James Flynn[9] during the recruiting meeting when he called for more young men to enlist, as married men, like William Mehigan, had responded to the call in adequate numbers. Seemingly there was a generational difference in southern Irish enlistment and it has been suggested that this was a factor in the development of separatist nationalism and the revolutionary fervour of 1916 and later the War of Independence.

The majority of the Irish soldiers, whether soldier, reservist or enlister, would have seen the war as a just one. It would have formed part of the *esprit de corps* in their army life. If economic factors induced a person into the army, it did not preclude him from thinking it was also the right and just thing to do. For those who enlisted after the war started, as early as November 1914 and certainly by that Christmas, it was clear that the war entailed massive casualties. However economically beneficial it was to join the army, there was the distinct possibility that one could be wounded or even killed. The *Cork Examiner* constantly published soldiers' letters endorsing the view that they were fighting for liberty in Europe and for Ireland. One letter was from a Blackpool soldier:

CORKMAN'S LETTER FROM THE FRONT

Quartermaster Sheehan, 1st Leinsters, a Blackpool man, writing from the front to Mr. James McMahon, Paradise Place, Cork, expresses himself in the characteristic fashion of the Irish soldier. He says: – 'Well, we will be on the move again in few days' time, and God only knows what part of the country we shall be in the next. Suffice it to say that the Huns do not at all like the division we are in. We were always able to wallop them whenever they chose to meet us. Even their gases do not stop our fellows, and we nearly always have the green flag flying near our trenches. They curse the Irish when they see it, and our fellows give them all they want, I assure you, when opportunity arises. Well, Mr. Tirpitz has resigned, I see. Gott strafe him anyhow. [Naval Secretary of the German government, he had resigned over the reversion to cruiser rules ordered by the German Government after the sinking of the SS

Arabic in August 1915 with the further loss of civilian life including American citizens.] I trust I will be spared to see ye about Xmas, and may victory be ours in the not distant future. I dare say your sons will be out soon, and I am proud they heard the call, and trust they will never be sorry for the step they have taken. It is a fine principle to fight for freedom, and may the Hun perish in his attempt to Prussianise the world. I wish I had time to give vent to my feelings.[10]

The industries of Blackpool also responded supportively to the war effort. There is evidence that both Murphy's Brewery and Goulding Ltd assured employees who wanted to enlist that their jobs would be retained for them on their return and gave a war bonus to their remaining employees as war inflation began to have an effect on prices in the wider economy. Gouldings even went so far as to offer supplementary payments to the wives and dependents of their employees who joined the army.[11] As mentioned before, eighteen employees from Murphy's enlisted in the British army, four of them from Blackpool. Over 200 joined up from Goulding Ltd, which was a nationwide company, but it can be estimated that between thirty and forty of them came from the Spring Lane plant which had a workforce of about 300, including William Mehigan. Based on those employees who died in the war, again a figure of between thirty and forty enlisted from the Cork Spinning and Weaving Company. The figure from Harrington's Paint Factory must have been proportionately similar. Mr William Harrington had a son, Lieutenant Charles Stanley Lawrence Harrington, 1st Battalion Connaught Rangers, who died in the war.

Murphy's Brewery, Gouldings and Harrington's (Shandon Chemical Works) contributed to the war fund. Sir William J. Goulding, as chairman of the company, donated a massive £10,000 (roughly €4 million) directly to the war effort. It has been established that at Murphy's Brewery there also existed from September 1914 onwards a voluntary weekly war fund to which the workers themselves could contribute by means of a permanent collection point on the brewery site.[12] There is no reason to suggest that the practice, and the others mentioned above, were not replicated throughout the industries of Blackpool, indicating the cohesive response of an urban community like Blackpool to the First World War.

There were benefits to the industries of Blackpool from the war. Murphy's Brewery rented stores to the British army on Pine St (off Coburg St) for £7 10 shillings per month in 1916 and later the same with some storerooms on Leitrim and Devonshire St (off Coburg St). They also increased their sales of stout and ales to the army in the Cork area during the war, which was crowned by their breaking of the Beamish and Crawford monopoly of supply to Victoria Barracks. In January 1915 management at the Brewery allowed the army, at request, to use their five-ton Garret steam engine (produced in 1914) and its trained driver. But it was not all positive: the Brewery had to refuse requests in 1916 to supply the Irish soldiers in France and Flanders due to restrictions. These restrictions also meant lower levels of alcohol in their products and importantly, more restrictive opening hours for all public houses due to Defence of the Realm Act (DORA) which meant sales were curtailed.[13] This resulted in lay-offs at the brewery during 1917.

However at Goulding Ltd the war offered the company not only the opportunity but the duty to increase their production and sales. This they could do once their supplies of phosphate from North Africa and America and pyrite from Spain had been assured safe passage by the efforts of the Royal Navy which the chairman of Goulding Ltd, Sir William Goulding, thanked publicly at the AGM in Dublin in August 1915. However, increased freight rates would at times disturb the importation of such vital raw materials during the war. At this meeting he also expressed the view that 'the whole of Europe is engaged in a life and death struggle, and the end of which none of us can foresee, except that in the end, whatever the sacrifices, we are going to win, and I hope, put an end for ever to the militarism which has been oppressing Europe for the last generation'.[14] Sir William recognised it as a duty for Ireland to expand its cultivation of land to make Britain and Ireland more food secure and acknowledged the cooperation between themselves and the government in this regard. Gouldings had been working with the Department of Agriculture and the technical institutions

in efforts to increase crop return from fertiliser use and these
experiments had proved successful. Goulding's plant in Spring Lane
was run by James Douglas with the help of Mr. A. Young (works
manager) and despite a fire in September 1915, which seriously
depleted production for three months, the factory would go on to
produce 10,000 tons of plant food in 1916. Some of the fertiliser
was exported to Britain and other countries as Gouldings was one
of the biggest fertiliser producers in the British Isles at the time.

The outbreak of the war proved a difficulty to the biggest
employer in Blackpool, the Cork Spinning and Weaving Company
at Millfield. They had been receiving their flax from Belgium but
obviously this ceased after August 1914. They surmounted this
problem with 'larger supplies than usual having been procured from
the South of Ireland' and 'other kinds of flax'. One of the sources of
flax was from Russia in 1916, which the government had helped to
arrange for the company, but after the revolutions there in 1917 the
company's yearly report noted that 'supplies from Russia have been
stopped owing to the unfortunate state of that country'.[15] Under the
management of J. H. Sutcliffe the factory employed 1,000 workers,
mostly female, working 20,000 spindles, and produced a number
of different fabrics like, 'Fancy Ticks, Flannelettes, Shirtings,
Sheetings, Zephyrs, Apron Chocks, Sun Blinds, Towelling, Bengal
Stripes, Galateas, Dungarees and Regattas, Bleached Calico and
Grey Calico' with the warm, non-inflammable flannelette one of
their most popular products.

Importantly the mill began to do 'a large trade for government
work and aeroplane yarns'. In fact, during 1917 the British
government, who controlled Irish flax, required of the company
that spinners 'spin Yarns only suitable for war work, and to reduce
production by stopping machinery in which Aeroplane Yarns
cannot be spun'. This effectively incorporated the factory directly
and totally into the industrial base of the war effort for the last
year and a half of the war. Linen produced at Millfield, Blackpool,
would be shipped to aeroplane manufacturing sites like the British
and Colonial Aeroplane Company at Bristol, England or Sopwith
Aviation Company and the Aircraft Manufacturing Company

outside London, where the linen would be sewed and wrapped around the fighter and observation planes of the Royal Flying Corps (later in April 1918 Royal Air Force). Not only did the women of the Flax Factory at Millfield have brothers, fathers, sons, friends and co-workers fighting in the war, they themselves were very much part of the home front that underpinned the British and Irish war effort.[16]

Not everybody was caught up in the mild British imperialistic fervour that swept over Cork city in the first few weeks and months of the war. A very small group of Irish Volunteers had rejected totally John Redmond's endorsement of the British war effort. To them only a national independent parliament could give such legitimacy for Irishmen to fight in France. Until then the real enemy remained the British colonial rulers. The formal break amongst the Volunteers in Cork occurred on 28 September 1914 with the Redmondites forming the National Volunteers and those opposed retaining the name 'Irish Volunteers'. The split had reduced the Irish Volunteers in Cork to a core of about 200 for the first year of the war.[17] As these were mostly rural members it would mean that the vast majority of the fifty-eight Volunteers from Blackpool joined Redmond's National Volunteers, and of them, it could be deduced from the urban and industrial nature of Blackpool and an estimate of 27,000 National Volunteers that enlisted in total, that around eighteen Blackpool National Volunteers joined the British army.

The handful of Irish Volunteers in Blackpool received a boost when one the leaders of the movement in Cork, Tomás MacCurtain, returned to Blackpool during 1915 and opened a shop at 40 York St/Thomas Davis St which had a mill and flax factory at the back. The Irish Volunteers, nationally and in Cork, were an isolated group for the first year of the war. Flor O'Donoghue, a prominent figure during the War of Independence, claimed that during this period they were treated like criminals.[18] Their parades were at times jeered and even stoned. The MacCurtain family experienced some of this hostility directly, as their granddaughter Fionnuala MacCurtain recounts in her biography of her grandfather:

> Some of the workers from the Flax factory [Millfield], whose husbands
> were in the British Army, used to swarm around the children and
> Elizabeth's [wife of Tomás] door at night shouting abuse. Elizabeth
> could understand why they were annoyed but believed that they were
> misguided.[19]

The authorities also harassed the leading members of the Irish
Volunteers, forcing some of them into exile. Terence MacSwiney's
pro-German *Fianna Fáil* paper was closed down in December 1914
and Tomás MacCurtain's house in Blackpool was raided a number
of times, usually in the early hours of the morning.

Despite it all, the Irish Volunteers persisted, most of them driven
by their deep love of the Irish language and culture which gave their
political movement an almost spiritual dimension. By the end of
1915 there were distinct signs that the Irish Volunteers were gaining
support within Irish society. The war was not only dragging on, it
seemed endless. The hope of victory by Christmas 1914 or within
the year had evaporated, leaving in its wake horrendous numbers
of casualties with little gain. Not only that but when the British
and Allied forces retreated and withdrew from Gallipoli and the
invasion of Turkey in late 1915, the British Empire suffered a very
bloody defeat. For James Connolly, socialist and Irish nationalist,
it was a herald of things to come: 'How about the Dardanelles
now? Was I not correct in my forecast? It looks blue for the poor
Empire.'[20]

4

Gallipoli and Loos: Defeat and the Long War

WHEN THE WESTERN FRONT had been truly established as a formidable military fortress of trenches by December 1914, discussions over other means of circumventing this apparent stalemate began to circulate in Britain. These views gained more traction when Tsar Nicholas of Russia asked for help in relation to the Caucasus offensive by Turkey in January and February 1915. Turkey had entered the war in late October 1914 after attacking some Russian ports and ships in the Black Sea. Turkey's government, led by Enver Pasha, had eventually favoured the Germans whom they thought would win the war and thus enhance Turkey's position as a powerful force in the Middle East as well as aiding its policy agenda within Turkey. One idea developed within British military circles, which had ultimate preference over others, through the able persuasion of Winston Churchill amongst others, was for an attack on the forts of the Dardanelles to open the straits permanently, allowing access to Russia and also providing the possibility of toppling the Turkish government by means of a naval bombardment of Constantinople. Such an event could have changed the war dramatically, bringing Greece, Bulgaria, and Romania in the Balkans to join the Allies while also persuading wavering Italy to do the same.[1]

The naval bombardment of the forts that protected the Dardanelles Strait began on 19 February 1915 but had a limited effect due to the flat trajectory of the naval guns against the Turkish forts and the ability of their more mobile artillery to escape.

Minesweeping the straits remained too dangerous for the navy and so on 18 March a large naval assault was launched on the whole defensive system of the Dardanelles. This too proved unsuccessful as three ships were sunk and three were disabled. Admiral of the Fleet John de Roebuck (from Naas, County Kildare) asked for land troops to neutralise the Turkish artillery and so began plans for the Gallipoli landings. The man responsible for the plan was Commander-in-Chief Sir Ian Hamilton. By 25 April 1915 he had amassed 30,000 troops for one of the biggest military amphibious attacks the world had seen.

The force consisted of one French division but was comprised mainly of Australian, New Zealand and British troops, which included a number of Irish regiments most notably, the 1st Battalion Royal Munster Fusiliers and the 1st Battalion Royal Dublin Fusiliers. Australia, New Zealand and Canada had all responded immediately in support of Britain's declaration of war, which was viewed by most of their inhabitants as a fair and just stance by the mother country. Ties were still very strong between Britain and the ex-colonies. Of all the Australians that enlisted in 1914 about 30 per cent of those had been born in Britain.[2] This figure probably included men from Ireland like Patrick and Robert Kieley, whose parents ran a flour and meal store at 29 York St/Thomas Davis St and Thomas Williams of Dublin Hill. Patrick Kieley enlisted at Perth, Western Australia, while Robert did so in Melbourne and Thomas Williams enlisted at Brisbane Queensland. Thomas Williams went to school at the North Monastery and had left his expectant wife, Ellen, and their one-year-old child, Hannah, in their new house on Dublin Hill, to join his brother in Australia to set up a new life. His twelve-year experience as a soldier with the Munster Fusiliers probably acted as a spur to his rejoining the army when the war broke out and it put him in good stead for promotion (he was made a corporal immediately with the 15th Battalion of the Australian Infantry Force (AIF)). By November 1914 he had become a sergeant within the burgeoning Australian army. Even though Patrick Kieley described himself as a mechanical engineer on attestation (he had described himself as an 'engine fitter' on the census of 1911 back in Blackpool), he did not join the Engineering Corps but instead served with the 11th Battalion AIF. He is representative of the first wave of Irish soldiers who enlisted from civilian life in 1914 to experience military action for the first time.

Sergeant Thomas Williams embarked for Europe with the 15th Battalion AIF on the HMAT *Ceramic* at Melbourne on 22 December 1914. He would soon join Patrick Kieley's 11th Battalion in Egypt where they would be informed of the new plans for the invasion of Gallipoli. By then the Australian and New Zealand forces had been combined as the Australian and New Zealand Army Corps, known as ANZAC. The plan was a two-pronged amphibious assault consisting of the main attacking force of the British and French troops landing on five beaches on the southernmost tip of the Dardanelles at Cape Helles, with the other prong 15 miles north at Ari Burnu and Gaba Tebe, which became known as Anzac Cove as the landing troops were ANZACs. After landing the British would advance up from the south meeting the ANZACs after they had successfully driven inland, thus gaining dominance of the Gallipoli peninsula and of the straits.[3]

Historians largely agree that the Dardanelles Strait was one of the most unfavourable places in which to launch a seaborne military attack and even more so in the choice of areas in which the Allies did land. Its gullies, ravines and gorges, which were covered in thorny, impenetrable scrub, were shielded by stony foothills that rose to 800 feet, as at Sari Bair, which had natural fortress-like qualities that the Turks, who knew the land, used so well.[4] The naval bombardments had alerted the Turkish army on the Straits, under the control of the German General, Otto Liman von Sanders, to the prospect of invasion and hence to strengthen their defences in the area. Liman von Sanders would write in 1928 that 'the preparation of the enemy were excellent their only defect being that they were based on reconnaissance that were too old and that they underestimated the powers of resistance of the Turkish soldier.'[5]

The initial landing troops for the ANZACs consisted of 4,000 soldiers, including Patrick Kieley's 11th Battalion which was part of the 3rd Infantry Brigade; while at Helles the first wave of 3,000 troops included the 29th Division with elements of Royal Naval Division.[6] All soldiers had practised disembarkation for a few weeks on the island of Lemnos. When the 1st Battalion Royal Munster Fusiliers and the 1st Battalion Royal Dublin Fusiliers left Mudros, a port on Lemnos, on 23 April they had 'TO CONSTANTINOPLE' written on the side of the ship, such was their optimism amidst the cheering crews and the music of the bands. Captain Geddes of the Munsters, however, later recorded: 'What struck me most forcibly was the demeanour of our men, from whom, not a sound, and this from the light-hearted, devil may care men from the South of Ireland. Even they were filled with a sense of something impending which was quite beyond their ken.'[7]

The ANZAC forces to the north were to land first as their commander, General Birdwood, wanted to use surprise and the cover of darkness to launch the attack, while at Helles it was to be preceded by a naval bombardment.

The 11th Battalion AIF's objective was on the left section and the capture of the height called Chunuk Bair. The first wave of the attack consisted of 500 troops from 9th and 10th Battalions with the remainder following, with the 11th and 12th Battalion landing in the second and third wave. According to the 11th Battalion's war diary they landed at 4.30 a.m. 'under heavy musketry + machine gun fire' and, seemingly, mostly in the wrong areas. In some cases they were facing fire from cliffs 200 feet high. Confusion reigned as battalions got mixed up with the only clear signal to move forward, up the hills through the thick scrub, against fire from the Turks who controlled the heights. One section of the 11th Battalion reached furthest inland, passing the inland crest of Baby 700, going towards Chunuk Bair, but were stopped by withering machine-gun fire. By now shrapnel fire began to rain down on the Australian troops. In other areas soldiers rushed entrenched Turkish positions but these were largely uncoordinated. These assaults were definitively halted by Turkish counter-attacks led by the future leader of post-war Turkey, Mustafa Kemal (Atatürk).[8]

By 3.30 p.m., under constant fire by rifle, machine gun and artillery, the ANZAC force began to dig in. They had no support from their own artillery. They were being pushed back to positions that would be their line of defence, rather than attack, for the next eight months. The beach was secure and by 6 p.m. 15,000 men were on shore, including two companies of 15th Battalion. The rest of Thomas William's battalion would not reach the shore until 9.00 a.m. the next morning. By that time it is estimated that there were at least 2,000 ANZAC casualties, with a similar number for the Turks. Patrick Kieley was reported missing and it was later established that he had been seen rushing forward from an Australian entrenched position, never to be seen again. He was the first man from Blackpool who enlisted after the war broke out to die. His battalion war diary stated that on that day they had 'cleared the heights of the Turks': they had, but not the further heights that overlooked them.[9]

It was much worse at Cape Helles. Four companies of Munsters, two of the 11th Battalion Hampshire Regiment and a company of the Dublin Fusiliers, had transferred to a collier, the SS *River Clyde*, which was nicknamed 'the Trojan Horse', as it had been specially modified with cut-out doors on the hull fitted with rolling-out ramparts for the troops to disembark onto smaller boats tied to the ship and then to shore. The Munsters were heading towards 'V' Beach, the cove at Sedd-el-Bahr, which was partially enclosed by cliffs and had two forts. The naval bombardment started at 5 a.m. and included the super-dreadnought HMS *Queen Elizabeth*. The *River Clyde* beached as planned at 6.30 a.m. with two companies of Dublin Fusiliers in tow on smaller boats. These boats were fired upon immediately and suffered great casualties as they struggled to get to shore. Five minutes later the doors opened on the *Clyde* and 'off went the men cheering wildly and dashed ashore' down the ramparts. Captain Geddes recalled:

> We got it like anything, man after man behind me was shot down but they never wavered ... Captain French of the Dublins told me afterwards that he counted the first 48 men to follow me, and they all fell. I think no finer episode could be found of the men's bravery and discipline than this – of leaving the safety of the *River Clyde* to go to what was practically certain death.

All the smaller boats (lighters) were filled with wounded or dead. Soldiers tried to swim ashore but were either shot there or drowned, weighed down by the heavy pack of rations and ammunition. The sea began to turn red. Captain Geddes, and all who survived the dash to shore, made for a sheltered ledge which gave them cover. He estimated that at this point they had lost 70 per cent of his company. They managed to secure the right part of the beach. Nearly all who had died by this point had not fired their rifle or seen a Turk. The naval guns took up the battle and the rest of the landing troops waited till dark to come ashore. Private Michael McAuliffe of Millfield Cottages, Blackpool, was among the fallen Munsters.[10]

During the night the Turks at times attacked the beach but were repulsed. Captain Geddes was wounded and retired back to ship. On the morning of 26 April a renewed effort was made to secure the whole cove. It was done against ferocious fire from the Turks and greatly strengthened entrenchments of barbed wire.[11] Corporal William Cosgrove, from Aghada, County Cork, earned a Victoria Cross for clearing barbed wire in the face of enemy fire. By 2 p.m. they had overrun the forts and were 1½ miles inland. The invading force was relieved at dawn on 27 April after staving off repeated Turkish counter-attacks. On the other four beach landings around Cape Helles, three were easily attained with little opposition. Slowly the four sections of the invading forces began to merge (the fifth beach (Y) to the north was evacuated) and on 28 April the Munsters were called into action again for a general advance towards Krithia. Here again, as at Anzac Cove, the Allies were put on the defensive by the tenacious counter-attacks of the Turkish army. So great were the casualties that the Dublin and Munster Fusiliers had to merge their battalions to maintain fighting formation and named themselves the 'Dubsters'.

On 12 May the 29th Division, which included the Munsters and the Dublin Fusiliers, were withdrawn to rest for five days. By then the front lines at Cape Helles and at Anzac Cove had formed into static trench-like formations similar to those of the Western Front.[12] Thomas Williams, with the 15th Battalion AIF at Anzac Cove, had been wounded on 26 April and spent the next two months in hospital. He was promoted to Company Sergeant Major. The rest for the 1ˢᵗ Battalion Munster Fusiliers allowed the men time to write home and Private Patrick Doyle from Walshe's Avenue, Blackpool (and of the Roche's Guards Band) did so. It was published in the *Examiner* and though it claimed that he had died in the assault, he had not:

> Just a line, hoping this will find you and all at home in the best of health, as it leaves me, at present. I suppose you have already heard how the Munsters and the Dublins fared out here. It was a terrible sight to witness the day we were taking a village called Siddel Bar. The two regiments mustering together charged the enemy and completely routed them – that was a six mile charge without a single stop; and glad I am to say that all the boys of the district are quite safe; there is only one chap that I saw dead, and his name is McAuliffe [Private Michael McAuliffe from Millfield Cottages] and he resides at Blackpool. I was very sorry for him, as he used to tell me that he was the only support of his mother. A younger brother of his is fighting in France. I met William Carroll out here, he has changed a great deal since I saw him last; he had become such a fine fellow, you would hardly know him if you met him now ... Our losses out here are a bit heavy, but as you know one cannot expect to get great gains without on the other hand having great losses. The Turks do not want to fight at all; it is the Germans that are urging them on. Well, you may be sure that we shall have those German officers one of these days. I hope that I shall live to see the end of this terrible calamity. The *Queen Elizabeth* is a fine ship, and her ton shells are very well able to find their mark. We advanced while near shore under the protection of her great guns. Well, hoping to hear from you soon. – Your fond Chum, P. Doyle[13]

Private Patrick Doyle
of Walshe's Avenue.
(*Cork Examiner*)

During June and July a new offensive in Gallipoli was devised with the additional help of three fresh divisions including the Irish 10th Division. The 10th Division included troops who were civilian recruits and were the first from Ireland to see military action. The main thrust of the new offensive was to push on from Anzac Cove but which coincided with a fresh landing further north at Suvla Bay to help circumvent the Turkish positions. At Helles Cape only diversionary attacks would be carried out to tie down reinforcements.[14] General Birdwood's own plan for the Anzac Cove attack also involved a diversionary battle for Lone Pine which turned out to be one of the most hard-fought struggles of the offensive if not of the whole campaign. The main assault would be divided into two objectives, one heading for Chunuk Bair and the other taking a wider loop through unknown country to Hill 971. Charged with taking Hill 971 was General Monash who had control of 4th Brigade which included Thomas Williams' 15th Battalion AIF. Twenty-ninth Brigade of 10th Division were assigned to Anzac Cove while the remainder of the division was to land at Suvla Bay. Their aim there was to take Kiretch Tepe Ridge furthest north, advance forward onto Tekke Tepe, and then to link up with Anzac troops at the end of the second day encircling the Turks on Hill Baby 700 and Battleship Hill. After eliminating the enemy positions, the Allies would head for Maidos and take control of the Dardanelle Strait.[15]

The plan relied on good coordination and strict timing to maximise surprise but this did not allow for the harsh terrain of labyrinthine pathways through unknown scrubland, rivers and gullies in the blazing heat. It started on 6 August and initially went well with the attack at Lone Pine ultimately successful and the New Zealanders heading towards Chunuk Bair without a major setback. However, by the morning of 7 August German Colonel Hans Kennegians stirred his Turkish forces to resistance in the area. Monash's 4th Brigade set out for the hills of Abel Rehman Spur on the same morning to take Hill 971. The route was maze-like, resulting in 15th Battalion, amongst others, winding up on heights believing they were in one area, while in reality they were in another, all the time being fired upon by the Turks. By midday on 7 August they were not in a position to attack.[16]

Of the three new divisions, half of 13th Division and 29th Brigade (10th Division), which included 5th Battalion Connaught Rangers, were diverted to Anzac Cove, landing on 7 August. The 11th Division had landed at Suvla on 6 August and had achieved their goals on the southern side but to the north they failed to make progress up Kiretch Tepe Ridge. The leading battalions of the 10th Division landed at Suvla at 5.30 a.m. on 7 August but due to the difficulties encountered by the 11th Division were forced to land further down the coast. This disturbed and delayed plans. They ended up on a coordinated attack on the southern side of Suvla Bay against Turkish forces on 'Chocolate Hill' and Green Hills. They succeeded, which showed that the New Army, which was composed of troops who were civilians who had enlisted after the war started, were capable soldiers. The evening of 7 August witnessed the remainder of the 10th Division, including the 6th and 7th Battalions of the Royal Munster Fusiliers, arrive at Suvla with General Mahon. Their aim was the capture on the still-untaken Kiretch Tepe Ridge and in doing so protect the left flank of the troops on the Anafarta Plain to the south.[17]

At Anzac Cove on 7 August, the New Zealand attack on Chunuk Bair failed. Monash now was given extra troops to hold the line he had reached on that day which allowed his 14th, 15th and 16th Battalions AIF to launch an assault on Abdel Rahman on 8 August, the objective before Hill 971. He was supposed to attack at 4.15 a.m. when the artillery barrage had lifted but nobody knew that Monash's forces were actually farther behind than expected. When the three battalions set off they thought they were climbing Abdel Rahman, but were in fact on another hill. They still received Turkish machine-gun fire from Alai Tepe, which remained unmolested by Anzac artillery. The leading 15th Battalion, which included Company Sergeant Thomas Williams, spread out into attack formation. Its commander sought help from 14th Battalion to counter the heaviest fire coming from the left but received only partial aid. The 16th Battalion were even further behind than the

14th to offer assistance. The war diary of the 15th records, 'the enemy having counter attacked in strength on our left front and left flank and our line being very thinly held + began to gradually fall back'. Contact was made with HQ and as Turkish shrapnel began to fall, the order to withdraw was given.[18]

Thomas Williams was shot in the chest and was one of the 200 wounded of the 15th Battalion alone and which had also suffered over 100 fatalities. Thomas managed, most likely by stretcher, to make it back to the shore where Irish troops of the 29th Brigade witnessed the arrival of the copious numbers of wounded being laid out on the beaches. He was placed on the hospital ship *Devanha* which set off for Alexandria in Egypt. He died four days later on 12 August on board ship from his wounds and was buried at Chatby Military and War Memorial Cemetery, Alexandria.[19]

The 6th and 7th Battalions of the Munsters had on the morning of 8 August succeeded in the northern sector of Suvla Bay in gaining an objective. The evening before, they began the climb of the 600-foot ridge of Kiretch Tepe with the preliminary goal of overtaking a Turkish strong point called the 'Pimple', which was held by about 500 Turkish troops with two guns. By the time they were within 100 yards of an entrenched Turkish position (well before the 'Pimple') it was too dark to attack and they dug in for a dawn charge. The navy helped secure their position and weaken the Turkish stronghold by bombardment and searchlights exposing the Turks to fire. The bayonet charge at dawn was led by Major Jephson and succeeded in overrunning the stronghold. In the process Major Jephson was mortally wounded and the place was named 'Jephson's Post' in his honour. The Munsters suffered 48 killed and 150 wounded in all and were too exhausted to advance further, hindered greatly by the heat and lack of water. One of the Munsters on that day who helped to protect the gained trenches from a westward attack was Private James Jones from Millfield Cottages, Blackpool.[20]

The advance across Kiretch Tepe Ridge was a strategically important objective as behind the enemy lines in that area were, firstly, water springs to aid the troops and more significantly, a very large Turkish ammunition dump for the peninsula as a whole. The next day, 9 August, the Munsters tried to advance but were beaten back as the Turks had strengthened their forces under Major Kendir, the ridge commander. What developed then were aggressive raids by each side on each other's trenches, which resulted in mounting casualties throughout the day. Private James Jones was killed in action at some point during the day. He was the fourth man from the small collection of houses at Millfield Cottages to die in the war which was just over a year old at this stage. He had a brother in the army and two others soon to be.

The attack at Suvla, as at Anzac Cove, had faltered. The commanding stretch of heights from Suvla running down parallel to the coast to Anzac Cove had not been captured. Another attempt was made on Kiretch Tepe Ridge on 15 August, which included the 6th Battalion Munster Fusiliers and 7th Battalion Dublin Fusiliers. This time they climbed past Jephson's Post to capture the 'Pimple' and took a dominating hold of the heights. This could have been a turning point. However, their right flank was exposed and no reinforcements came.[21] In a few days they were driven back by tenacious Turkish fighting. The last Allied offensive of the Gallipoli campaign came on 21 August at Scimitar Hill, on the southern side of Suvla Bay, coinciding with an assault on Hill 60 at Anzac Cove; again, the objective was to unite forces and advance after both were taken. The 29th Division, including the 1st Battalion Munster Fusiliers, who had been transferred by ship to Suvla from Cape Helles on 20 August, were to be part of the attacking troops at Scimitar Hill, while the 5th Battalion Connaught Rangers of 10th Division formed part of the ANZAC attacking force for Hill 60.

The 5th Connaught Rangers had been at Anzac Cove since 7 August and had suffered continual casualties while helping the wounded, especially on 8 August, and carrying out other duties, such as trench improvements and water carrying. The attack on Hill 60 was to be their first attack and their objective was the capture of the Kabak Kagin Wells. It started at 3.30 p.m. and ten minutes later the first company of Rangers dashed forward and were 'clear through the gap + with great dash made for the wells and trenches'; they then were followed by D Company 'in successive lines at 4 paces distance all cheering with fixed bayonets but no firing was allowed until the line was won'. [22] They rushed the trenches successfully and then wheeled to the right, cleared the Turkish communication trench and forced the Turks out. Soon these trenches were under artillery fire. On the right, however, the New Zealanders were fairing badly against entrenched Turkish positions on Hill 60 itself. Some of A Company of the Rangers managed to support the Kiwis in a trench on the hill which then prompted more of the Rangers at the Wells, under Captain Jourdain, to come to their aid.

The Rangers attacked up the hill and were met with withering fire from the Turks. The war diary records that

> the charge was most brilliantly and gallantly carried out + although the losses were severe the Battalion held on gallantly throughout the night of the 21–22 August [Strangely enough the anniversary of its formation] + the next evening were relieved with the exception of 10 Officers + 50 men + marched back to the bivouac of two nights ago behind the S.W.B. [South Wales Borderers] entrenchments. They had done splendid work in digging saps to the New Zealand trenches and to the <u>WELL</u> + the position was secure when they had left it.

The diary also recorded that 46 were killed and 167 were wounded in the attack with 47 missing and that total casualties for the 5th Connaught Rangers up to that point were 401 excluding sick. Ranger Patrick Murphy from Spring Lane, and a Roche's Guards Band member, died of wounds on 23 August. Another Ranger, Thomas Murphy from St John's Square, Blackpool, who worked at the Flax Factory, was also involved in the attack. He died in hospital on the island of Lemnos on 16 November 1915.

The assault on Scimitar Hill at Suvla Bay had commenced a half an hour earlier at 3 p.m. with an artillery barrage. It provoked a Turkish counter-artillery shelling which resulted in the scrub in the area being set alight, indicating the parched nature of the land. This significantly affected the attack. Each of the 1st Battalion of the Munsters were told to bring no pack but instead 'carry a piece of biscuit tin 6in scale for marking captured trenches. 200 rounds SAA [single-action ammunition]'. The charge was met with frontal

Private Patrick Murphy,
Connaught Rangers. (*Cork Examiner*)

Private Denis Donovan, 1st
Battalion Royal Munster
Fusiliers. (*Cork Examiner*)

and enfilading fire but a section of the attackers managed, briefly, to take the summit of the hill. However, 'shrapnel and machine gun fire ripped into the Irish troops and they broke and ran back down the Hill. Dead and wounded lay all over the western slopes' as the scrub burned.[23] There would be more attempts on Hill 60 but these too were repulsed by the Turks. Casualties were very high with 5,000 dead or wounded out of the 14,300 troops. The Munsters had 400 casualties, nearly half of the battalion. Among those who fell was Private Denis Donovan from Madden's Buildings, Blackpool; he had arrived at the Dardanelles on 1 August 1915.

Overall casualties among the Allies for the August offensives were 40,000 and the breakout at Anzac Cove had not been achieved. Military historians have subsequently poured scorn on the Allied commanders who led this offensive and the whole campaign and pointed to their failures at one point or the other. The bravery and courage of the soldiers is well documented against Turkish forces that were unremitting in their steadfast defence of their homeland under the inspirational leadership of Mustafa Kemal. After 28 August there were no more Allied offensives but instead their forces hunkered down as if under siege. Commander-in-Chief Ian

Hamilton was replaced by Sir Charles Munro who recommended withdrawing to the British government. This was accepted and the troops at Suvla and Anzac Cove were evacuated in December without incident. The soldiers at Cape Helles had to wait until January 1916. The Irish troops were heading to Salonika in Greece.

In all, 410,000 British and Empire soldiers and 79,000 French troops passed through the Gallipoli campaign of which 205,000 and 47,000 respectively became casualties.[24] British estimates put the casualties for the Turks at 251,000 but this may have been higher. For Australia and New Zealand the sacrifice made by their countrymen at Gallipoli has been interpreted as a transformational act, turning them from colonies to independent nations. The first Anzac Day was commemorated in Australia on the anniversary of the landings, 25 April 1916.

Many Blackpool men fought at Gallipoli and survived. Royal Marine Engineer Timothy Kelly, who lived on Spangle Hill, had his left hand injured in June, which put him out of the rest of the Gallipoli campaign. Included among this 'band of brothers' were two actual brothers: Denis and David O'Connell from Spring Lane. Denis was wounded at Cape Helles but survived. However, the injury he sustained probably undermined his health and he died subsequently of tuberculosis at home in Cork, aged twenty-five, on 1 November 1916 and was buried at Rathcooney, the local cemetery for Blackpool. He was thus the eighth soldier from Blackpool to die as a result of the Gallipoli campaign, six of whom were killed in action. Denis and David had two other brothers in the army in 1915, one of whom has been mentioned before: James O'Connell. He was taken prisoner at Étreux in August 1914 and was in a camp in Germany. The fourth brother was Michael O'Connell who joined the 2nd Battalion Leinster Regiment on the Western Front in February 1915. The 2nd Leinsters were part of the 6th Division which had been stationed in the south of Ireland, in Munster, at the start of the war and were positioned on the Ypres Salient in trenches opposite Wieltje, a couple of miles from Ypres itself. My grandfather Gus Birmingham was a driver for the 2nd Brigade Royal Field Artillery which were part of the divisional artillery of the 6th

Division. After the war he would settle at Scourragh Hill at the top of Spring Lane and quite close to the O'Connell household. He would more than likely been on duty on 1 August 1915 when the war diary of the Leinsters records: 'Considerable shelling of Wieltje and forward trenches with field guns.' This must have provoked a retaliation as the next day B Company of the 2nd Leinsters received heavy shelling which resulted in eleven casualties and two killed.[25] Private Michael O'Connell was one of those killed. His father, also called Michael, received a letter from Fr P. J. Maloney, the Leinster's chaplain, which was published in the *Cork Examiner* on 9 August 1915:

BRAVE CORK SOLDIER
KILLED WHILE HELPING COMRADE

Mr. Michael O'Connell of 48 Spring lane, Cork, has received a letter from Rev. P. J. Moloney, Chaplain of the 2nd Leinsters, giving details of the gallant death of his son, Private Michael O'Connell of that regiment. One of his comrades had been wounded, and O'Connell was assisting him out of the danger zone, when he, himself, was struck by a German bullet which killed him. 'He died' says Father Moloney, 'literally in the act of performing a heroic act of charity. The good God will assuredly bless him and reward him. He lived long enough in the trench for me to anoint him there and give him the last blessing – R.I.P. His C.O., his officers and comrades join with me in sending you their hearty sympathy in your great loss. We had a Requiem Mass behind the trenches for himself and another comrade killed at the same time – this morning (August 3). He is buried next to the Church of St Jean near — . We have erected a small cross near his grave.'

Such letters were very common and they were regularly printed in the *Cork Examiner*, especially during the first year and a half of the war. When his son Denis died in November 1916, Michael O'Connell senior from Spring Lane became the first father from Blackpool to lose two sons because of the war.

After the failure of the Allied offensives at Gallipoli in August, attention once more was paid to the Western Front for a break-through. The Germans were on the defensive here, given their

Private Michael O'Connell, 2nd Battalion Leinster Regiment. (*Cork Examiner*)

military focus on the eastern front. Knowing this, French Commander-in-Chief General Joffre wanted a renewed offensive in the west as the French army had 200,000 more men than in December 1914. He planned the biggest bombardment of the German lines since the war began with the help of even the guns of the fortresses scattered all over France. The plan involved a two-pronged attack each side of the 'Noyon Bulge' with one front at Champagne and another at Artois. Joffre believed it would win the war. The French government acquiesced to his plan believing that without it the Russians would be in danger in the east. They also demanded a quick cessation if success was not immediate. Joffre and General Foch put pressure on the British to join the offensive with their area of attack assigned to the north of Artois at the Loos sector. Even though the British commanders disliked their allocated area, believing it was too open to German observation of the assault, they too acquiesced due to Kitchener's belief that without a show of support to Joffre, the French were in danger of going weak and even signing a separate peace deal with the Germans.[26]

The start date was 25 September and in the British sector at Loos, a four-day bombardment was carried out, which lost the element of surprise but was believed to have a greater ability to destroy the German ramparts. For the first time the British used gas in an attack which allowed them also to widen the front of the assault and use six divisions instead of two, making it the biggest of their war yet. It was also the first time on the Western Front that a newly trained division was used in an offensive. The 2nd Royal Munster Fusiliers were again involved but this time only in support of the assaulting troops of 1st and 2nd Brigade. They were at Corons de Rutoire, west of Hulluch. At 5.51 a.m., 5,243 cylinders of chlorine gas were opened and 150 tons discharged until 6.30 a.m. despite the fact that weather conditions were not assuredly favourable. The gas did aid the attack in the northern sector at the Hohenzollern Redoubt but in other areas the result was decidedly mixed: at times it returned to cover some British trenches while in other areas it hovered in no-man's-land.[27]

The infantry attacked at 6.30 a.m. Despite suffering significant losses the British forces managed to infiltrate the first line of the German defences and were at one point through to the second, but as reinforcements were too far behind, they failed to exploit it. The Munsters suffered some casualties in getting to the supporting trenches after the assault had begun. The communication trenches were filled with wounded, some of them due to chlorine gas even though the troops had been issued with gas helmets and blankets. One company of Munsters under Major Considine decided to aid an attack by 2nd Brigade at 'lone pine' who were being held up by German machine-gun fire and thus endangering that sector's whole attack. They were completely routed: 118 were killed or wounded. As the historian Thomas Johnstone wrote, 'It was a heroic attempt but a complete waste of gallant men.'[28] The rest of the battalion moved forward and occupied captured trenches which they consolidated. They remained there until 29 September.

The offensive was renewed the next day using two new divisions, the 21st and 24th, which were in reserve. What occurred to them has been likened to the charge of the Light Brigade at Balaclava during the Crimean War: they attacked over open ground with little preliminary bombardment against the German second line which had been reinforced and made equivalent to front-line defences. Out of 10,000 troops there were over 8,000 casualties within an hour. The German wire was not cut and the offensive was severely stalled.[29] The newly organised Guards Division – which included the newly formed 2nd Battalion Irish Guards of which William Higgins from Kilbarry, Blackpool, was a member – were brought into the attack. Their aim was to capture the 'Chalk Pits' followed by the Scots Guards who were to take '14 Bis' with the Irish Guards providing covering fire. The attack started at 4 p.m. on 26 September and their objectives were attained relatively easily which buoyed both Guards battalions to advance further. They, however, met terrific fire from Bois Hugo and Pinots and were forced to retreat back to the captured positions. The Irish Guards suffered 324 casualties of which 146 were killed or died of wounds.[30]

The main Loos offensive had faltered as the German second line of defences had been reinforced and proved too good to overcome. The British, however, maintained an aggressive front to help consolidate the gains they had made and prepared for a renewed offensive. However, the Germans brought their elite corps, the German Guards Division, to the Loos sector after they had secured Vimy Ridge. On 8 October the Germans began their counter-attack with a four-hour bombardment. It started at 12.30 p.m. and was aimed mainly at the 1st Division sector which included the 2nd Munster Fusiliers, who were holding trenches to the right of the Chalk Pit, which the Irish Guards had previously captured. In the Munsters War Diary it records that,

> This bombardment lasted until 4:30pm at that hour the Germans delivered a series of attacks directed against our trenches on Hill 70, the Chalk Pit and Wood and further to our left each side of Hulloch ... The Battn, which had not suffered so much from the bombardment as had doubtless been expected by the enemy, assisted in repelling their attack on Hill 70 by a vigorous rifle and machine gun fire.[31]

The surviving German troops retreated to the safety of their trenches. Killed during the day was Michael Allen from Narrow Lane in Blackpool. If, as seems likely, that he was Michael Donovan's brother-in-law, who had been killed at Aubers on 9 May, then his sister Sarah living at Narrow Lane would have been informed of another bereavement to her family within the space of six months. Two days later on 10 October, Munster Fusilier Cornelius O'Brien from Seminary Road (around the corner from Narrow Lane) died of wounds. Also from Seminary Road and involved the fighting

Acting Sergeant Thomas Tyson, 2nd Battalion Royal Munster Fusiliers. (Cork Examiner)

with the Munsters was Acting Sergeant Thomas Tyson. He would subsequently die in England on 7 March 1916 from wounds sustained during shelling in the trenches the previous day, 6 March. He had been a butcher by trade.

Aggressive, localised fighting continued along the Loos sector in the weeks after the battle as the BEF continued to consolidate and even improve the line. The 2nd Battalion Irish Guards again became involved in such action, opposite the Hohenzollern Redoubt, when on 12 October they became one of the first to use Mills bombs after a batch of 8,000 was delivered. These hand grenades were a sign of the technological development that continued to occur within the British army as the war progressed.[32] The war necessitated new devices which gave birth to new inventions. One of the saps (a shallow trench which jutted into no-man's-land for reconnaissance) taken over by the Irish Guards was called 'Cork Street'. On 21 October, according to the Irish Guards' war diary, a bombing attack was planned by the Guards in order to keep the Germans 'at bay whilst a new barricade was being built' and help straighten their front line. They made a 'detailed reconnaissance of the front with a periscope' and it was decided that there would be two separate bombing parties attacking from the right and left followed by four more bombers to protect the two men who were to construct the barricade. At intervals of two yards would be riflemen connecting the front of the attack to base trench and whose task it was to keep the operation supplied with bombs or sandbags as required.

Guardsman William Higgins, from Kilbarry, was killed during the operation and the following is a description of what occurred that night:

Sergeant William Higgins (*back row, third from right*) from Kilbarry with his fellow Irish Guardsmen. (*Cork Examiner*)

20 Oct. Casualty return for preceeding 24 hours: – 1 Killed, 9 wounded.

21 Oct 1am Both right and left attacks started off. The leading men had been cautioned to go very slowly and quickly and to use every endeavour to approach without being seen: in fact they were to stalk the Germans but immediately they were discovered they were to rush the enemy and drive him back. The advance throughout very slow for the leading men lay down a distance most of the time. It was 1.40am before contact was gained although only this happened at about 70* or 80* [yards] distance from our barricade from where the start had been made. As soon as contact was gained Capt. HUBBARD fired a volley of 3 VERY [Verey] pistol lights (one of them failed to explode) followed at 30 seconds interval by another volley of 3. This was the signal agreed upon for units on our right and left and for the artillery to cooperate.

1.40am To take each attack in turn. At 1.40AM the leading bombers of the left attack met a German bombing party about 60* or 70* [yards] from our barricade from which the advance had commenced. At this moment 2/Lieut. Tallents was about 20* or 30* [yards] behind them and just at a point in the old trench where there were some old iron girders, apparently the remains of an old dugout roof of a brigade which had existed over the trench. This marked the objective of this attack, as it was at the junction of WEST FACE and GUILDFORD STREET. Our bombers who had never had an opportunity of throwing many [indecipherable] and live bombs back at training were really out classed by the German bombers, and they were all either killed or wounded or driven back on to 2/Lt. Tallents. This officer together with 7493 Pte J. Higgins and Pte. BROPHY made a most gallant stand at the iron girder, but they were eventually driven back to our own barricade, Pte BROPHY being killed and 2/Lieut TALLENTS and Pte HIGGINS both being wounded. The Germans attacked and for some 30 minutes there was a very sharp struggle behind the barricade and it was doubtful whether we would be able to retain possession of it. 2/Lt. TALLENTS, though wounded kept the men at their posts and united them to resist the attack, frequently exposing himself on the top of the barricade so as to make a longer and more accurate shot with a bomb. Meanwhile as many of our bombers had become casualties ... as the supply of bombs were running out it was decided that it would be unwise to make a second attack to push the Germans back, but as soon as more bombs began to arrive from Bde. HQ a second attack was made which drove the Germans back and kept them successfully at bay whilst the barricade was built and the communicating trench to it was dug out ... After the attack had started Capt. HUBBARD sent forward 2/Lieut. F. SYNGE to take command in place of 2/Lieut. Tallents who was removed to the dressing station. Shortly after arrival 2/Lieut. Synge was slightly wounded in the head but he remained at his post and never delayed his efforts to get the position consolidated and stable until he too was removed to the dressing station after dawn. By this time the barricade was completed and the communication trench back was sufficiently cleared to complete the work to be continued in daylight.

To return to the right attacks. At 1AM it started and it progressing slowly. The leading bombers reached a part about 80* [yards] beyond our lines before they met the enemy and exchanged a few bombs with them. Practically no serious opposition was encountered on this side and a new barricade was built some 50* [yards] in front of our line.

Some difficulty was experienced in opening up the old communicating trench back from the new barricade to our lines owing to a tangle of old wire and other debris. The men were also slow at getting to work on this, with the result that dawn arrived to find the cover far from complete. The men however had just sufficient cover to enable them to continue work in a crouching position + before many hours of daylight had passed they made it all good. The sniping on to this trench was very brisk and came from different directions. The result of which were some casualties including 2/Lt. R HAMILTON who was shot through the jaw shortly after dawn while supervising the work. He was at once taken to Chateau VERMELLES, but he died about one hour after admission. He was buried in the afternoon in the British Cemetery VERMELLES.

The total casualties in this affair were 2/Lt. HAMILTON Killed, 2/ Lts Tallents and SYNGE wounded, and about 60 other ranks Killed, wounded or missing. About 2500 or 3000 bombs were thrown, practically all in the left attack.[33]

Sergeant William Higgins was buried in British Cemetery Vermelles along with 2nd Lieutenant R. Hamilton, as mentioned in the report.

After the main Loos battle this type of desultory fighting petered out by the end of October and the Loos front quietened down for the second winter in the trenches. In total 61,000 British casualties were sustained in the battle, 50,000 in the main fighting area between Loos and Givenchy with the remainder in subsequent attacks. Of these casualties, 7,766 men died.[34] The failure and the criticisms of the Loos offensive led to the resignation of British Commander-in-Chief Sir John French, who was then replaced by General Douglas Haig. The war continued with little appreciable gain but at great human loss and suffering. Societies all over Europe were beginning to strain at the effort. Their governments, however, were as determined as ever, or even more so, to carry on for the sacrifice of their dead could be redeemed only by a victory.

John Redmond visited the Irish troops at the Western Front in November 1915 (accompanied by his son, Lieutenant William Redmond, DSO of the Irish Guards). This was a visit of the leader of the Irish nation-in-waiting.

He inspected the Irish Guards in a village which had been shelled from time to time, so that there were sandbag shelters in the cottage gardens ... Mr Redmond walked down their lines and spoke a few words of greeting and praise and gratitude to these tall fellows who fought on the way to Hill 70 with the Guards Division on September 27th.' He visited all the Irish regiments except one and stated on his return that they were 'full of confidence and cheerfulness ... full of fight'.

He also reported that in most cases they made a parade to hear his remarks, headed by the pipes playing 'O'Donnell Abu' and 'God Save Ireland' (a Fenian song regarding the Manchester Martyrs). Redmond purposefully emphasised the optimism of all the Irish troops at the front to counter the growing pessimism at home but the confidence of the Irish troops was not the only thing that 'filled my heart with hope': it was the sight in the trenches of Flanders of 'a battalion of the Ulster Division from Belfast side by side with the Dublins'.

I found that so far from any friction having arisen between them, they were like comrades and brothers. I pray God that it may go on (cheers). I pray that wherever an Irish battalion goes into action, there may be a battalion of the Ulster Division alongside of them (more cheers). I need not point out the moral to you. This is the way of ending the unhappiness and the discord and the confusion of Ireland (cheers) when Irishmen come together in the trenches and risk their lives together, and spill their blood together. I say there is no power on earth when they come home that can induce them to turn as enemies one upon the other (cheers).[35]

Redmond also reminded his audience of the devastation that he witnessed in Belgium and the cause of the war when he as leader of the Irish people met the King of Belgium. He told the King that 'Ireland poor and weak. Ireland weak, but yet Ireland, determined at any cost, at any sacrifice, to stand by the independence of the Belgian Nation.' The King acknowledged with gratitude the help Ireland was giving and it was reported that 'there were tears in his eyes when he said how deeply he had been touched by learning that the little children of Ireland, in very poor parishes had given their pennies to help in the relief of the Belgian refugees and starving people.'[36] Redmond finished his speech by boldly announcing that 'Ireland for ever would be disgraced in the history of the world, if having sent these men to the front, they could not raise the remaining resources to fill every gap that may arise in their ranks.' However, Ireland was changing, something Redmond must have sensed. The strains of the war were emboldening not only those who wanted peace and rejected the war, but those who wanted war with the old enemy, England. In 1916, southern Ireland would begin to shed its old political skin, and a 'terrible beauty' would be born.

5

Blackpool, Easter Week 1916 on the Western Front and the Somme

OBVIOUSLY THE WAR DID not greatly affect the daily routine of life within Blackpool. People worked the same long hours, bought their necessities in the local shops, went to church on Sundays, if not other religious meetings and observances, and of course, socialised in their spare time, be it sporting or otherwise. In January 1916 they could have seen Blackpool's Packey Mahoney take on Private Clarke at the Boxing Tournament in the Opera House. It was also noted that 'Sergeant Sullivan, the well known Blackpool heavy weight, is at home on leave, and is anxious for a match with Mahoney, which will probably be staged at a later date.'[1] There were two serious floods in Blackpool during the war years. The first was in December 1914 when over fifty houses were inundated with water from the River Bride, particularly affecting Great Britain St/Great William O'Brien St and York St/Thomas Davis St and the houses off it. The *Cork Examiner* commented that 'the area which has suffered is inhabited by very poor people and the existing conditions converts their frugality into privations and sufferings'. It called upon the Corporation to clear up the area and protect Blackpool from future flooding.[2]

Significant city-wide floods occurred again in November 1916 and again Blackpool suffered damage. In the previous month, nine-year-old David Power from the Commons Road was playing by the river near his home and fell in. He was swept away under Blackpool Bridge and drowned. Fire seems to have been a common occurrence as the prevalence of horse transport necessitated straw, a very

Postcard from the front, sent by Irish Guardsman Paddy Foley
to his younger brother, John, at Dublin Street, Blackpool.
(Tom Foley)

combustible material. Both Casey's and Barry's stables of Blackpool
went on fire in 1915. As mentioned in chapter 3, a serious fire at
Gouldings at Spring Lane in September 1915 troubled production
for three months. Then in August 1917 fire broke out at the
Cork Spinning and Weaving Company at Millfield but though it
hampered production for a while it did not stop it.

Many a woman in the Flax Factory had a loved one in the army and the Post Office on York St/Thomas Davis St would have been visited every week by the women and other family members of Blackpool to receive their separation allowance from the government. The Foley family of Dublin Street received seven shillings and four pence per week (about €200 today) for the absence of their son Paddy, who was active with the Irish Guards in France. For most the money was a necessity to ease the 'frugality' of their lives but some of it might have gone back into the war effort directly through Church and civic collections for Belgium and Poland, for the Red Cross, the Soldiers and Sailors Association or Soldiers and Sailors Help Society, all of which had branches in Cork. There was an organisation specifically set up to aid the soldiers and dependants of the Royal Munster Fusiliers, the regiment of the majority of soldiers from Blackpool. This organisation called for donations of tobacco, pipes and cigarettes for the soldiers but also warm clothing. Food would have been included, more urgently so for the prisoners of war in Germany. A depot was opened at 37 Grand Parade which was open weekdays from 11 a.m. to 3.30 p.m. and run by a Mrs Peacock. It forwarded parcels to the soldiers at the front. It made the following appeal to the 'willing members of the county and city' in December 1915:

> All the battalions at the front require shirts, socks, mittens and muffles (drab shades): muffles to be 58 inches long and 10 inches wide. The mittens should have short thumbs and no fingers and to be 8 inches long from the wrist to the knuckles. Socks to be 11 inches in the leg and 11½ inches in the foot. Any of these articles sent to the Depot will be forwarded without delay to the men.[3]

Many women in Blackpool knitted during the war. They also talked about the war for it was intimately connected to all their lives. Going to work or to the shops, news, rumours and gossip about the war would have abounded. People would have been informed of who had joined, who had been injured and, of course, whose son or husband had died. Most notifications of a loved one's death was by letter. By mid-March 1916 twenty-one soldiers and one sailor

Rev. Joseph Scannell of Farranferris Seminary and chaplain to the Irish Guards. (*Cork Examiner*)

from Blackpool had died in the war. These figures suggest that over forty Blackpool soldiers had been wounded and hospitalised by this stage. Grieving families would have been visited and St Nicholas Church, at the centre of Blackpool, would have become a communal focus in coping with the suffering as the names of those soldiers who had died were read out on Sundays.

Priests had a role not only in bringing consolation to the grieving families at home but also in ministering to the troops at the front line. Fr Scannell, a teacher at Farranferris College, became chaplain to the Irish Guards and would earn a Military Medal, the third highest award for bravery in the British army. Also from Farranferris College, Fr Duggan enlisted and became a chaplain in the army. As mentioned previously, Fr Charles O'Connor, Blackpool's parish priest, joined up and ministered to the 9th Battalion Royal Dublin Fusiliers in the 16th Irish Division. In February 1916 he had a letter published in the *Irish Catholic*, a Church publication, which was subsequently reprinted in the *Cork Examiner*, calling on more Catholic priests to enlist:

> Sir – I have just opened my copy of this week's *Irish Catholic* and seen Cardinal Logue's urgent appeal for more Army Chaplains, and your own admirable leading article on his Eminence's letter. Both will, I have no doubt, 'awaken,' as you say, 'a responsive echo in many fervent sacerdotal hearts.' There is one question, however, which most priests who are thinking of becoming Chaplains ask themselves – namely, 'What kind of a time has the priest in the Army.' ...
>
> No priest is, nowadays, at any rate, 'snubbed' or in any way deliberately inconvenienced or hampered in the Army ... When I came to France last December I was sent to the 18th Casualty Clearing Station, where there were but three Catholics out of some eighty men, and only one Catholic officer, the Commanding Officer, out of eight.

Here, again, I found the same thing as in Wales [where he trained] – genuine respect for the Catholic 'padre' – all Chaplains are called 'padre' in the Army – and every possible facility for my spiritual work ...

I am now with the new Irish Division, and chaplain to the 9th Dublins. We are practically all Catholics, and all I need say is that it is absolutely a pleasure to be with them. I am treated with the utmost respect, have every possible facility for Mass, Confessions, Benediction, Rosary, etc., and can do absolutely as I please. I was never so happy in my life ...

Is the work really too hard? I have had experience of both field hospital work and regimental work. I was chaplain, as I have said, to the 18th Casualty Clearing Station. It accommodated some 250 or 300 patients. In times of rush – as during the fighting at Loos – as many as 1,200 were there at the same time, but I was never there for one of these rushes. I was at the same time chaplain to the 23rd Casualty Clearing Station, another hospital some two miles away, and about the same size as the 18th. Moreover, I used to visit a convalescent home, a mile and half in the opposite direction, where there were always about 250 patients. All this looks very big indeed, but was I killed with work? Well, all I shall say is that I had ample time for innumerable little excursions around the neighbourhood by cycle, horse and motor. With a regiment the work is somewhat different. I have a great many more Confessions, but one hour every evening, and two and a half on Saturdays, with perhaps five or six hours on the day before going into the trenches, is the most I shall ever have. The men have their military duties to attend to, and the chaplain's work, of necessity, is comparatively very light. When in rest billets a priest is on vacation practically all the time, except for the Confessional hours, which, be it remembered, he alone arranges ...

In a word, a Catholic Chaplain has to-day a very good time in the Army; he is respected by all, loved by his Catholic soldiers, has every facility for his spiritual work, has ample leisure time, the consciousness of 'doing his bit' in the great war, and does more good in a week than he would do in three months at home ...

– I am, yours faithfully,

C. C. O'CONNOR.[4]

By the end of the war the British army would have 649 Catholic priests serving as army chaplains as well as over 100 Church of Ireland chaplains, 25 Irish Presbyterian ministers and 22 Methodist preachers.[5]

Another institution dealing with the casualties of war was the Irish hospital system which included the local hospital, the North

Infirmary, just a few minutes' walk from Blackpool. Here, with a range of hospitals within the city, they nursed the wounded back to health. The following extract gives an indication of the number of wounded they were dealing with at one particular time:

WOUNDED SOLDIERS IN CORK

One hundred wounded soldiers arrived in Cork yesterday. They arrived in the city from Dublin and were conveyed by the Great Southern and Western Company's ambulance train, in charge of Dr. Winter, of the Dublin Division of St. John's Ambulance Brigade, assisted by two VAD [Voluntary Aid Detachment] nurses of the same division. The train contained 60 sitting and 40 cot-cases, and these were allocated to the City Hospitals as follows:- North Infirmary, 15; South Infirmary, 23; Mercy Hospital 27; Victoria Hospital, 19: Cork Steamship Company Hospital, 12, and Eye, Ear and Throat Hospital, 4. Dr. Winder, solr., Cork, was in charge of the transport arrangements, and there were in attendance a number of motor cars belonging to local motorists and ambulances supplied by the Cork Steam Packet Company and military authorities ... The wounded were most carefully dealt with and handled with great skill by the stretcher bearers and at the same time with such expedition that the train was emptied and the men set to their various destinations in something under an hour and a half.' [6]

Most, if not all, of these soldiers would have been from non-Irish battalions.

The Board of Management had a small dispute amongst themselves on the issue of opening the grounds adjacent to the hospital to act as a recuperative outdoor walking area. The problem was that the area was lined with graves and gravestones, and the suggestion was deemed a 'sick joke' by one member. The outcome of this dispute is not known but from the reaction garnered at the first meeting it would suggest that it was not taken up. The following is a description of a more harmonious time that of Christmas at the North Infirmary in 1916:

XMAS IN NORTH INFIRMARY

It has been a busy Christmas time in this institution. In the records of this old city hospital the largest number of intern patients was treated during the month. Many of the cases were of a serious character. The city and county had contributed 78 to the roll by Christmas morning, which, with 27 wounded soldiers, made a grand total of 105. With all the wards occupied, the house hustled with activity, affording continuous work to the staff of doctors, Sisters and nurses. The great Festival was ushered in by the celebration of midnight Mass by the Rev. Father O'Regan, C.M. As the strains of the 'Gloria in Excelsis Deo' poured through the corridors the beautiful music reached many of the poor sufferers, reminding them in joyous tones of the events of Bethlehem on the first Christmas morning twenty centuries ago. The ordinary patients were provided for, as usual, by the Trustees of the infirmary, and the wounded soldiers had their wants liberally looked after by Mr. A. M. Winder, hon secretary of the 'Comforts Committee' of the Cork branch of the British Red Cross Society.[7]

The hospital also trained nurses for active duty in France and contributed to the 4,500 Irish nurses who would go to France and other countries to tend to the wounded and dying. At the end of the war the matrons of both the North and South Infirmary were invited to attend a special ceremony presided over by King George V in gratitude for their services during the war; however, both declined as they believed no thanks were necessary as they were just doing their duty.[8]

The war not only brought death and injury to the men of Blackpool, it heralded greater economic hardship in the guise of inflation. By 1916 half of the Gross National Product of most belligerent countries was spent on their military engagement in the war.[9] This was paid by inflationary finance which lowered the standard of living for everybody in society except those directly involved in munitions work, which was minimal in Ireland. The farmers in Ireland benefited to an extent but not the industrial workers who were least immune to price rises on all commodities. Worker discontent at places like Murphy's Brewery and Goulding's Chemical Factory at Blackpool were eased by war bonuses which in places like Murphy's increased as the years went by. It certainly helped to prevent strikes by the workers and by November 1917 it amounted to 10 shillings a week.[10] Such practices might have been, and probably were in some form, enacted throughout the industries of Blackpool during the war.

Worker disquietude was evident all over Ireland and Britain, and probably all over Europe during the war. Higher taxation was another economic burden people had to bear. Industrial unrest in Britain reached its peak in May/June 1917.[11] The patriotic consensus behind the war held in Britain despite the economic hardship and the loss of life and limb because there seemed to be no alternative. Opposition to the war in Britain, and generally in Europe, was taken up by some socialists and by communists who wanted to remake the whole of national society and even international society. Such views during the war remained marginal, or at best minority, but they would succeed in Russia. There was, however, a conservative alternative to the war in Ireland: extreme nationalism and their vision of a Gaelic Ireland reborn. This vision had been fostered by cultural groups like the Gaelic League, which tried to spread the Irish language and Gaelic culture, and its sporting equivalent, the Gaelic Athletic Association. Its political manifestation had, up to this point, been relatively minimal. Sinn Féin had been moribund in Cork since 1911 and the Irish Volunteers had less than 10 per cent of the overall Volunteer membership in Ireland in December 1914. However, towards the end of 1915 – a year and a half after the war had started – there were signs of change.

Firstly, the immediate prospect and possibility of invasion had abated. This threat had been a constant theme at recruitment meetings in Cork but this began to lack credibility when the contours of the war began to appear firmly established on the Western Front in France and with the Royal Navy still firmly in control of the seas. This was certainly the feeling that imbued Limerick Bishop O'Dwyer's public letter in November 1915 in defence of Irish emigrants to America who had received public abuse from some Liverpool people as being 'shirkers' from the war as they awaited an emigrant ship from Liverpool docks. Bishop O'Dwyer was the first from the Irish 'establishment' (or the establishment-in-waiting) to break rank and claim publically that the war was not 'our war' and was of no interest to those ordinary folk from the west of Ireland who were leaving for America. This division between a rural Ireland steeped in a Gaelic folklore and culture, and the more anglicised urban centres was made more explicit when the Bishop dismissed the war as concerning only 'cosmopolitan considerations'.[12] Such a fracture in interpreting the war became more prevalent in independent Ireland. The letter was a great fillip to those opposed to the war and particularly to those opposed to Irish involvement in the British army. A few weeks later, in early December, the prominent Irish constitutional nationalist Tom Kettle was speaking at a recruiting meeting in Cork but was heckled and interrupted by a group of men questioning the basis of the war. This was new.[13] In February 1916 a letter was printed in the *Cork Examiner* questioning Ireland's role in the war. Cracks in the public consensus began to appear.

Secondly, and related to this probing of Ireland's role in the war, was the question of what the Irish soldiers were sacrificing their lives for: where was Home Rule? A year after the war started there was still no sign of Home Rule being implemented and less hope of it as the war appeared to be very static. Doubts and distrust began to grow, fed by British army intransigence over the formation of a distinct southern Irish Division with its own Irish identity, followed by its (and the existing Irish regiments') apparent lack of recognition in the military field. John Redmond would not join the British Cabinet in national government in May 1915 for fear of too close an association with the British government. The Irish Unionist leader Edward Carson did, which increased southern fears of Unionist manipulation of the strings of power. The British government had no intention of implementing Home Rule during the period of existential threat posed by the war as it was deemed too bold a political experiment. The longer the war lasted the more the war's grinding gloom would fray the faith of moderate Irish nationalism in the war effort.

These dynamics were clearly evident in the fate of the two Volunteer movements of Irish nationalism. As mentioned before the Volunteer movement split at the outbreak of the war with the vast majority siding with Redmond and the setting up of the National Volunteers, as distinct from the Irish Volunteers who were against the war. Initially, the Irish Volunteers were mainly a rural-supported organisation, which suggests that of the fifty-eight Volunteers from Blackpool, over fifty of them became National Volunteers. Following national figures and also including the fact that Blackpool was an industrial urban area, then as many as fifteen or sixteen would have joined the British army and more likely ended up in the 47th Brigade of the 16th Irish Division which had been identified with Redmond's National Volunteers. Denis O'Riordan from 12 Commons Road, was a Volunteer who enlisted. For the remaining Blackpool National Volunteers, they were part of an army-in-waiting for the new Home Rule nation. As the war dragged on the National Volunteers began to lose focus. Their natural leaders would have probably joined the war effort by enlisting but, importantly, the British government never endorsed their self-perceived role as a home defence force. An offer was made to this effect in Cork in early 1915 with duties involving guarding two bridges over the River Lee that led towards the Royal Naval base in Bantry, but after initial acceptance it was later withdrawn and not followed up on. Such inaction must have sapped morale within the National Volunteers and might have contributed to a wider questioning of the bona fides of the government towards the whole Home Rule project. By the end of 1915 the National Volunteer activities in Cork had become almost non-existent.[14]

While the National Volunteers were decaying during 1915, the Irish Volunteers were becoming stronger. Their outright rejection of the war and Irish involvement in it was gaining an increasing resonance within the wider Irish public and especially in rural Ireland. Their strong showing at the funeral of the old Fenian O'Donovan Rossa in August 1915 heralded a new stage in their development. Tomás MacCurtain organised their commemoration of the Manchester Martyrs in Cork in November and managed to march 1,200 Irish Volunteers down Grand Parade. However, only 150 to 200 of these Volunteers were from the city. Leaders of the Irish Volunteers, like Patrick Pearse, had been planning a rebellion since the start of the war and had sought German help in this regard. In early 1916 a cache of arms destined for the Irish Volunteers was found at Kilbarry Railway Depot off Dublin Hill, Blackpool.[15]

The Rising started, as is well known, on Easter Monday 24 April in Dublin city, where it remained largely confined until its quashing a week later on 30 April. It was an abortive national rising which had stalled due the countermanding orders from conflicting elements within the Volunteer leadership in Dublin and also because the expected German help never arrived. Roger Casement's efforts in Germany to garner support for an Irish rebellion from among Irish captured soldiers had failed. He was arrested near Banna Beach in Kerry after returning to Ireland by means of a German U-boat with the message to call off the rebellion precisely because of German unwillingness to support the rising. The Germans did, however, supply a ship full of arms and ammunition, called the *Aud*, but it was discovered by the British navy and *Aud*'s captain subsequently scuttled it off Cork Harbour. The Irish Volunteers in Cork city, under the leadership of Tomás MacCurtain and Terence MacSwiney, ended up being surrounded by the army at their headquarters at Sheare St. The stand-off was diffused by the Bishop of Cork, Bishop Colohan, and the Lord Mayor, when the Volunteers agreed to give up their arms to a neutral party for safe keeping. Not a shot was fired but no arrests were made, at least not immediately.[16]

The Rising in Dublin and the subsequent execution of its sixteen leaders has been rightly seen as the foundation stone for the birth of the new Irish state and nation which came into existence in 1922. The violent insurrection and the perceived martyrdom of its leaders created a breach in the Home Rule consensus that had lasted fifty years. Flor O'Donoghue, an Irish Volunteer from Cork, wrote of those who sought independence from Britain as being at a loss at how to do so before the Rising but inspired thereafter by the Rising and its leaders' example. It was a new dimension to Irish politics that was able to feed off the growing disillusionment with the war as it staggered from one catastrophe to another. The violent abyss of the war in Europe created dynamics that made the Rising in Dublin possible and helped propagate its subsequent interpretation as some kind of political but also spiritual redemption of the Irish nation. The lingering distrust and suspicion between Irish nationalism in all its guises and the Unionists and British were only amplified in the post-rebellion Ireland of martial law. Even southern Unionists began to harbour fears that Redmond's Home Rule was only a stalking horse for an Irish Republic and a complete rejection of Ireland's 750 years of union with Britain, fears that became increasingly true with every month after the rising that Home Rule was not implemented. The British government shared these fears.

The political project for complete independence within Ireland was never guaranteed success and only developed its obvious dominance through the conscription crisis of April 1918. One suspects that cities and places like Blackpool were the last areas to come under its sway and it must be remembered that loyalty to Redmond and the Irish Party was never fully eclipsed. Of the 120 leading members of the Irish Volunteers eventually arrested in Cork after the Rising only one came from Blackpool, the recently returned Tomás MacCurtain.[17] The majority were from the county. Redmond must have felt the political ground shake under his feet as he heard of the rebellion and immediately denounced it as a betrayal of the Irish soldiers who were fighting for a Europe in which a Home Rule Ireland would play its part and, as such, a betrayal of Ireland itself. He likened the rebellion to a 'German Plot' that made Ireland a cat's paw to German machinations.[18] He subsequently toned down such language after the execution of the leaders of the rising and the sympathy it aroused. But the Irish soldiers were angry too and endorsed Redmond's sentiments.

Joseph O'Donnell from Great Britain St/Great William O'Brien St was with the 9th Battalion Royal Munster Fusiliers in the 16th Irish Division and had arrived at the front in February 1916. In May the 9th Munsters were manning a line of trenches south of Hulluch on the Ypres Salient when on 21 May members from the battalion 'suspended from the neck from a tree' an effigy labelled 'Sir Roger Casement'. It was brought in the next day as 'it appeared to annoy the enemy + was found to be riddled with bullets.'[19] Roger Casement was hanged for treason in London two months later in July 1916. A letter from an Irish soldier 'from the trenches' was reprinted in the *Cork Examiner* on 18 May 1916 which claimed that those who rebelled were 'blackguards' and that 'such fine regiments out here fighting and doing such good work for their native country and say we should have a slur thrown on us over those couple of worms, who would be afraid to stand in our boots for a few days, never mind twenty months ... as everybody knows the flower of Ireland is fighting here'. However, Tom Kettle, with the 7th Dublin Fusiliers, rightly feared that the Rebels (and physical-force separatism) would usurp the constitutional nationalist movement that he and others had participated in, and that those Irish nationalists who supported the British war effort would be marginalised and eventually written out of the national narrative.

During the week of the rebellion in Dublin, Irish soldiers – including soldiers from Blackpool – were losing their lives in France and elsewhere. Timothy O'Brien was from Sunday School Lane and according to the 1911 census the O'Brien family had a railway background with Timothy's father, Patrick, and brother, Jeremiah, railway workers. They also seemed to have been a bilingual family, able to speak both English and Irish. Timothy had emigrated to Lancashire sometime after 1912 where he worked probably in a factory as a general labourer. When the war broke out he enlisted in Manchester on 1 September 1914 and joined the 8th Battalion of the Loyal North Lancashire Regiment which had been formed in Preston, Lancashire, that same month and was part of the 25th Division. Timothy was in France with his battalion by the end of September 1915.

Before moving to the trenches in front of Mont St Ely on 20 April 1916, the war diary of his battalion noted that on 6 April: 'Inter platoon races were held each team consisting of 8 men, distance 500 yrds. The Machine Gun Team won after a very close race. No. 11 Platoon being second.' On 8 April D Company gave a 'very successful' concert in the evening. The trenches they occupied on 20 April for three days were in a very bad condition and needed a lot of repair. On the night of 22 April they expected a German mine to blow up and most of the battalion 'were "standing to" all the night – the water and the mud was very bad indeed. The mine however was not exploded.' The next evening, April 23, they were relieved 'very satisfactorily' by the 1st Battalion Wiltshire Regiment

James Dwyer from Walshe's Avenue, a stoker on submarine *E22*. (*Cork Examiner*)

and the battalion went into reserve at St Eloi. Private Timothy O'Brien was killed in action on 23 April. One of the dangerous times for any battalion at the front was when they were being relieved as such movement, and maybe greater exposure in the process, brought the enemy's attention to their quarter and drew shelling and sniping.[20]

In coordination with the Easter Rising in Dublin the German Navy became active off the east coast of England when they shelled Lowestoft on 24 April 1916. James Dwyer from Walshe's Avenue in Blackpool was a stoker on the *E22* submarine which had been launched as recently as late August 1915. On Wednesday 25 April 1916 (the first anniversary of Gallipoli landings) *E22* was part of a patrol line that was sent to intercept a German naval force, however, *E22* itself was torpedoed off Great Yarmouth, Norfolk, by *UB 18* with the loss of thirty crew members with only two surviving. James Dwyer was among those who died, as was his crew mate Patrick Flynn from Ballinassey, Dungarvan, County Waterford. The commander of *UB 18*, Lieutenant Otto Steinbrinck, enhanced his reputation by sinking *E22* and subsequent shipping and became one of the 'aces' of the war, gaining a 1st and 2nd Class Iron Cross. *UB 18* had a number of commanders during the war and sank in total 128 ships. However, on 9 December 1917, as it rose to the surface at the entrance to the channel, it was spotted by the trawler *Ben Lawer*, which was minesweeping for a coal convoy, and which immediately rammed the submarine just behind the conning tower. The U-boat sank and became one of four U-boats to be sunk by a trawler in the war. Otto Steinbrinck survived the war and lived until 1949.[21]

On 27 April the 16th Irish Division in the trenches at Loos opposite Hulluch faced the brunt of what was the second biggest gas attack by the Germans of the war thus far. At the front line were the 49th and 48th Brigade, which included the 9th Battalion of the Munsters. Eighth Battalion of the Munster Fusiliers was with the 47th Brigade in support. At 4.35 a.m. heavy rifle and machine-gun fire was aimed at the Irish held trenches which brought the men to 'stand to' in expectation of an attack and then the bombardment started with a simultaneous release of chlorine gas in front of the Irish trenches and tear gas behind, amidst the artillery. The chlorine gas created a cloud which the gentle breeze eventually pushed over the Irish lines. Heavy casualties ensued due to the density of the gas cloud which made the experimental gas helmets ineffectual. The German infantry then attacked through the gas and smoke and gained some parts of the Irish trenches.[22] After very hard fighting the enemy were pushed back out but not before they had taken some prisoners. They made good their retreat by blowing a mine between two existing craters, named by the Irish 'Tralee' and 'Munster'. Two hours later the Germans repeated the attack with more gas but this time the troops from the 4th Division Barvarians failed to make the line and fell back. This was helped by the wind blowing the gas back over the German trenches. This happened again two days later on 29 April when the Germans repeated the attack but again the Irish troops drove them back.

The 16th Irish Division, however, suffered heavy casualties with a total of 570 killed, 338 by gas, and over 1,400 wounded. The 9th and 8th Battalions of the Munster Fusiliers did not suffer the most amongst the battalions of the Division. However, after the month of May in the trenches, which involved a significant amount of German localised attacks and counter-attacks by the Munsters, the 9th Battalion was disbanded and amalgamated with the 8th Battalion of the Munsters in early June, owing to the depleted number of soldiers in its ranks. The 9th were commended by High Command.[23] It is not known precisely how or when Private Joseph O'Donnell or Private David Mulcahy, of 9th and 8th Battalions respectively, received their wounds but they both succumbed to their injuries:

Private David Mulcahy, 8th Battalion Royal Munster Fusiliers. (*Cork Examiner*)

on 3 June at Calais with respect to Private O'Donnell and on 29 July at Tottenham, Middlesex, with regard to Private Mulcahy. The hospitals in which they were treated were a distance behind the front line, which suggests that they both received their wounds some time before they died. They had lived quite close to each other in Blackpool, Joseph O'Donnell in Great Britain St/Great William O'Brien St while David Mulcahy resided on Seminary Road and had worked in the Flax Factory.

The 16th Irish Division stayed in the Loos sector until late August and suffered many casualties while there. They were moved to participate in one of the most famous battles of the war, the Battle of the Somme. It is a battle that is largely remembered for the opening day, 1 July 1916, when Kitchener's[24] newly enlisted soldiers were decimated in an attack that saw over 19,000 killed and 38,000 wounded. It was the worst day in British military history, unifying British communities in collective grief that is still remembered. Protestant Ulster shared that grief as the Ulster 36th Division sustained enormous casualties, over 5,000 in two days, in a brave attempt to achieve their goals but with little success against unbroken wire and well-entrenched German positions. It was the same fate for nearly all the British battalions that day. The battle, however, would last another four and half months. It had originally been conceived as a predominantly French offensive that was supposed to reverse the massive German offensive on the French at Verdun, begun in February 1916. The BEF involvement enabled the French to broaden their frontal attack and it was they who selected the Somme area which disregarded British plans for a Flanders offensive in August 1916. The British government acquiesced to French demands for fear of a French military collapse and Commander-in-Chief of the BEF, General Haig, eventually believed that a major breakthrough could be achieved at the Somme.[25]

Because of the near continual battle at Verdun, the French army's role in the Somme offensive was reduced from thirty-nine divisions to a more supportive twenty-two, which gave greater prominence to the British involvement in the battle, which amounted to nineteen divisions. The problems encountered on the first day and subsequently were due to the insufficiency of artillery to the area of front that was attacked. Many of the shells were duds and two-thirds of them were shrapnel rather than high explosive. These factors, coupled with poor accuracy of shelling, left the German front line, with its dugouts in some cases 40 feet deep, well intact to withstand the frontal assault of novice troops coming up a slope against it. The French did better in their sector because their bombardment was heavier. The Germans suffered 10,000 to 12,000 casualties on the first day. The offensive continued with the aim increasingly one of attrition and weakening of German morale rather than the grand expectations of winning the war, which was the BEF's belief at the start. Another coordinated offensive began on 14 July which had better results with German lines being captured but it was along a smaller sector and it soon stalled.[26] Thereafter large attacks were launched by the British side to straighten the line in preparation for another general offensive and it was within this context that the southern Irish troops of the 16th Division became involved in the Battle of the Somme in early September 1916.

The 16th Irish Division established themselves on 1 September in the Guillemont area in support of the 20th Division. At this time the 2nd Leinster Regiment, with their 24th Division, were in the process of repulsing a German counter-attack on Delville Wood (or Devil's Wood as it was referred to, due to the horrific sights of mutilation amongst the trees) northwest of Guillemont. This wood had seen a tremendous amount of fighting in July and would be noted for the high casualties that the new South African soldiers suffered in helping to take the wood. But on 27 August the Germans re-entered the area after a bombardment by them that demolished all the trees there except one which remained there after the war. The 2nd Leinsters were part of the two brigades of 24th Division sent into Delville Wood to reinforce the 14th Division in their defence of the area. They relieved 1st Battalion Middlesex Regiment on 30 August at 6 p.m. at Charlton Trench in very wet conditions. At 2.30 p.m. the next day the Germans broke through on the left of the front line. The Leinsters responded with a combined bombing attack with the 13th Middlesex to regain the line at 9.30 p.m. but it was unsuccessful. However, 1st Company of the Leinsters succeeded at about midnight in regaining a portion, on the left, of the original front line.

The next day, 1 September, the Leinsters tried to extend the captured portion to the right by bombing raids but due to the strength of the Germans at Wood Lane and Orchard Trench, it ended in failure. Another attempt 'at 9:50am ... up PLUM STREET was unsuccessful.'[27] However by 6.30 p.m. the Royal Berkshires attained Orchard Street. Henry Clarke, originally from Battersea in London but who lived with his wife Bridget at St John's Square in Blackpool, died on that day. He was among thirty-two other men from the Leinsters who were killed between 31 August and 2 September when the battalion were relieved of duty. There was also thirteen recorded missing and 118 wounded for this short period.[28] By 2 September the Germans had been cleared from the Wood. A report on the battle for Delville Wood was published in the *Cork Examiner* on 5 September which made the insightful comment about the war that

> victory in this war is going to be attained by the side which has the pre-ponderance in artillery and the mastery of the air, to ensure employing that superiority to the fullest advantage. Let me not be misunderstood as trying to minimise the splendid part the infantry is playing; but they can only follow the guns. To attempt more is to court disaster.

On 2 September the 47th Brigade of the 16th Irish Division were told to prepare for the attack next day on Guillemont, a couple of miles south of Delville Wood, in support of 20th Division. This brigade included 8th and, back from Gallipoli, 1st Battalion Munster Fusiliers. The task assigned to the 47th Brigade was the northern part of the village of Guillemont. The Royal Field Artillery (RFA) began a heavy bombardment of the German lines at 8.15 p.m. on 3 September. Amongst the BEF artillery that day were the field guns of 6th Division (which was a Cork-based division before the war) in which my grandfather Gus Birmingham participated. The Guillemont/Ginchy sector had withstood many an attack before. At zero hour (i.e. the time assigned for the beginning of an operation, usually an attack) precisely, the artillery instigated a creeping barrage, which was a barrage timed according to expected advances of the infantry, to act as forward cover. The 6th Division RFA took some credit for the development of this technique.[29]

The 5th Battalion Connaught Rangers and the 7th Battalion Leinster Regiment led the attack followed by the 8th Battalion Munster Fusiliers and the 6th Battalion Irish Regiment. The leading battalions gained their objectives with fighting that earned the 16th Division its first Victoria Crosses, those awarded to Thomas Hughes of the Rangers and Lieutenant John Holland of the Leinsters (from Counties Monaghan and Kildare respectively). The 8th Munsters and the Irish Regiment swept through the forward battalions and so completed the capture of Guillemont. It was a notable success and one of the few gains made by the BEF on 3 September but the brigade had 1,147 casualties out of only 2,400 soldiers involved.[30] It was probably here that Private William Mehigan of the 8th Battalion Munster Fusiliers sustained the injury that invalided him out of the war and back to his home in Spring Lane, Blackpool.

The following is a letter from William Redmond MP, brother of John Redmond, and an officer in the 16th Irish Division, written to a friend in Cork. Fr Charles O'Connor, a priest who ministered in Blackpool before the war, is mentioned.

> You will have heard before this of the splendid success of the Irish Brigade at Guillemont. I write you a line to say that while all were magnificent, the Corkmen by all accounts were second to none.

Sergeant Cahill won the D.C.M. months ago for gallant conduct in the trenches. The brigade chaplains – Fathers O'Connell, Wrafter, Burke, O'Connor, Cotter, Doyle, and Kelly – have won the intense respect of all ranks for their devoted conduct. You Cork people will be especially glad to hear of the Cork chaplains, Father O'Connell, Cotter, and O'Connor. At the Battle of Guillemont they, like the other chaplains, were unremitting in their zeal and gallantry. They went, so the men say, everywhere, ministering to the wounded and dying. I was myself with Fr O'Connell at an advanced dressing station, and he worked without ceasing amongst the prisoners as well as amongst our own men. Afterwards he left the dressing station, and, I am told, spent the whole night working right up in the front line. He returned next day, not having one moment's rest. He would be annoyed if he knew I was telling you this, but it is only right I should. Fathers Cotter and O'Connor worked in like manner, and Fr O'Connor was put out of action by gas. Chaplains of all denominations were splendid, but our own were second to none. Ireland should be proud of them and of all the splendid brigade. With my warm remembrances to you, your wife and brother, and all friends in Cork. – yours very truly, William Redmond, Attached to Headquarters, 16th Irish Division B.E.F.[31]

Fr O'Connor survived the war but the effects of the gas injury he sustained would linger with him all his life.

On the same day that 47th Brigade helped take Guillemont, 7th Division (Bombardier Moore from Spangle Hill was with its artillery) failed to hold Ginchy, a village a little northeast of Guillemont. This time the other two brigades of 16th Irish Division, the 48th and 49th, were tasked with the next assault on this stronghold. On 4 September, the 1st Battalion of the Munsters, who had joined the 16th Division in May after their tour of Gallipoli, were ordered to occupy Bernafay Wood and the second line of trenches behind Guillemont. Relief of the 8th Battalion King's Royal Rifle Corps took all day and the war diary records: 'The road and shelters were heavily shelled at intervals during the day. At about 20:00 the enemy bombarded heavily causing many casualties.' The shelling involved a direct gas shell hit of battalion HQ which killed seven officers 'including the C.O., who bravely refused to be evacuated'. By the end of the day the Munsters had lost nine officers and twenty-two ordinary rank, which included Patrick Doyle from Walshe's

Avenue, Blackpool. He had landed at Helles on 25 April and wrote a poem about his experiences, lamenting his fallen comrades, which was published in the *Cork Examiner*. It was now his comrades who would lament the passing of this Roche's Guards man.[32]

After another failed attack on Ginchy on 6 September, the 16th Division began their preparation for the planned assault three days later. Commander-in-Chief of the Division, General Hickie, ordered 48th Brigade to lead the attack, supported in part by 49th Brigade which also supplied battalions to help 47th Brigade in taking a series of trenches, called the 'Quadrilateral', on the southeastern side of Ginchy itself which would protect the 48th attacking right flank. The 1st Munsters suffered some casualties from 'friendly fire' from their own artillery as they moved up to the starting trenches on 8 September. They were to lead the attack of the 48th Brigade with the 7th Irish Rifles, which were then followed by two battalions of Dublin Fusiliers. Bombardment of the German lines began at 7 a.m. on 9 September and lasted until zero hour at 4.45 p.m. which allowed the Germans to prepare and also return shelling, no doubt causing casualties amongst the waiting Irish troops. The 47th Brigade experienced machine-gun fire as they got out of their trenches to secure the 'Quadrilateral' and it soon became obvious that the bombardment in their sector had not been effective, with one enemy trench, thought moribund, giving great resistance. The 47th were not only repulsed but had to withstand a series of counter-attacks all day which would mean for the 8th Munsters the loss of 81 out of the 200 they could muster for the attack. In the early hours of 10 September the Brigade was relieved to Trones Wood.[33]

The main attack by 48th Brigade was faring better due to the swiftness of their fighting movement after the artillery barrage was lifted. The Irish Rifles gained the German trenches quickly but were forced into a heavy mortar fight with a remnant of the German defenders. They were eventually scattered and the Rifles achieved their objective by 5 p.m. On the right, however, the 1st Munsters encountered a serious check with the first two waves of attacking soldiers wiped out by machine-gun fire. The remnant of the battalion wheeled to the right, dug in and acted as protecting flank for the supporting battalions while also preventing German envelopment of the Irish attack. 'It was a brilliant feat of minor tactics in the face of stout resistance by men of the 1st Battalion'.[34] The 8th Battalion of the Dublin Fusiliers then passed through the Munsters at the same time as the 9th Dublin Fusiliers went right through the captured positions of the Irish Rifles. Tom Kettle was killed during this forward rush by the 9th Dublin Fusiliers. Both battalions of the Dublin Fusiliers stormed the village of Ginchy and captured it. Their success nearly endangered the whole attack as the Irish Rifles and Fusiliers joined in and pushed beyond Ginchy itself, thus overextending the frontal attack but officers soon reeled the forward troops back in to consolidate and secure the captured village. It was necessary as the Bavarian Regiment counter-attacked at 6.20 p.m. and again at 9 p.m. but they were repulsed.[35]

Ginchy was a great victory for the 16th Irish Division. The following letter is from Sergeant C. Warren of the 8th Dublin Fusiliers to his brother in Tipperary, which conveys a sense of the jubilation of the Irish troops after Ginchy:

> I suppose by this time you have heard about our great deeds. I was through it all, and, thank God, came safely through the rain of shells and bullets ... It was a deed that will live in Irish history. To use our Brigadier's words: 'Colonel Bellingham, officers, N.C.O.s and men, I am proud to command you. Yesterday you performed a feat of valour that has earned the admiration of all the troops in France. The fact that you, immediately previous to this, lay in shallow trenches and shell holes under heavy shell fire without scarcely a meal – never a hot one – proves a spirit of endurance that was magnificent. Then came the ordeal. A task was set you that two divisions had failed to do. You accomplished it through the inferno of shell fire, machine guns and rifles, and, despite the heavy casualties, you had carried the position in record time, but it was only through your own grim determination and splendid courage, I was for a moment afraid you would lose ground owing to the relief being late, but I am proud to say you held on to the position through the long night. I know now that when you are again called upon I can depend on you to do whatever is required.'
>
> Further, we were proud men that day, proud of ourselves, and proud of old Ireland. It was a Scotch and an English division that had failed to do the job before, and it lay to Paddy to finish it off. We had to dig

ourselves in before daylight, and be there all day. There was a certain time given us as platoon commanders to get up and advance. There was no signal, only get up, give the lads the tip, and off we went, not a man faltered. We were in a certain formation, but owing to casualties and the rough nature of the ground, we advanced in a regular mob. I think it was best; it frightened the Germans. As I looked around for the first two hundred yards I could see every man's face as pale as death, but fired with a grim look that boded no good to anyone they met. The moment we caught sight of the Germans, there were no more pale faces. We set up a yell, and dashed forward and cleared the wood and the village inside of an hour. I was in the seventh line, but before we reached them, found myself in the first, and when we got to our final objective I was proud to see a lot of Blackrock boys around me, all belonging to different Regiments.[36]

The 16th Irish Division were relieved on the morning of 10 September by the 3rd Guards Brigade. The Munsters recorded 13 officers and 210 ordinary rank casualties. Private Jeremiah Dwyer of the Munsters from York St/Thomas Davis St was among the fallen.

Though the 16th Division marched joyfully behind their pipers back to billets at Vaux-sur-Somme, in quieter moments they would have reflected on the heavy toll exacted. During the fighting on the Somme the Division lost 1,167 soldiers. Added to the 1,496 who had died from February to August in the trenches at Loos, it amounted to a third of the division, not including those who were wounded, seriously or otherwise. Many of these men were active nationalists at home and the numbers mentioned above match those who were active in the IRA during the War of Independence. Such losses could not be replaced and the Irish Party lost valuable and respected men throughout Ireland. The 16th Irish Division had faced eight months of war on the Western Front; they still had over two more years of the war to go.[37]

Guillemont and Ginchy were notable victories during the Somme offensive but they were tactical ones whose aim was to straighten the line for the next large-scale attack planned for 15 September, later called the Battle of Flers-Courcelette. This would be the last major offensive of the Somme from the British forces and again there would be hopes that it would defeat the German army and mark its terminal decline. Significant aspects of this offensive were that it saw the debut of the Canadian and New Zealand armies on the Somme and also the first use of the tank in warfare. Forty-nine 'land-ships' would be used in the battle and the 28-ton, machine-gun- and cannon-equipped, iron-clad 'creepy-crawly' gained the attention of all the battalions as they made their way stealthily to battle, their noise disguised by the activity of British aeroplanes overhead. This included the 1st and 2nd Battalions of the Irish Guards with two soldiers from Dublin St amongst them, Paddy Foley and John Hyland.[38]

Seven tanks were allocated to the two Canadian Divisions, the 2nd and 3rd, who would open the attack on 15 September. Thirty-nine-year-old Jeremiah Murphy, whose parents lived on Spangle Hill, was a member of the 3rd Battalion Canadian Pioneers of 3rd Division. Jeremiah had previously been a soldier with the Royal Dublin Fusiliers and served during the Boer War and in India but he had left the army and emigrated to British Columbia in Canada where he became a miner. His soldiering and mining experience were clearly combined for the pioneer units of the army; their primary task was to consolidate forward areas captured by the infantry and involved tunnelling, mining, wiring, railroad work, deep dug-out building and keeping trenches in repair. The pioneers could also be called upon to join the infantry in attacking or defending.

The offensive involved two armies that would attack along a 10-mile line with the expectation that at its centre, at Flers, a hole would be punched in the German line to allow the cavalry through and take the important town of Bapume. The Canadian Divisions were allocated the northern sector with the objective of Courcelette, a village northeast of Flers, and to the south the Guards Divisions aimed at continuing the advance of the 16th Division at Ginchy. Zero hour was 6.20 a.m. on 15 September and the battle opened with a tremendous roar of artillery and the din of tanks. Again a creeping barrage by artillery would be used. The 3rd Canadian Division were charged with providing flanking protection to the 2nd Division's attack on the main German defences of Courcelette. The attack went well with the 2nd Canadians gaining their objectives and eventually capturing Courcelette.[39] The tanks prompted some German units to surrender on sight but their overall effectiveness was fairly limited. They were, however, a great morale boost to the troops. Of the six tanks used by the Canadians (one of their allocation was in reserve) only one reached its objective and helped clear a strategic factory building of German soldiers while the other five broke down, some due to shell fire.[40]

The 3rd Division's attack managed, in places, to gain trenches directly west of Courcelette and eventually linked up with the 2nd Division in Courcelette itself. That night the Engineer Corps 'directed the pioneer battalions to work on communication trenches and strongpoints' which was carried out as the Canadian infantry fought off a series of counter-attacks by the Germans north and east of Courcelette.[41] Down south at Ginchy, the 1st and 2nd Irish Guards were able to take the German first line with the help of the Coldstream Guards despite getting mixed up during the attack. They consolidated their gain while the 1st Irish Guards and the Coldstreams probed forward to gain their second objective, the next German line, which again they attained. Despite more forays forward this would be the limit of the Guards advance on the first day. A notable fatality in this area of fighting was the Prime Minister's son, Raymond Asquith of the 3rd Battalion Grenadier Guards. Forty-six were killed among the 1st Battalion Irish Guards and a similar number in the 2nd Battalion Irish Guards in the attack. Guardsman Paddy Foley from Dublin St, Blackpool, received a shell wound on his left heel in the attack and was moved to 48th Clearing Station, then to 12th General Hospital for four days and finally to a convalescent depot at Rouen for another short period. Gains had been made along the front but not as much as had been expected (the villages of Morval, Lesboeufs and Guedecourt remained untaken) and not as much as the Canadians had achieved.

The 3rd Canadian Infantry Division were then given the task of taking a stronghold on the German line called the Zollern Redoubt, which lay forward of their original flanking attack west of Courcelette. They attacked the enemy on 16 September but the first phase failed to establish the eastern platform for the assault on the redoubt due to the opening bombardment overshooting its objective. The trenches halfway to the redoubt were taken. Another midway point, Moquet Farm, was captured, which had seriously troubled the Australian forces before. That night the Canadians were relieved by troops of the 2nd British Corps, including Moquet Farm where trouble would continually menace the troops until 26 September as the Germans had taken refuge in the tunnel system there. The Canadian pioneers were, however, ordered to build a trench immediately from the old line to the new and it is probable that Jeremiah Murphy from Spangle Hill, Blackpool, was killed on 17 September while fulfilling this task. His body was never found and he is commemorated at the Vimy Memorial.

The Irish Guards too were relived in the early morning of 17 September and were bivouacked at Trones Wood on 21 September. They, with the rest of the army, were regrouping. The Canadian had 7,230 casualties for the week. The offensive had stalled by this stage and plans for a renewal of the attack laid. Morval and Lesbouefs, villages in front of the Guards' line, still had to be taken. Trones Wood was being shelled at times. On 24 September the war diary for the 2nd Irish Guards records: 'Mass celebrated in [the] Wood by Father Casey, several shells were put into the wood during the morning, causing quite a number of casualties mostly in No.1 Coy due to our shell.'[42] This seems to indicate a case of 'friendly fire'. The shelling caused thirteen wounded and two killed. Guardsman John Hyland from Dublin St, Blackpool, died of wounds on that day. An attack on 25 September by the 1st Irish Guards was a success and helped to capture the village of Lesbouefs. Second Battalion Irish Guards relieved them the next day. But, even though headway was made, again there was no breakthrough. During the fifteen days of fighting from 15 September, the Irish Guards battalions lost over 1,000 men killed or wounded, but according to their historian they were undeterred, buoyed by their successes in gaining some of their military objectives.[43]

Thereafter the Germans brought in more troops and artillery and though the Allies made some advances, the offensive on the Somme finally ground to a halt on 19 November. There had been a gain of 7 miles from the front line in July which cost the British and colonial armies 420,000 and the French 194,000 casualties. German losses may have been half a million. Thirty million shells had been exchanged and still the Germans managed to hold their front intact through the continual creation of more trench line defences. Their staunch defending witnessed over 330 counter-attacks. The battle did, however, release pressure on the French army at Verdun. This attritional warfare also damaged German morale whose army experienced the brunt of a stronger and more coordinated British army. Innovations like the tank, in turn, improved Allied morale, though it would take time to make them more militarily effective. The Battle of the Somme prompted the German army to retreat voluntarily to the well-prepared Hindenburg Line in 1917, shortening their front line. The strength of the Allies on the Somme also drove the Germans to increase their armament supply and was a factor in reactivating their policy of unrestricted submarine attacks, which would have a vital bearing on the war and would have a direct consequence on places like Blackpool with its many merchant seamen.[44]

Five men from Blackpool died at the Battle of the Somme and when thinking of 1916 it is a worth noting that the Somme impacted on communities in the south of Ireland albeit to a lesser degree than in the north. When Augustine Roche, Irish Parliamentary Party MP, died in December 1915, his funeral was marked by an almost unanimous chorus of respect from the various bodies and shades of opinion in Cork and even further afield. Members of the 9th Battalion of the Munster Fusiliers, which contained soldiers from Blackpool and specifically from the Roche's Guards Band from Spring Lane, wrote a letter publically praising him for his 'generosity to the poor' and claimed 'they knew him well', and would 'revere' his memory. They declared pride in following a man with 'good and manly Nationalist principles' and concluded that 'when we are back victorious after we do our little bit [we will] "fall in" again under the old banner and with the old Party'.[45] A year later Ireland had experienced the Rising, the execution of its leaders, and then the Battle of the Somme in the summer: it would appear that Edwardian Ireland died with Augustine Roche. There were reports in January 1917 of soldiers in Cork city being attacked.[46] The war continued to polarise Irish society and soon Ireland would become almost unrecognisable to the Irish soldiers at the front. This new emerging Ireland would eventually, in turn, fail to recognise them.

6

The Naval War and Blackpool
1914–1918

THE NAVAL WAR OF THE Great War can often be overshadowed by the scale of destruction and number of casualties inflicted in places like Gallipoli and the Western Front; however, the Royal Navy's importance in securing the British Isles during the war and pro-actively undermining German morale through its successful blockade should not be underestimated. The naval war was truly a global one with naval operations and engagements witnessed in the seas around Europe but also Mesopotamia, the Atlantic, North and South, and in the Pacific Ocean. Cork men – and some women – participated in all major operations, whether with the British Royal Navy or the merchant navy, so vital to these islands. They were stokers and firemen in the engine rooms, as well as the trimmers who supplied them with coal, they were boatswains who maintained the ship, gunners and cooks, and some were officers. From August 1914 to November 1918 Cork sailors, including those from Blackpool, manned the smallest boats from tugs, trawlers and drifters to the newest, like submarines, and the biggest, like the Royal Navy's famous dreadnoughts and battlecruisers. They laid mines off Cork and other areas, mineswept, blockaded and searched ships, loaded and unloaded troops, brought foodstuffs and equipment to neighbouring countries and to the army in France, and fought in the biggest naval battles of the war, such as Jutland and Coronel.

Those who joined the Royal Navy came from the traditional centres of maritime life in County Cork. Being a port, Cork city was the biggest recruiting centre in the county and the Royal Navy had their recruitment office at Morrison's Island at the centre of the

city. Within Cork city Blackrock and Ballintemple seemingly were
strong recruitment areas but Blackpool gave its fair share too. Two
thirds of those Cork merchant sailors who died came from the city.
Recruitment to the Royal Navy seems to have been more evenly
spread throughout the county. Castletownbere and especially
Queenstown (later called Cobh) became important Royal Navy
ports and logistical centres during the war.

Even though the naval race (i.e. the competitive building of
warships) between Britain and Germany was a feature in the
interplay of causes that contributed to the outbreak of the war
in 1914, neither navy had a detailed plan of how such an event
would be conducted. The strategies that came to characterise the
war were to an extent improvised. British public opinion (certainly
mirrored in Ireland) expected an aggressive war by the Royal Navy
with its Grand Fleet of 22 dreadnoughts, 9 battlecruisers, 40 pre-
dreadnought battleships, 121 cruisers, 221 destroyers and 73
submarines against the German High Seas Fleet of 15 dreadnoughts,
5 battlecruisers, 22 pre-dreadnought battleships, 40 cruisers, 90
destroyers and (surprisingly) only 31 submarines.[1] With such
dominance it was hard to suppress a belief in another Nelson-like
victory similar to Trafalgar. Public opinion was to be disappointed
as the Navy, mostly under Admiral Sir John Jellicoe, took a very
cautious attitude towards engagement with the High Seas Fleet.
Jellicoe was aware of certain aspects of the German fleet's greater
technical capabilities but he was more concerned about the Royal
Navy being lured into a submarine and torpedo ambush that would
leave British naval dominance shattered and its ability to sustain the
war fatally undermined. This defensive policy was endorsed by the
Admiralty for, as Winston Churchill said of Jellicoe, 'he was the
only person who could have lost the war in an afternoon'.[2]

What was initiated by the Royal Navy at the start of the war was
the 'distant blockade'. This entailed locating the Grand Fleet at Scapa
Flow in Scotland as far away from German submarines as possible.
The Royal Navy could cordon off the North Sea through controlling
the waters between Scotland and Norway and by extensively
mining the Dover Straits in tandem with keeping a Destroyer force

in the English Channel. This forced German submarines to go via Scotland if they wanted to roam the wider oceans and thus limited their 'hunting' time. It also proved to be very successful in limiting merchant sea trade with Germany. Only 4.1 per cent of merchant shipping escaped detection through this cordon.[3] The success of this policy eventually contributed to undermining German civilian morale and their army's ability to sustain a long war. In the meantime it emboldened German retaliatory efforts through, primarily, their infamous U-boats.

The German navy was just as cautious as its British counterpart, fearing not only the Royal Navy's superior fleet but, to a certain extent, its very tradition as master of the seas. The Germans never attacked troop or supply shipments across the Channel. The strategy that the High Seas Fleet developed was to try and engage the Grand Fleet partially, to whittle away its superiority so that eventually, on terms favourable to itself, it could strike at and defeat the Royal Navy comprehensively.

In the first few months of the war the Royal Navy was concerned about its numerical superiority being jeopardised, not due to the High Seas Fleet but to enemy mines, and increasingly, to the relatively new weapon, the submarine. German mines were superior to British ones and were extensively planted around the British Isles. It has been estimated that 48,000 mines were laid around the waters of Ireland.[4] The first major naval sinking in the war was the HMS *Amphion* on 6 August 1914, two days after Britain declared war, when it struck a mine in the North Sea after it had successfully destroyed a German minelayer. Six Corkmen lost their lives with the 144 other crew members and the 18 German prisoners of war. Further Cork casualties occurred on 22 September when the destroyers HMS *Cressy*, *Hogue*, and *Aboukir* were sunk off the coast of Holland, this time by a submarine, the *U 9*. The most significant naval fighting of 1914, however, was in the far seas of the southern Pacific Ocean.

The main role of Germany's East Asiatic Squadron, under Graf von Spee, was in protection of Germany's small colony of Tsingtoa in China. This colony was soon overrun by a small Anglo-Japanese force and Spee decided to sail his squadron, consisting of two armoured cruisers and three light cruisers, back to the High Seas Fleet on the North Sea. He ordered, however, the light cruiser *Emden* to act as a raider in the Indian Ocean and its environs where for seven weeks it sank 70,000 tons of Allied shipping. The *Emden* was finally put out of action on 9 November by the Australian ship HMAS *Sydney*.

Spee's squadron sailed to Easter Island and then to Valparaiso in Chile and was joined by two other light cruisers which were patrolling North American waters. Sir Christopher Cradock was the Royal Navy commander of two old armoured cruisers HMS *Good Hope* and *Monmouth*, the light cruiser *Glasgow* and the armed merchant cruiser *Otranto* in the South Atlantic when he was informed of Spee's movements. He sailed, eager for a fight, not waiting for the pre-dreadnought *Canapus* as reinforcement despite knowing the comparable inferiority of his squadron. They sailed through the Strait of Magellan and encountered Spee on 1 November 50 miles off Coronel on the Chilean coast just before 5 p.m. Around 8 p.m. *Good Hope* was blown up with Cradock on board and an hour later at 9 p.m. HMS *Monmouth* also went down. The *Glasgow* and the *Otranto* escaped. A crew member of the *Glasgow* wrote a letter home on the battle which was printed in the *Cork Constitution* on 19 December 1914:

> The fight commenced at a range of 12,000 yards. The merchant cruiser *Otranto* was immediately sent out of range. Flames were seen on the *Good Hope* and *Monmouth*. In a quarter of an hour the former dropped out of the line, being partly disabled, and soon afterwards a tremendous explosion occurred, which must have blown nearly half the ship away. It was growing dark, but the *Glasgow* continued to fire as long as the crew could see a dark object. When unable to see any longer the *Glasgow* drew away and asked the *Monmouth* how she was getting on. She replied – 'I am making water badly, forward, and want to get my stern to sea.'
>
> The *Glasgow* kept up with her for a time until the Germans came up again, when the *Monmouth* signalled to the *Glasgow* to separate and get away if possible in the darkness. The *Glasgow* put on full speed and was soon out of sight. The *Monmouth* was overtaken by the Germans, who

opened fire again. The *Glasgow* counted 75 flashes before everything was quiet again. Out of hundreds of shells fired at the *Glasgow*, only five took effect. Not a man was killed, and only seven slightly wounded. The conduct of the officers and men was magnificent. Everyone praised Admiral Cradock for the way he took his fleet into action against big odds.[5]

There were no German losses but of the 1,600 Royal Navy casualties twenty-five were Cork sailors, three from the *Good Hope* and twenty-two from the *Monmouth,* including Stoker Joseph O'Sullivan, a blacksmith helper before the war from the Commons Road, Blackpool. Spee's squadron soon faced the same prospect at the battle of the Falklands on 9 December when, after surprising a reinforced British squadron at Port Stanley, in the ensuing chase the Royal Navy eventually sank all of Spee's ships.[6]

The Royal Navy's focus on the South Atlantic prompted the German High Seas Fleet into some action and in December 1914 Admiral Franz von Hipper's battlecruiser squadron ventured forth and bombed Scarborough, Whitley, and Hartlepool on the English east coast killing 122 civilians.[7] However, when Hipper tried to attack the British fishing fleet at Dogger Bank on 24 January 1915 he was confronted by a Royal Navy squadron under the command of Admiral Sir David Beatty which sank one German cruiser, SMS *Blucher*, and seriously damaged another, SMS *Seydlitz*. The German navy learned valuable lessons from this clash and carried out improvements on its ships which increased their armour and further compartmentalised their interiors to improve fire control. Such measures would have an effect in later engagements. After Dogger Bank the German High Seas Fleet's caution increased and it began to concentrate its naval efforts on its U-boats as its main weapon in the naval war.[8]

Germany's incremental use of the submarine was both a retaliatory tactic to the Royal Navy's blockade and because in the few months of the war it had proven effective. The British Admiralty announced that the North Sea was a 'War Zone' in early November and by 4 February 1915 Germany had declared unrestricted submarine warfare in all the waters surrounding these islands. During January 1915 German U-boats were lurking in the Irish Sea but after this declaration they no longer abided by 'cruiser rules', that is, surfacing and allowing the targeted crews to scramble to safety. Now they would attack without warning. There were some assurances given to neutral shipping, mainly to placate the United States. In March Britain and France declared an even tighter blockade, blockading neutral ports, such as those belonging to the Scandinavian countries and more particularly Rotterdam in Holland which acted then, as now, as a gateway to Europe.

Merchant ships were being sunk regularly but more shocking to world opinion, and especially American opinion, was the sinking of the Cunard Line passenger ship *Lusitania* on 7 May 1915 by *U 20*, 14 miles off the Old Head of Kinsale in Cork with the loss of 1,198 lives, including 128 Americans and six people from Cork, four of whom were crew members. The rescue operation was carried out from Queenstown and many local boats and fishermen were involved in bringing the 761 survivors to safety. It was only in September 1915 that Germany bowed to American pressure after the sinking of the liner *Arabic* the month before (again off the Old Head of Kinsale) and again reverted to cruiser rules.

There had been a raid by the British in late August 1915 on German patrols at the Heligoland Bight where, with the help of some of the Grand Fleet's battlecruisers, three light cruisers were sunk. The High Seas Fleet was not involved as the tide in the Jade estuary was too low for movement. The Royal Navy had also been active in the Mediterranean with its initial attempts to force the Dardanelles Strait by naval ships alone, and then aiding the army in its invasion through transport and naval shelling. At the same time, the Royal Navy was continuously involved in maintaining the successful blockade of Germany maritime trade as well as transporting and protecting troops, animals and supplies to and from France. However, the German High Seas Fleet became more active in the spring of 1916. This was due mainly to the U-boat campaign's reversion to cruiser rules but also because of the appointment of Admiral Reinhard Scheer as commander of the fleet in February 1916. The High Seas Fleet began to venture out once a month. As mentioned before, during the Easter Rising in Dublin in April it shelled Lowescroft in England. It was prevented from bombing Great Yarmouth (when Stoker James Dwyer of submarine *E22* from Walshe's Avenue, Blackpool, lost his life) and the operation against Sunderland in early May was postponed.

Room 40 O.B. (Old Building) at the Admiralty was the very successful hub of British naval intelligence where German intercepted communication was deciphered and passed onto the Grand Fleet. Admiral Jellicoe was notified on 30 May 1916 that the High Seas Fleet would be active, and the Grand Fleet sailed to meet it. After a chance encounter the next day at 2.28 p.m. the first shells were fired by the German guns at 3.49 p.m., which started one of the most dramatic events of the war, the Battle of Jutland. About 150 British and 100 German ships were involved and when Scheer's fleet finally slipped through the clutches of the Grand Fleet in the darkness of the next morning, over 8,000 heavy calibre rounds had been fired in engagements that were very intermittent and very short.[9]

Within seven minutes of the opening salvo HMS *Indefatigable* received two hits from the SMS *Von der Tann* and blew up.

> The explosion started with sheets of flame followed by a dense, dark smoke cloud which obscured the ship from view. All sorts of stuff was blown into the air, a 50 foot steamboat being blown about 200 feet, apparently intact though upside down.[10]

Captain Sowerby and all but two of the 1,000-strong crew died, including forty Cork sailors. Amongst them was Stoker Timothy Crowley from Blackpool. This would be the biggest number of Cork fatalities for a single ship during the war. It was nearly matched by the sinking of the HMS *Defence* close to 6 p.m. after a battlecruiser chase. The following eyewitness report by a gunner on HMS *Warrior* gives an insight into the battle and the *Defence's* sinking:

Timothy Crowley, a stoker on
HMS *Indefatigable*.
(*Cork Examiner*)

Maurice Riordan from Watercourse Road, a stoker on HMS
Defence. (*Cork Examiner*)

On Wednesday, when we had been steaming for six hours, the sound
of gun firing was heard, and the flashes of the guns were observable
about ten minutes later. Both squadrons were evidently approaching
each other at the rate of twenty knots. At 5.50p.m. 'action quarters' was
sounded. At 5.55 the following order came down from the fire control
turret, 'Enemy cruiser, three funnels, bearing green 90, range 15,850
yards, deflection 10, left salvos control.' Twenty seconds later the gong
rang, and a fraction of a second had not elapsed before a double gong
sounded for range-finding. The first two shells having given us the range,
the starboard gun of the fore turret thundered out, the shell crumpling
up the hindermost of the three funnels of the enemy. A direct hit was
then signalled, when, suddenly, two more light cruisers were signalled
to port, and the *Defence* and the *Duke of Edinburgh* were left to deal
with them. The latter vessel had to intercept a minelayer that had made
its appearance. All at once a huge fountain of water rose twenty yards
ahead of us, and we then knew that we had to deal with something
bigger than light cruisers. Two shells of at least 12-inch calibre fell
ahead of the *Defence*, and three seconds later a salvo cut her amidships,
and she crumpled up and sank. The *Black Prince* was the next to go.
Two great shells carried away her funnels and fore turret, and a second
salvo hit in the magazine, and she blew up. Our turn had come, for
far away in the horizon we could see three tripod masts. By now the
enemy light cruisers were burning fiercely and had ceased to fire, but

one after another 12-inch shells dropped on either beam of us. At last the enemy, out of our range by 3 miles, found their mark. The first shell smashed our motor boat hoist into splinters, the second shell hit the starboard side in line with the turrets; the third hit the quarterdeck, just abaft the bulkhead door, ploughing downwards, and wrecking the dynamos, and putting the whole ship in darkness. The gun turrets, too, were almost useless, as the ammunition hoist had gone. Another shot put the port and starboard engine rooms out of action, killing 20 men. After five minutes the vessel was on fire, and a number of men were out of action from the effects of the asphyxiating gas shells which the enemy were now using. At 6.30 we were a hopelessly battered hulk, and waiting for shells that would probably finish us, when the *Warspite* passed between us and engaged the foremost enemy battle cruiser with deadly effect. The first shot from the *Warspite* lopped off the foremast of the leading enemy battle cruiser. The next overturned both foregun turrets, and in five minutes the enemy vessel was absolutely ablaze from end to end, enveloped in a cloud of dense smoke. The second battle cruiser, which had been concentrating her fire on the *Warspite*, turned to starboard, smoke belching from her funnels, and endeavoured to pick up her main squadron, but it was not to be. Two shells from the *Warspite* blew every funnel she had got to pieces. A third shell made a great rent in her stern. A fourth ploughed up her deck and burst against the foremast, bringing it down. Two minutes later this vessel also was on fire, heeling over, with the *Warspite* still pounding her, and ripping great gashes in her starboard side and bottom. The last we saw of her was nothing more than a broken hulk. Slowly the *Egadine*, which was a hydroplane, parent ship, towed us towards port, passing the Crescent, with all the survivors of the *Queen Mary*, *Invincible*, *Ardent* and *Fortune* on board. For ten hours we were towed, and it was not till five o'clock next morning, when our quarter-decks were awash, that we had to abandon the old *Warrior*.'[11]

Thirty-two Cork crew died among the 900 sailors of the *Defence*, including Stoker Maurice Riordan from the Watercourse Road in Blackpool.

In all, ninety Cork men lost their lives at the Battle of Jutland, being among the 6,097 Royal Navy casualties after 14 ships were sunk; 11 German ships were sunk and 2,551 German sailors died. This is probably the greatest loss of life amongst Cork sailors in a naval battle in the history of naval warfare. It was the single worst day for Cork in the whole of the Great War on land or on sea. A number of ships, including the *Indefatigable*, were destroyed by a single salvo. It was later found that cordite, shell propellant, which had been overexposed to enable rapid fire, had itself caught fire and in turn ignited the magazine hold. The German Admirals, Scheer and Hipper especially, were hailed by the German public as victors of the Skagerrak. The *Cork Examiner* acknowledged the defeat and reported on the anxious enquiries from many Cork families seeking news on the fate of their loved ones. The *Examiner*, however, urged its readers to take heart from the gloom of defeat as the Royal Navy would have its revenge.[12] However, it did not, at least in battle, for it did not get the opportunity, as the German navy largely stayed in harbour until the end of the war. British naval superiority was still intact after Jutland and their shipbuilding capabilities greater, which still meant the Royal Navy was master of the seas and it would prove to be so until the end of the war. The German High Seas Fleet would briefly set out in April 1918 but its most lasting contribution to the war effort remained in tying up Royal Navy resources.

The continued dominance of the Royal Navy after Jutland led to what has been called one of the most epochal decisions of the war, the German's renewal of unrestricted submarine warfare in February 1917. It was a decision that would bring the destructive power of the war directly to the everyday lives of many Irish communities, including Blackpool. Admiral Scheer had advocated it as early as July 1916. But with, on the one hand, food riots in Germany after the failure of the potato crop (coupled with an even more draconian blockade due to a food agreement between Britain and Holland in December 1916) and the growing Allied military might demonstrated at the Battle of the Somme, and on the other, the projection that, with achievable monthly targets of shipping sunk, Britain could be knocked out of the war in five months, the Kaiser's government succumbed. What gave the Germans this belief were better U-boats with more torpedoes (more than twelve as opposed to four at the start of the war) and, more significantly, many more submarines in operation. With Britain out of the war the Western Front would collapse, the Germans forecast, even before America could fulfil its stated threats and send its comparatively small army over the dangerous Atlantic to Europe. It was a mistaken policy: not only did it fail to cripple Britain by underestimating its adaptability, it provoked President Wilson to declare war on 6 April 1917, two months after Germany announced global unrestricted submarine warfare. It immediately provided US naval logistics to the war effort, and US troops would eventually be a decisive factor in attaining Allied victory during the last hundred days of the war.[13]

The renewed German U-boat campaign was a serious threat to Britain and Ireland. At the start of the war British merchant shipping accounted for 43 per cent of world trade. By the end of 1916 this had contracted by only 4 per cent. Within a few months of the campaign the new Prime Minister Lloyd George was warned that if trends continued, Britain would be forced to sue for peace by the end of 1917. British and world shipping sunk in the initial months of the campaign doubled, even tripled, average figures from 1916. The last fortnight of April was dubbed 'black fortnight' as tonnage sunk reached its highest in the war, with over 550,000 tons of British and over 330,000 tons of world shipping sunk in the whole month. Anti-submarine weapons were largely ineffective. Intensive destroyer sweeps yielded few results; hydrophonic technology was still at an embryonic stage, and though an effective depth charge had been developed by 1916 with a depth charge discharger by 1917, mines remained the most effective method of inflicting direct damage to U-boats. Of the 188 U-boats sunk in the war, fifteen were in Irish waters. What saved British merchant shipping was the introduction of the convoy system.[14]

This entailed a number of merchant ships sailing together under the protection of the Royal Navy. The Admiralty had been reluctant to introduce it as it was believed that such a large target made rich pickings for any U-boat. It had, however, worked in smaller operations in the English Channel and other areas, and when it was introduced with a certain amount of desperation on Atlantic routes after June 1917, it proved dramatically successful. Of the 5,090 ships escorted for the remainder of 1917 only 63 were lost, compared with the 373 sunk in April 1917 alone. Merchant tonnage losses remained relatively high until the end of the war, mainly because of independent or lone sailings, for what convoys did was give more open sea for the U-boats to search in and even if the convoys were found some U-boats turned away to look for easier prey. Lloyd George claimed he himself forced the Admiralty to adopt the convoy system and, if so, then he had the support of the US navy in the guise of Admiral Sims. America provided 27 per cent of the Atlantic convoy protection that was the lifeline to the war effort.[15]

Cork merchant sailors also suffered from the U-boat onslaught. Merchant sailors were recognised as being a vital cog in the war effort and the majority of them saw themselves in that light too. Certainly Ebenezer Pike, the owner of the largest merchant sea fleet in Cork – the Cork Steam Packet and Cork Steam Ship Companies – was a prominent supporter of local organisations in aid of the war effort. Cork was one of the biggest ports on the island and, as already mentioned, Blackpool was very much connected to it, primarily through the cattle trade. It also had a significant number of merchant sailors residing there. The last three months of 1916 had seen six merchant ships sunk with Cork crew on board; four were sunk by submarines and two by mines. There was only one other sunk in 1916 with a Cork merchant sailor on board. In 1917 there were forty-six ships sunk with Cork crew; forty-two by U-boat and four by mines. In 1918 this would decrease to twenty-three, of which twelve were sunk by subs and one by mine, all within the first six months of the year except for one, indicating the success of the convoy system. Some of the ships had substantial numbers of Cork crew members.[16]

The first, and the worst, to affect Blackpool and Cork, was the sinking of the SS *Bandon* by *U 44* off the Waterford coast on 13 April 1917 with the loss of twenty-eight sailors, of whom twenty-seven were from Cork, including four from Blackpool. The *Bandon* had set sail from Liverpool on 12 April bound for Cork loaded with general merchandise. It was a Cork Steam Packet ship. The ship was torpedoed around 4.30 p.m. the next day and it sank within a few minutes. Four crew members survived, including the captain, P. F. Kelly, who recalled the fireman, John Walsh, letting go of the life-saving collapsible deck seat and grasping a large rope fender of the motor launch, but just as he did so the *Bandon* took a heavy roll, with the result that he lost his grip and was drowned. John Walsh was from Great Britain St/Great William O'Brien St. Also from that same street to lose his life was Batt Collins and, from Madden's Buildings, Simon Louro, both with wives and a number of children. William O'Sullivan, a cattleman from Walshe's Avenue, also went down with the ship. Cork city was in shock at the news and all corporation buildings lowered their flags in mourning. The *Cork Examiner* reported on the disaster only obliquely but as sinkings became more regular it reported them more extensively.[17]

The next U-boat attack to affect Blackpool was the torpedoing of the SS *Bellucia* on 7 July 1917. The *Bellucia* was not a Cork ship but operated by Bell Brothers of Glasgow. It was carrying flour and wheat from Montreal in Canada to London in a convoy when, at about 3 p.m. on 7 July, and 2 miles from the Lizard (the tip of Cornwall) it spotted a U-boat periscope (*U 31*). Almost immediately after the sighting, a torpedo struck the port side of the engine room, killing the third engineer, the chief steward and two firemen, one of whom was Eugene O'Leary from Thomas Davis Avenue. The *Bellucia* did not sink at once and the rest of the crew got clear in life rafts and were rescued soon afterwards. The sinking ship was blown inshore where it grounded and keeled over. Holes were cut in its exposed side and most of its cargo extracted.[18]

Thomas Davis Avenue experienced another casualty with the sinking of the SS *Ardmore* on 13 November 1917. Again this was a Cork Steam Packet ship, this time en route from London to Cork carrying general cargo; at 10.30 p.m. in the Celtic Sea it was struck by a torpedo fired from *U 95*. It sank almost immediately due to the explosion of one of its boilers with the loss of nineteen sailors, all from Cork, from a total crew of twenty-seven. Those who escaped managed to do so by means of a life raft which survived (though damaged by the powerful suction caused by the sinking of the ship).

Seaman Denis Collins, who lived next door to Eugene O'Leary in Thomas Davis Avenue, died as did Patrick Barry from Dublin St, Blackpool. (Patrick's father, Thomas Barry, was also a merchant marine sailor.)

The SS *Kenmare* had escaped previous attacks by U-boats, having been fired upon as early as June 1915 and being missed by a torpedo in October 1917. Along with a lot of merchant ships during the war, it became defensively armed with a cannon on deck, which enabled it to avoid a preying U-boat in November 1917. But its luck ran out in the Irish Sea en route from Liverpool to Cork on 2 March 1918 when it was torpedoed by *U 104*. There were only six survivors from a crew of thirty-five. One of the rescued was Tim O'Brien from Green Lane, Blackpool, and the following is a report of his experience:

> He was in his bunk at the time [7pm], in the steerage over the propeller, and was thrown by the force of the explosion some yards. The lights went out immediately. Four other firemen were sleeping in the rooms. There was some confusion in the darkness but he succeeded in getting a flash lamp and his lifebelt and made for the deck followed by James Barry. When he got on deck the ship was sinking fast. Along with Mr Evans he got into one of the lifeboats and floated off the ship. As they were leaving the ship they grabbed the donkeyman and pulled him into the boat. At this time the captain was on the deck shouting instructions as to the lowering of the boats. After leaving the sinking ship they rescued the carpenter and a gunner from the water. Meanwhile 25 of the crew had put off in a boat which became upturned and from which only one man, the steward, was rescued. They found him with his head through the bottom of the boat, and extricated him with great difficulty, he being powerless to assist, as one of his arms was broken. They remained in the vicinity for a quarter of an hour in the hope of picking up other men.
>
> For about ten minutes cries were coming from the water for assistance, but owing to the wreckage, they were unable to get to their drowning comrades. At about seven o'clock in the morning they were picked up by a small cruiser [*Glenside*]. They were then nearly dead with the cold, the majority being only half-clad. He (O'Brien) was in his shirt and trousers. The night was very cold, and a heavy sea was running. [They were landed at Dublin.][19]

Michael Coleman, fireman on the
SS *Kenmare*. (*Cork Examiner*)

Joseph Jones, Connaught Ranger,
drowned after sinking of SS *Leinster*.
(*Cork Examiner*)

Tim's fellow fireman, Michael Coleman from Great Britain St/ Great William O'Brien St, did not survive. The *Cork Examiner* reported 'heart-rending scenes' at the offices of the Cork Steam Packet Company on Penrose Quay 'when relatives of members of the crew formed a constant stream of callers to ascertain if any news was to hand respecting those who, in many instances, meant everything to the families they left ashore'. Eighteen of the twenty-nine drowned sailors were from Cork. The war was not over for the merchant seamen from Blackpool and two more would lose their lives before it ended. Eleven days after the sinking of the *Kenmare*, the SS *Castlebar* sank off the north coast of Ireland for an unknown reason with all hands lost. It was en route from Glasgow to Limerick with bagged grain. Fireman Michael O'Keefe was on board and was the third merchant sailor from the small laneway of Thomas Davis Avenue to die in the war. On 12 May the SS *Iniscarra* was torpedoed by *U 86* ten miles off Ballycotton with the loss of twenty-eight crew members (twenty of them from Cork) including Denis O'Shea of Great Britain St/Great William O'Brien St. In all, ten merchant seamen from Blackpool would die in the war out of a total of 207 from Cork city and county. These were men who left their homes to go to work and never returned. Their service to the war effort was vital and is commemorated as such at Tower Hill in London.

There was one more terrible twist in the war on the mercantile navy that would have a repercussion in Blackpool: the sinking of the SS *Leinster* by *U 123* on 10 October 1918, less than a month before the end of the war and only six days after Germany had started the process of surrender. This is one of the worst maritime disasters in history to affect Irish people as over 500 people lost their lives on a passenger ship that was transporting troops and civilians to Britain from Dublin. Lance Sergeant Joseph Jones of the 3rd Battalion Connaught Rangers was drowned. His body was recovered and subsequently buried in Whitechurch Cemetery, County Cork. He had lived at Upper Quarry Lane, Blackpool.

Most of the U-boats mentioned above, including *U 123*, did not survive to the end of the war. The HMS *Jessamine*, for example, depth-charged and destroyed the *U 104* (which had sunk the SS *Kenmare*) in April 1918 in St George's Channel. Mines, however, were a greater danger to the U-boats. After the Battle of Jutland the Royal Navy successfully maintained the naval blockade on Germany that was slowly undermining its civilian morale. It continued to patrol the seas surrounding the British Isles protecting and guarding. On 15 August 1917 the following brief mention appeared in the *Cork Constitution*:

DESTROYER LOST
————

MINED IN NORTH SEA

London, Tuesday

The Admiralty announces:– One of His Majesty's destroyers has struck a mine in the North Sea and sunk.

The captain, two officers, and 43 men were saved. All the next-of-kin have been informed.

– P.A. War Special.

William Sullivan (*far right*) who was active in the Zeebrugge raid posing with fellow Cork sailors including (*second from right*) William Kelly from Great Britain St/Great William O'Brien Street who served on HMS *Inconstant*. (*Cork Examiner*)

This referred to the destroyer HMS *Recruit II* which hit the mine on 9 August. Among the 53 who were killed in the blast was long-time navy man and stoker Michael Hegarty from Ballyvolane Road. There were also two other Cork sailors who perished, Con Connolly and John Donovan from Rosscarbery and Union Hall respectively.

The Royal Navy attempted one more major operation in April 1918 when it raided Ostend and Zeebrugge on the Belgian coast to disable them as submarine bases. It was a very daring raid but it ultimately proved a failure. It was a disappointing war for the Royal Navy in comparison to Nelson's time. As one historian has commented on Admiral Jellicoe, 'he fought to make a German victory impossible, rather than a British victory certain.'[20] By neutralising the U-boat threat the Allied navies had defeated a war-winning ploy by the enemy. British shipping carried over a million Dominion soldiers without loss and hundreds of thousands across the Channel. It transported over 23.7 million people, 2.25 million animals and 46.5 million tons of British military stores during the war.[21] It successfully enforced an economic blockade of Germany which, ultimately, fatally undermined the German war effort. Such success received a symbolic vindication when the German High Seas Fleet scuppered itself at Scapa Flow in June 1919 after the Treaty of Versailles.

7

Bravery of Blackpool Soldiers as the War Continues – 1917

EVERY WAR PRODUCES HEROIC acts by soldiers and the First World War was no different. Acts of valour and conspicuous gallantry were recognised by the British army through the public awarding of various medals. The highest honour was the Victoria Cross (VC), and next were the Distinguished Service Order (DSO) for officers and the Distinguished Conduct Medal (DCM) for other ranks. Below them were the Military Cross (MC) for officers and the Military Medal for the other ranks and then down to the lowest recognition for gallantry, Mentioned in Despatches, which was when a valiant act by a soldier was publically recognised by a senior officer. The Irish soldiers who went to war were probably imbued with romantic notions of gallantry and heroism, certainly more so than their counterparts in other areas of the British Isles, given the political culture of Ireland which was enhanced by the development of the Irish Volunteers prior to August 1914.

Constitutional Irish nationalism had subsumed as best it could a reverence of the Irish rebellious past into its wide political topography. Speeches by Redmond and others extolled the military, and also the manly, virtues of the Irish soldier going to war and purposefully framed the act as a continuation of a proud Irish military history that stretched back hundreds of years. It was a context that was understood by the soldiers themselves and the general Irish public. It would have been the framework in which the Irish involvement in the Great War would have been sequenced in a Home Rule Ireland led by John Redmond and undoubtedly the new roads and housing estates of that state would have borne

Sergeant Denis Donovan from Watercourse Road, Mentioned in Despatches. (*Cork Examiner*)

John Cronin, of HMS *Thunderer*, from Thomas Davis Street. (*Cork Examiner*)

testimony to this Irish military participation, the most extensive ever in its history, then or since. Instead the language and rhetoric of military valour and manliness only helped to polarise a divided Irish society that began to cleave open after the Easter Rising. Was not Patrick Pearse's 'blood sacrifice' and his political/spiritual apotheosis the only counter to the abysmal vortex of the Great War for those indifferent, wearied and, of course, opposed?

Regarding heroism in the war itself, as one Cork soldier remarked in a letter to a friend, if the British army recognised all the acts of outstanding bravery during the war, they would not have any metal left to make ammunition for the guns.[1] Blackpool soldiers also came to prominence for their acts of valour and the following are only the ones I have been able to confirm: as mentioned before, Sergeant William Foley gained a Military Medal for the stand he took at Étreux in August 1914 when the 2nd Battalion Royal Munster Fusiliers heroically delayed a German army in the BEF retreat after Mons. He became a prisoner of war and spent the war years in a German prison. Sergeant Denis Donovan, of the Leinster Regiment

Sergeant Cornelius (Con) O'Callaghan DCM, 2nd Battalion Royal Munster Fusiliers. (*Cork Examiner*)

in the 16th Irish Division, was Mentioned in Despatches in February 1916.[2] He was from the Watercourse Road. The Division during that time were adjusting to trench warfare with the help of French soldiers on the Ypres Salient and had to withstand a number of localised German attacks. Unrelated directly with the war, the *Cork Examiner* brought its readers' attention to the heroic act of sailor John Cronin of York St/Thomas Davis St in saving a drowning woman whilst boarding his ship the HMS *Thunderer* at Lowestoft. He jumped in, fully clothed, to save her. He was a member of the Roche's Guards Band and his family ran a shop in Blackpool.[3] Another member of the Roche's Guards Band, Patrick Condon of Bullen's Alley, received a Military Medal for the gallant part he played in the Battle of Cambrai in late 1917 with the Royal Munster Fusiliers. Another to receive a Military Medal was the Rev. J. Scannell, chaplain to the Irish Guards and who was, and continued to be after the war, a teacher at Farranferris College.[4]

One of the highest awards for bravery was given to Sergeant Cornelius O'Callaghan: he earned a DCM for the part he played in what one historian has called 'The Great Raid', made on German trenches by the 2nd Battalion Royal Munster Fusiliers on 25 June 1916.[5] The 2nd Munsters were at Le Brebis at the Loos sector north of the 16th Division and various major raids were enacted at this time in a diversionary ploy in preparation for the Battle of the Somme on 1 July. According to the 1911 census, Con O'Callaghan was a general labourer, married to Ellen, with a baby daughter and living in Broad Lane, off Great Britain St/Great William O'Brien

St, where he would live subsequently. On the night of 25 June 1916 he had his face blackened and had a white bandage or signifier placed on his shoulder along with the 160 others of the raiding party. They were divided into two groups of eighty which were further subdivided into four groups of twenty. They had already practised at night on dummy trenches. The real German trenches were only 100 yards from the Munsters' line and on the previous night tape markers had been surreptitiously laid out to aid access and escape across the terrain. All the raiders had revolvers and, on average, seven bombs and those designated to enter the trenches carried a bludgeon as well.[6]

The raiding party climbed into no-man's-land halfway between the German and Allied trenches and awaited the bombardment which arrived at 11.10 p.m. The attack commenced at the sound of well-aimed machine-gun fire which came soon after the shelling. The bombardment had broken the barbed wire to allow access to the trenches but there the raiders met heavier resistance than expected. Once the initial posts were overcome casualties were light for the next fifteen minutes or so. The Germans had expected a raid but not one as big as this. Bombs and bludgeons were used extensively and later Lieutenant Colonel W. B. Lyons noted that 'the Irish soldier is fond of this form of weapon. They are perhaps too deadly if prisoners are desired.'[7] There were no prisoners that night. It was estimated that forty Germans were killed. The withdrawal involved the carrying back of wounded soldiers under heavy fire and in total seventy Munsters were either killed or wounded. The Divisional Commander commended the Munsters in their feat and it earned the raiders one VC, four DCMs, two MCs, and nine Military Medals. The following appeared in the *London Gazette* 27 July 1916:

> 4/6403 Sjt. C. O'Callaghan, 2nd Bn., R. Muns. Fus., Spec. Res.
>
> For conspicuous gallantry during a raid. He led his party with great dash down the hostile trenches, and held his own against the determined efforts of the enemy. He was badly wounded during the withdrawal, but stuck to some equipments he had captured.

2nd Lieutenant. Francis Mooney,
1st Battalion Royal Dublin Fusiliers.
(*Cork Examiner*)

He was only one of the 23,000 soldiers to receive a DCM during the war.[8]

Francis Mooney from the Commons Road might have been as brave but not as lucky when the 1st Battalion of the Dublin Fusiliers attacked trenches opposite their front line east of Sailly (near Ginchy) on the Somme on 28 February 1917. He was killed in action in a manoeuvre that attained some of the Dublin Fusiliers' military objectives.[9]

The war was relentless. It gave rise in Britain and France to a growing sense of impatience and demands for a victorious ending. Such pressures contributed to the replacement of Herbert Asquith as Prime Minister in Britain by David Lloyd George and also the toppling of the French premier, Aristide Briand, in March 1917. The Germans were on the defensive on the Western Front and tactically retreated to the greatly fortified line known as the Hindenburg Line. They concentrated more resources on the eastern front which resulted in the overrun of Romania in late 1916 after defeating the Serbian army. The French responded to their mounting pressure with a new plan of attack, the Nivelle Offensive, named after the person who devised it, the new commander-in-chief of the French forces, General Robert Nivelle. His plan envisaged a massive French attack on the River Aisne that had the genuine expectation of smashing the German army within forty-eight hours. Nivelle convinced Lloyd George to persuade the BEF to instigate a diversionary attack and BEF command agreed to do so at Arras one week before the mid-April date for the French offensive.

The Battle of Arras lasted from 9 April to 16 May 1917 and involved British, Canadian, New Zealand, Newfoundland and Australian troops. Its aim was to draw German troops away from the French sector at the Aisne and capture the German-held high ground that dominated the plains of Douai. The southern part of the attack at Bellevue did not proceed as well as expected as the Germans here employed 'elastic defences' which meant troops would temporarily retreat, regroup and then counter-attack. In the central and northern sector, however, the British and Canadian troops were more successful, with the Canadians capturing Vimy Ridge, one of the more famous feats of the war.[10] Daniel Donovan, from the Commons Road, Blackpool originally, was with the 50th Battalion of the Canadian Infantry in that attack. He had emigrated to Canada sometime after April 1911 and ended up in a town called Vanderhoof in Alberta province. He had been a general labourer in Ireland (he was also able to speak Irish) but by the time he enlisted in the Canadian army in late 1915, he had become a fireman. His battalion arrived in France on 11 June 1916.

After the first phase of the BEF offensive it became clear that the Nivelle plan was failing. This led in turn to significant mutinies within the French army, indicating a weariness that was afflicting French society and its army. The BEF felt compelled to persist in their offensive to help shore up the French sector. The offensive in Arras, which lasted until 16 May, consisted of a series of battles that consolidated the gains already made, like at Vimy Ridge, and also gained more ground, but at high casualty rates. The Canadians suffered 11,004 casualties at Vimy Ridge. There was no breakthrough despite the better use of the creeping barrage and counter-battery shelling by the Royal Field Artillery. The Germans too had improved defensive techniques.

After the Arras offensive there were further attacks by the Allies to consolidate the gains made but also to prepare the line for the major offensive planned for the Ypres Salient in August. Daniel Donovan's 50th Battalion Canadian Infantry were the leading troops in their part of the Battle of Lens in early June. The Canadians were tasked with breaking into the German salient between Avion and the outskirts of Lens. The 4th Division, which included 50th Infantry Battalion, were to lead the capture of a number of fortified positions behind the Vimy–Lens line including the village of La

Coulotte, a brewery and an electricity generating station. The 44th Battalion attacked La Coulotte and the brewery on the right while 50th Battalion's target was the generating station on the left.[11]

The war diary for the 50th Battalion records that, at midnight, 'The barrage opened partially at the zero hour (12am) and simultaneously 15 officers and 435 ORs "went over". Casualties 1OR [Ordinary Rank] killed.' Both the 44th and 50th Battalions met stiff opposition but by 2.35 a.m. it was claimed that a few companies of 50th Battalion had achieved their objectives. By 8.30 a.m. they had taken control of the generating station but it was a tenuous control, as it was under well-observed enemy shell fire and, importantly, the 44th Battalion on the right had been forced back to their original lines after attaining their objectives only temporarily. Sniping was a major problem as the troops found it difficult to entrench due to the hardness of the ground. By 3 p.m. 'casualties had become serious' within the 50th Battalion and reinforcements were called for but none arrived. In turn, the Canadians were unable to prevent German reinforcements from arriving and at 6.45 p.m., who, after a 'short but intense bombardment', counter-attacked 'using bombs chiefly' and forced the remnants of the 50th Battalion to withdraw with their wounded to their old position. At the end of the day amongst the 50th Battalion there were 129 wounded, 32 counted as missing (probably prisoners or dead), and 30 killed. Private Daniel Donovan died that day.[12]

Though this attack did not succeed, the Canadian soldiers had gained a reputation over the preceding months, coupled with the large-scale raiding carried on thereafter in the Lens region, which proved them to be doughty soldiers; they would be increasingly employed as elite or storm troops in BEF-led attacks.

The next major operation in which the Canadian Corps were involved was the Third Battle of Ypres. The 16th Irish Division and the 36th Ulster Division had had a cooperative success at the Battle of Messines on 7 June. This was a preparatory battle for the Third Ypres offensive and the Irish troops, both unionist and nationalist, managed to capture the important Messine Ridge including the village of Wytschaete. It was a battle famous for the man-made earthquake caused by the explosion of nineteen massive mines underneath the German lines which shook the earth and killed 10,000 German soldiers and, it was claimed, could be heard in London. There were relatively very few Irish casualties but a notable one was Willie Redmond MP, brother of John Redmond, an irony considering that the Redmonds held a redeeming hope in the war as a means of reconciliation between the two traditions in Ireland and to which the Battle of Messines would have been a shining example of cooperation. The success of the 16th Irish Division at Messines brought them to prominence and they too were assigned as storm troops for the coming offensive in Flanders.[13]

Commander-in-Chief of the BEF General Haig's advocacy of the offensive at Ypres in August 1917 was based on a belief that a 'wearing out fight' was necessary before the lines could be breached, which could then be exploited to give a serious, if not fatal, setback to the German army. The great optimism of a war-winning breakthrough evident at the outset of the Somme campaign had certainly become more circumspect. The Ypres Salient was chosen because of the exposed position of the BEF to the German army who were able to inflict high casualty rates in the static warfare of the trench system. It was also a major consideration that the bases for the Gotha bombers, which were attacking London, were in Flanders and that the Belgian coast harboured the 3rd Fleet of German U-boats, whose overall threat to merchant shipping was of grave concern in the spring and summer of 1917. Others factors in persuading Lloyd George and the British government to give their backing to Haig were that the Russians, under a new government headed by Kerensky, were fighting on the eastern front since July and a Ypres offensive would not only hinder Germany's eastern transfer of troops, it would also bolster the brittle morale within the French army and government (a near continuous factor in BEF thinking). Haig envisaged the BEF and allies taking control of the Belgian coast and even pushing the Germans back to the Dutch border, a very serious setback.[14]

The battle started on 31 July, led by General Gough's Fifth Army which initially consisted of nine British divisions amounting to around 100,000 men. The 16th Irish Division were brought to the front and held in reserve for the second phase of the attack expected two or three days later. The first objectives of advancing 4,000–5,000 yards, however, were not reached despite fighting along a shorter front than at the Somme, using four times more shells in the bombardment, having air superiority and forty-eight tanks. The Germans had this strategically valuable area well protected with numerous well-hidden concrete pillboxes for machine guns and again used the tactic of elastic defence. The Germans also used a new gas, mustard gas, which was more effective in debilitating advancing troops though less lethal than chlorine and the even deadlier phosgene. The BEF suffered 27,000 casualties on the first day which was half the sum at the Somme but managed to gain 18 square miles as opposed to the 3.5 miles the year before. They captured Pilcken Ridge but not the Gheluvelt Plain which the Germans retook. The heavy rain that started to fall on the first day was a factor and when it continued for the whole of August it would define the battle as a hell of mud and blood. British bombardment had wrecked the land's drainage system, turning the area into a morass of mud which frustrated every soldier in the grinding heat of battle.[15] Irish soldiers testified to the utmost horror of the Third Ypres offensive, claiming that Messines and even Ginchy and Guillemont were easy compared to soldiering in Flanders in the autumn of 1917.

The 16th Irish Division were in reserve and their planned attack was delayed until a renewed offensive battle was scheduled for 16 August, an attack on Langemarck. They remained at the front area all that time and suffered heavy casualties while they acted as reinforcements and carrying parties, and undertaking fatigue duties. They were in full view of German artillery.[16] The 6th Battalion Connaught Rangers 'marched via Ypres and the Menin Gate to the old British reserve line' to release the 2nd Dublin Fusiliers in the trenches left of the St Jean–Weltje Road and found the trenches in a 'terrible condition'. By the night of 2 August they were on the reverse slope of the Frezeberg Ridge. The next day they were heavily shelled while it rained all day, making the trenches a misery. The morning of 4 August was relatively quiet but as the war diary records:

In the afternoon E.A. [Enemy Aircraft] were very active 14 planes being observed over our lines at one time. At 4pm heavy shelling was reported on our front line occupied by the 6th Royal Irish and D Coy prepared to reinforce but the intended attack was broken up by our own barrage. During the night shelling was again heavy and the battalion had its first experience of the new mustard gas employed by the enemy the shell being cleverly mixed with whizz-bangs.[17]

Private William Henry was killed during that day with the Rangers. He had a soldiering background; he was born in India and his next of kin were from Walshe's Avenue in Blackpool.

The 6th Connaught Rangers did not take part in the Battle of Langemarck on 16 August 1917 but their casualties up to 18 August were 250 men. For the 16th Irish Division, as a whole, the rate was just as high even before their participation in the next attack, suffering over 2,000 casualties.[18] The 36th Ulster Division suffered 1,500 casualties. The Battle of Langemarck increased this for both divisions but especially the Ulster Division as the battle made gains but successful counter-attacks by the Germans recaptured some of them. The plan of attack was now switched from General Gough to General Plumer of the Second Army, who took longer to prepare for the assaults and used a greater amount of artillery with the more limited aim of taking the Gheluvelt Plain. This was successfully achieved in three successive battles of 'bite and hold' attacks where each gain was limited but incremental. These attacks commenced on 20 September with the capture of Menin Road Ridge, then Polygon Wood on 26 September and finally at Broodseinde on 4 October. What helped the BEF was that September was exceptionally dry but the rains returned in October and turned the landscape into a quagmire once again.

The victory at Broodseinde on 4 October was notable as it dealt a significant blow to the German army and its command. German losses were very heavy and the 5,000 prisoners of war, a significant number at this stage in the conflict, was an 'unmistakable sign of demoralisation'.[19] It was a 12th Division assault and included Australian and New Zealand troops. Jeremiah Patrick Baldwin, whose father, Edward, resided at 26 Dublin St in Blackpool at the time, was with the 3rd/10th Battalion Middlesex Regiment, who were with the 4th Division in the attack which also included the 2nd Battalion Royal Dublin Fusiliers. The Middlesex Battalion were 'in support to 2nd Seaforths who were the attacking Battalion. The two forward Coys B + C coming under the orders of the 2nd Seaforths for zero hour, 6:00am, on the 4/10/17. 2 Platoons of B Coy being detailed as left plank guards + to keep in touch with the Dublin Fusiliers.' Their objective was 19 Metre Hill and the attackers managed to take the trench line, called 'Beek', prior to the hill before those advancing were pinned back by withering machine-gun fire. The Germans counter-attacked at 3 p.m. and came close to overrunning the gained positions but an artillery barrage, aided by covering fire from 11th Division on the left, enabled the Middlesex and Seaforth battalions to retain their achieved ground. Eventually more ammunition and reinforcements were brought up and they consolidated their position overnight. Private Baldwin was killed in action during the day. The 3rd/10th Battalion Middlesex Regiment would be relieved during the night of 5 and 6 October.[20]

The initial success of the attack on 4 October at Broodesinde tempted the British commanders to enlarge and exploit it and while General Gough gave orders to do so, the news of 4th Division's (which included the 3rd/10th Middlesex Regiment) repulse by the Germans at 19 Metre Hill prompted him to rescind the orders. The continuing rain from 4 October hindered the Allies for the remainder of the offensive. Victory at Broodesinde opened the way for an attack on the Passchendaele Ridge, another tactically vital area. This time the attacks on 9 and 12 October were more hurried in preparation, especially for the artillery. For the first time the German barbed-wire formations were not significantly damaged and led to heavy casualties for the BEF. The 12 October attack is deemed one of the blackest days in New Zealand military history. Many historians agree that General Haig should have ceased the offensive at this stage but he persisted.[21] He gave the main responsibility for the capture of the Passchendaele Ridge and its environs to the Canadian Corps under the command of General Arthur Currie. After some preparation he launched a number of large-scale assaults starting on 26 and 30 October and 6 and 10 November, which succeeded in capturing the village of Passchendaele and some, but not all, of the Ridge.

The attack on 26 October was led primarily by the 4th and 3rd Divisions (whose exploits on the Somme have been described in part already) but it also linked up with a brigade of the 63rd (Royal Navy) Division. This division had an unusual history as it was comprised of infantry who had initially been navy recruits but whose surplus now were employed by the army. Robert Spillane from Spring Lane in Blackpool, and who had worked in the Flax Factory at Millfield, was part of this division, being with the 2nd Royal Marine Battalion, which formed part of the 188th Infantry Brigade that was attacking on 26 October. It began at 5.40 a.m. and soon the 2nd Royal Marine had helped the Brigade to attain their objectives of Varlet Farm and Banff House, but in the centre they were held up between the village of Wallenden and Bray Farm. They were forced to dig in before their objective of Source Trench. After dark, Banff House had to be conceded. On the day there were 308 casualties amongst the 2nd Battalion Royal Marines, including Robert Spillane who was killed in action.[22]

The battle at Passchendaele continued until 28 October with success for the 3rd Canadian Division in the northern section but less so in the southern end. The renewed attack on 30 October aimed to complete those failed objectives and create a platform for an attack on Passchendaele but again it was met with great resistance from the German defenders which prevented a significant sector being taken; however, the Canadians did get close to the village of Passchendaele itself. On 6 November the Canadians finally captured the village and other objectives which set up the last attack of the campaign for 10 November with the aim of gaining control of the remaining high ground north of the village in the vicinity of Hill 52. Here the Canadians had the help, amongst others, of the 2nd Battalion Royal Munster Fusiliers.

At the start of October the 2nd Munsters were at Clipon Camp near Dunkirk preparing for an amphibious assault with the 1st

Division on the coast of Belgium in anticipation of success in the early battles around Passchendaele on 9 and 12 October. By 15 October these preparations had been called off and they reverted to semi-open warfare training instead. Sergeant Con O'Callaghan DCM was with them, having recovered from the injury he sustained in July when the Munsters' camp was shelled. On 8 November the Munsters moved to Irish Farm via Ypres and prepared for the attack. They were in line at Source Farm and ready at 4.10 a.m. on 10 November. To their right were the South Wales Borderers, also part of 1st Division, while the main advance on the ridge would be to the south led by the 2nd Canadian Infantry Brigade.[23]

The shelling began at 5.55 a.m. Five minutes later the Munsters attacked, following a creeping barrage. Objectives were attained relatively easily and quickly though there was 'stiff fighting' around Vat and Veal Cottages and 'sniping from all directions'. Many prisoners were captured in the process. At 7.15 a.m. a German Battalion was seen massing for a counter-attack and, according to the Munsters' war diary, 'they could be seen from a long way off and could have been beaten off by rifle fire but owing to mud not a single rifle was in action'. Two SOS signals were sent from Vat Cottage to notify artillery for a supporting barrage but owing to misty conditions that morning they were not seen.

The Munsters became 'perturbed' when they could not link up with the Welsh troops to their right. This was due to the Welsh Borderers' advance being pushed further to the right by German enfilading fire within 30 yards of their starting trench. This left their attack in disarray and forced the Munsters to retreat from their captured ground as the Germans began to exploit the gap. Enemy aircraft also enabled accurate shelling of the Munsters' position and it was during this period that 'a large number of officers and NCOs were knocked out'.[24] The Munsters rallied again to retake Tournant Farm but little else. They were reinforced by the 1st Gloucestershire Regiment in the afternoon and relieved from the front at 10 p.m. that night owing to their heavy casualties. Sergeant Con O'Callaghan DCM, from Blackpool, was killed in action during the day which also saw the Munsters suffer over 400 casualties out of a fighting force of 650. His body was never recovered and he is commemorated at Tyne Cot Memorial, Zonnebeke, Belgium.[25]

The attack on 10 November was called off despite not attaining all of the Passchendaele–Westrozebeke Ridge. The capture of Passchendaele inflicted 12,000 casualties on the Canadians but it left the BEF less exposed to German gunfire. However, General Haig would eventually think that their gains made the salient deeper and more angular and, ultimately, untenable. The human cost of the Third Battle of Ypres was 275,000 casualties for the Allies while the Germans estimated their casualties at 200,000, although some put it at double this amount.[26] Such losses, even at the conservative figure, were much harder to bear for the Germans and such attrition would contribute to the German decision to launch a series of all-out offensives in March 1918, after the Russians had pulled out of the war and the Americans had not arrived in large numbers. It was a decision that decided the war.

The Third Battle of Ypres, or Passchendaele as it became increasingly known, left an indelible mark on British memory of the war. The mud and the wasteland of the battle, coupled with the excess and futility of losses at the Somme, have been perceptions that have passed down the decades in British society. Poets would use it to denounce all wars. There was a spark of hope at the Battle of Cambrai in late November 1917 when aided by a quantity of tanks the BEF managed for the first time since 1915 to break through the German lines. It proved momentary as the Germans counter-attacked very successfully, sealing their lines and pushing the attackers back by early December. The Irish Guards fought at this battle, as did the 2nd Royal Munster Fusiliers and it was with them that Patrick Condon received a Military Medal for bravery. He was from Bullen's Alley in Blackpool and was a Roche's Guards Band member.

However, more sombre news would reach Blackpool before the end of the year. On 20 December, Lance Corporal James Lee, originally from the Common's Road in Blackpool, was shot and seriously injured while with the 3rd Canterbury Regiment of the New Zealand army, who were manning lines at the Polderhoek sector on the Ypres Salient. It is probable that James had been either on a reconnaissance mission into no-man's-land or a small raid on the German trenches and was shot on his return. It shattered part of his pelvis. As he was in the care of the New Zealand army, he did not return to his mother, Annie, in Cork for hospitalisation but ended up at Brockenhurst New Zealand Soldiers' Hospital near London.[27] For the Lee family on the Commons Road it would be a very anxious Christmas worrying over the seriousness of the injury to their son James.

Up to this point as many as seventy-five other soldiers from Blackpool had been wounded due to their participation in the war. But it would be a sadder Christmas for families of the thirty-eight soldiers, the six Royal Navy sailors and the eight merchant seamen from the locality who had lost their lives. Such a toll had an impact on communities like Blackpool that is often forgotten or unremarked upon. It was a burden that weighed on communities not only in Cork city but throughout Ireland and Britain. It was a burden that for many called into question the war itself.

8

Blackpool and the Last Year of the War – 1918

AFTER THE WATERLOGGED horror of Passchendaele started to become known, it added to the growing sense of gloom about the war in Britain. The winter of 1917/18 has been described as the nadir in this respect and one can imagine a fatalistic despondency developing when plans were afoot to carry the war into 1919 and even 1920. This was beginning to have repercussions within British society as one contemporary, socialist R. H. Tawney, observed amongst the working classes in December 1917:

> Three years ago the war was popular, a thing for which people were glad to make sacrifices. At present, as far as I can see, it is not. I doubt one would get a hearing at a working-class meeting if one spoke of the principles at stake. One would get laughed down![1]

Such antagonism had become evident in Ireland as far back as late 1915 and Bishop O'Dwyer's public letter was just as dismissive of the 'principles' involved. The war was not a short one and it needed the forces of endurance and commitment both in Britain and Ireland. In Britain it was the middle classes who would ultimately maintain and actively repair the national consensus and support for the war. They would do this, not despite suffering more proportionately than other classes through loss of life and the economic burden they carried, but because of these sacrifices. The war not only had to be just, it had to be won.[2]

In Ireland the Catholic middle classes never had the same proportional investment in the war and thus could not fulfil the same role as buttress to the war effort. In contrast the nationalist, Catholic, labouring classes of urban Ireland, like Blackpool, had contributed greatly in soldiers and sailors to the war during the first two years which probably caused a painful disjuncture for a period as Ireland's political stance morphed into one of outright rejection of and antagonism to the British Empire. It could be argued that the seemingly interminable nature of the war made swathes of home-based Catholic nationalists susceptible to a reinvigorated cadre of separatists, inspired by the Easter Rising, and their message of the anti-war alternative of a free, Gaelic Ireland. This susceptibility was greatly aided by food shortages and the fear of famine which Ireland, and in particular Cork city, suffered during 1917, reaching its greatest crisis between the autumn of 1917 and early 1918, a point replicated in Britain itself. Shortages of potatoes, milk, butter and meat for certain periods prompted impromptu organisations, in most cases in tandem with or linked to prominent separatist nationalists like Tomás MacCurtain, to protest, demanding an end to dead-meat exports, and general food self-sufficiency. Price inflation was also a major concern with accusations of war profiteering rife as the cost of goods like potatoes doubled in a year and a half. This in turn produced a spate of strikes in Cork city demanding better pay. In 1917 there were six strikes in Cork but in the first six months of 1918 there were nineteen alone with a further eleven during the rest of that year. There was a successful strike at the Cork Spinning and Weaving Company at Millfield, Blackpool, in early July 1918. A long war simply asked too much from an Irish society that had been too politically intractable from the start. It cracked under the strain and the rupture brought forth latent forces that would sweep Ireland towards a Gaelic separatist ideal and the War of Independence.

The Rising in 1916 put an end to recruiting meetings in Ireland. There would be no more special trips to Blackpool by tram for the army.[3] This left a civic gap which the more extreme nationalists amply filled especially when their leaders, including Tomás MacCurtain, were released from prison in June 1917. Count Plunkett, father of executed leader Joseph Plunkett, won an electoral contest in Roscommon in February 1917 indicating this change of opinion within Ireland. Sinn Féin was reactivated in Cork during 1917 and in May won another electoral seat in Longford, which prompted a victory procession of about 1,500 people in Cork. As this parade proceeded down the streets of Cork the marchers sang songs like 'The Soldiers' Song' (the Irish version, 'Amhrán na bhFiann', would become the national anthem) but some bystanders sang, in return, 'Tipperary' and 'Keep the Home Fires Burning'.[4] Éamon de Valera won Willie Redmond's seat in Clare in July and William T. Cosgrave won a by-election in Kilkenny in August. The Irish Parliamentary Party had wedded themselves to Britain in the war effort and had largely had to abandon the anti-British rhetoric which was inherent in Irish nationalism. This too was exploited by Sinn Féin who portrayed Irish troops as being mere cannon fodder for the British war machine. Arthur Griffith even suggested that, like the famine, the war was a kind of Irish genocide.[5]

The rise of Sinn Féin and radical nationalism in Ireland in the post-Rising era has been likened to an expression of religious nationalism, which, in the context of the war in Europe where industrial nations were pouring all their resources into annihilating each other, was very understandable.[6] This was not led by the Irish Catholic Church but the Church did follow popular feeling. Bishop Colohan of Cork refused to meet the Irish-Canadian soldiers when they marched through Cork in February 1917. When Éamon de Valera came to Cork in December 1917 he spoke to a large crowd on Grand Parade about the Sinn Féin movement, and by inference himself, being like Moses leading the Israelites to the Promised Land and away from the evil clutches of the pharaoh, i.e. the British Empire.

The speech is a snapshot, but an interesting one, of the changing position of Sinn Féin in Ireland. The continuing uncertainty over Home Rule and the partition issue exposed Redmond and the Irish Party to de Valera's charge that 'they had sacrificed the young men of Ireland to help those hypocrites'[7] who claimed to be fighting for liberty and the freedom of small nations but denied Ireland's right to self-determination. It must be remembered that there had been an expectation that the war would only last a year at most and that Home Rule would then be implemented, i.e. sometime in the autumn of 1915. It was now December 1917 and there was little prospect of it being implemented soon. In fact, the two efforts the government made in the wake of the 1916 Rising to reach a Home Rule settlement had ended in failure and acrimony, further demoralising all. De Valera also tried to reassure his audience regarding the extremism of his position by claiming that it had been Redmond who had 'turned away from the path he was chosen to follow' and all Sinn Féin was doing was 'going back from the bypaths to which they [the people] had been led ... to simply ... the bedrock of nationality'[8] and referenced Parnell in another part of his speech to add weight to Sinn Féin's claim as the real people's party and not Redmond's party.

De Valera also called on the people to persist with Sinn Féin as 'they might only make slow progress – even just as the Allies only made the progress of eleven inches of ground – but it was progress, however,'[9] a sardonic comment that alluded to the widespread disillusionment and frustration at the stalemate of the war, but which also implied that the war was a distant event without any emotional resonance with the Irish people. It was an attitude that informed the polarising rhetoric of Sinn Féin at this time and again was implied when de Valera brought up the subject of unity behind the movement. This unity was needed in the face of British government divisiveness as they were trying 'to get the Catholic Church opposed to their movement. They [the British government] hated the Catholic Church as much as they hated Irish nationality and nothing would please them better than these two enemies of theirs, and friends of each other, should fall out for their amusement.'[10] But in regard to the Irish soldiers who were fighting in France he made this veiled reference: 'Oil and water would not mix, and neither could those who gave allegiance to England unite with those who gave allegiance to Ireland and Ireland only.' The process of alienating the war in Europe from what it was to be Irish, as an experience for hundreds of thousands of Irishmen and their families, was gaining political traction in Ireland as Sinn Féin grew ever more popular.[11]

Irish society also became more sectarian during this process which became evident with the matter of conscription. Britain had introduced conscription in January 1916 and the issue had hovered over Irish politics ever since. It finally became a reality in April 1918 after the massive German offensive in March of that year. By and large, Protestant Ireland accepted it while Catholic Ireland, with the Catholic Church very much involved along with Sinn Féin and also the fading Irish Parliamentary Party, successfully opposing its introduction. Only an Irish Parliament could impose conscription on the Irish people, it was deemed. The success of the campaign instituted Sinn Féin as the political guardians of the Irish Catholic people and eight months later, in December 1918, the general election demonstrated it. Even though the Irish Party had opposed conscription as well, it could not prevent the decline of a party that had become too associated with the war and the British effort in that war. John Redmond died in March 1918, some say a broken man. His brother, Willie Redmond, had died in the war and the political project that he (John) had led for the last seventeen years receded before his very eyes. The war had changed everything.

The middle classes helped to buoy sagging morale in Britain and the ending of food queues at shops in February 1918 also helped continued commitment to the war effort.[12] There was good news on the war front for the first time: the Egyptian Expeditionary Force (EEF) was defeating the Turks in Palestine. The EEF under General Murray had made some progress on the Sinai Peninsula and into Palestine against the Turks until they were checked at Gaza. After a further defeat, General Murray was replaced by General Edmund Allenby, who had been Third Army Commander in France. Allenby asked for more troops and received the 60th (London) Division and the 10th Irish Division from Salonika. The 10th Division had been involved in fighting the Bulgarians intermittently over the year and half they had been stationed in the Balkans. James Donovan was with the 6th Leinster Regiment of the 10th Division and had been with them since the landing at Suvla Bay at Gallipoli in August 1915. His brother, Daniel Donovan of the Canadian Infantry, had been killed near Lens in France in June 1917. They were from the Commons Road, Blackpool.

The front line in Palestine was from the sea at Gaza to east of Beersheba, and Allenby planned to attack Beersheba on 31 October 1917.[13] Two regiments, the 6th and 1st Leinster Regiments, were allocated the vital task of water supply in the parched lands of southern Palestine. A water pipeline had been constructed under General Murray's orders from Egypt into the area but 30,000 camels were still needed to carry the 34,000 water containers, or 'fanatis' as they were called locally, to the front-line troops and, of course, to where they advanced. James Donovan was part of the 6th Leinster Regiment that did this job for two weeks, night and day. The attack at Beersheba was a success in what was the beginning of a series of victories that took the EEF to the gates of Jerusalem by December. For the 6th Leinsters, the work at Beersheba in loading 30,000 camels with water and then transporting them to their destinations was conducted in searing heat. In October their war diary recorded that 1 officer and 215 ordinary rank were admitted to hospital, 162 from malaria and 53 other cases. Malaria had been rife in the ranks during their stay in the Balkans and the troops had been weakened by it. The 6th Leinsters fell into line again with the 10th Division on 6 November and were in support when the 31st Brigade of the 10th Division took Hareira Redoubt on 6–7 November.[14] On 8 November the Leinsters marched back to Kat Camp at Karm which was about 10 miles across the desert, a march that exerted a physical toll on the regiment. At some time Private James Donovan was admitted to hospital where he died of pneumonia on 15 November 1917. Jeremiah Donovan, a general labourer from the Commons Road, would be the second father from Blackpool to experience the loss of his two sons, James and Daniel, in the war.

On 8 December the EEF attacked the Turkish lines defending Jerusalem from the Hebron side and the next morning the keys of the city were handed to Irishman Major General John Shea. General Allenby entered the city formally on 11 December. For the first time in the war real progress could be seen, however minor it was

Lance Corporal John O'Driscoll, Royal Engineers (Spring Lane Band Member). (*Cork Examiner*)

in the overall context. The attack on the Turkish position continued on 26–27 December which saw the 10th Division attaining Zeitoun Ridge. The Turkish position was pushed back 15 miles which secured Jerusalem.[15] The EEF regrouped and rested until the latter half of February 1918 when they advanced eastwards and captured Jericho. The 10th Division was involved in fighting that pushed the lines 8 miles further back in early March and were again part of a general offensive on 9 March tasked with taking Tell 'Asur. The attack was successful and throughout the operation 'the Divisional Signals Company was able to maintain telephone communication from Division H.Q. through brigade to battalion command posts, and from these even forward to observation posts (although they ran out of cables at critical times).'[16] At some point in the campaign while working with the Cables Section of the Royal Engineers, John O'Driscoll from Thomas Davis Avenue, Blackpool, received wounds from which he died on 11 March 1918 in Egypt. The 10th Division would soon cease to be mainly Irish in composition as many of its battalions were transferred to the Western Front to face the decisive German Offensive which started on 21 March. They were replaced by Indian soldiers.

Though the British army and navy were operating in far regions of the world like Central Africa, Egypt and Mesopotamia (Iraq), their main organisational and training centres remained, obviously, within the British Isles. A number of men linked to Blackpool died, either through accident or more likely natural causes, while fulfilling their role in the creation and maintenance of a modern army and navy. H. James, whose wife, Catherine, lived at 79 Great

Sergeant Michael Twomey, a career soldier with the Royal Munster Fusiliers. (Ann Griffiths)

(L–r): cousins William Kelly of HMS *Inconstant* and Private Christopher Twomey, Royal Munster Fusiliers. (Ann Griffiths)

Britain St/Great William O'Brien St, died on 1 December 1915. He had been with the 51st Reserve Battery of the RFA, which was stationed at the arsenal at Woolwich in Kent, England, and trained for artillery home defence amongst other duties. Seven doors down from Catherine James lived the Twomey family. Michael Twomey was an old Munster Fusilier man but at forty-seven years of age in 1914 he was too old to go to the front. He was posted to the Royal Munster Fusiliers Depot at Tralee where he helped impart the vast experience of soldiering he had picked up in India and during the South African War to the new troops. His son, Christopher, was also in the army, although his nephew, William John Kelly (who had lived with the Twomeys in Blackpool at least since 1911) was with the Royal Navy on board HMS *Inconstant*. Michael Twomey died in Tralee on 5 March 1918. Exactly a year earlier on 5 March 1917, Patrick Sullivan died in Cork from pancreatic cancer. He came from the seafaring port of Queenstown and joined the Royal Navy in 1884, aged twenty-two. In 1904 he left the service but

Sapper Timothy F. Kelly, 171ˢᵗ Tunnelling Company. (*Cork Examiner*)

rejoined when war broke out and helped man the armed merchant cruiser HMS *Pataca* and then the HMS *Zaria*, which acted as a patrol depot ship based near Scapa Flow in Scotland. His wife, Lizzie Sullivan, lived at Watercourse Road.

Timothy F. Kelly had recovered from the hand wound he received in June 1915 at Gallipoli while working with the divisional engineering section of the Royal Marines. By February 1917 he had been transferred to the Royal Engineers and was a sapper with the 171ˢᵗ Tunnelling Company which was at the Western Front. In mid-March 1918 this Tunnelling Company was working for the 33ʳᵈ Division in an area opposite Messines in Flanders. Timothy's brother, William Francis Kelly, had died of wounds on 24 November 1917 fighting with the 2ⁿᵈ/8ᵗʰ Battalion London Regiment (Post Office Rifles). He had been a post office worker at the General Post Office in Cork before the war. The brothers originally came from Rathmore Buildings, near Victoria Barracks, but when Timothy enlisted in early 1915 he had already been residing at 8 Spangle Hill with his wife, Bridget, and children. As the Western Front consisted of a vast network of subterranean routeways, huts, dormitories, latrines, etc., the tunnellers were employed to create such underground villages and towns. The 171ˢᵗ Company could have had over 300 personnel working with them at any one time and worked with different divisions at different times.

In the week prior to 21 March the 171ˢᵗ Tunnelling Company were constructing a number of underground accommodation areas for the 33ʳᵈ Division, with some of these rooms as much as 50 feet deep.

With Russia out of the war definitively in November 1917 due to the Bolshevik Revolution (this was confirmed in a treaty signed in March 1918) the German army were now allowed to concentrate more heavily on the Western Front. Ludendorff, Commander-in-Chief of the German army, along with General Hindenburg decided to launch an offensive in March 1918 that would match in scale the initial onslaught in August 1914. Despite knowing the logistical disadvantage of launching the offensive in March (the ground would still be wet after the winter), Ludendorff feared a build-up of American troops, which amounted to only 220,000 soldiers in mid-March 1918 (of which 139,000 were combatant).[17] Thirty-eight divisions were transferred from the east by the Germans which increased their Western Front's divisional strength from 147 to 191 and amounted to 3.5 million troops. This eastern transfer represented half of the BEF army and a total of 178 Allied divisions faced them. The German army had more planes than before, better light and heavy machine guns and their advancing infantry, including specially trained stormtroopers carrying light mortars, were ordered to make the attack, regardless of casualties. Artillery was there to support them, not lead the way.[18]

Ludendorff chose to attack the BEF because he believed the French army too big and with too much area behind it to retreat and regroup. He also thought the BEF less skilled and selected the line between Cambrai, St Quentin and La Fère to be the main thrust of the initial attack, with the aim of bursting through the line, then turning northwards to crush the remaining forces in this area against the sea. The BEF's front was more thinly held as its portion of the front had been extended by 25 miles in January 1918 and had fewer men than in 1917. The 16th Irish Division held a 7,000-yard (i.e. nearly 4-mile) sector of the line, a ridge in front of Épehy to Ronssoy, in which the Germans planned to attack.[19] The Germans amassed three divisions and three reserve divisions opposite the Irish sector in which the main focus of the attack would be to the southern Ronssoy section where the Irish troops linked up with the 66th Division from Lancashire. The southern section was held by the 7th Royal Irish Regiment and the 7th/8th Inniskillings in a defensive formation that had been adopted by the BEF generally in 1917 and which had largely imitated German army methods. Training by the 16th Division in these defensive tactics, however, was not thorough by this stage and they had spent a long winter engaged in arduous trench repairing. They had been out of the line for only three weeks since their arrival in France in December 1915.

Ludendorff launched the German attack, called 'Michael', on 21 March in what was not expected to be the decisive blow but certainly the biggest in a series of hammer blows that would destroy the Allied armies. A dense fog formed during the early hours of 21 March, which helped the infantry attack at 9.30 a.m. after a four-hour German bombardment. It was a catastrophic day for the 16th Division as it was for other Allied divisions. The Germans attacked the flanks of the Irish position and within an hour the southern section had collapsed. The heavy bombardment destroyed the 7th Irish Regiment's front-line post defences and the fog greatly aided German infiltration. Ronssoy was soon overrun, followed by the adjoining village of Lempire in the afternoon.[20] The remnants of the 7th Irish Regiment were forced back west of Ronssoy, being harried continually by machine guns and enemy aircraft. A portion made a stand and fought till forced to surrender and the rest were pushed further back to St Emilie where one officer and forty ordinary rank arrived at 7 p.m. Among the seventy-four soldiers who were killed with the Irish Regiment that day was nineteen-year-old Frederick William Oakley from 31 'Distillery Court' Thomas Davis St/York St.[21]

The northern area of the Irish line did better with a notable stand made at Épehy by the 2nd Battalion Royal Munster Fusiliers, who had joined the 16th Division in January 1918. Reminiscent of their stand at Étreux in August 1914, the Munsters again halted an advancing German army, allowing the surrounding BEF army to make a more orderly retreat. They too, however, were forced to retreat at 5 p.m. One of the noted failures of the day was the fact that the reserve troops were held too far behind to be of use, which allowed the German advance to maintain a greater momentum. There were also mistakes made as when the 1st Munsters and the

Private Frederick William Oakley,
7th Battalion Royal Irish Regiment.
(Gerry White)

6th Connaught Rangers were initially called upon to counter-attack, the order was soon re-scinded in the rapidly changing battlefield; the Munsters received the countermanding order but the Rangers did not and proceeded to attack. Seventy-nine Rangers died that day.[22] The battle had abated down by nightfall and the remnant of the 16th Division regrouped at St Emilie and Villers-Faucon: 531 ordinary rank and 32 officers had been killed, 10 per cent of its fighting force.[23] When those who were wounded and taken prisoner in the attack are included, the 16th Irish Division had in effect ceased to be an operating division. Along with the 36th Ulster and the 66th Divisions, the 16th suffered one of the highest casualty rates by the BEF that day.[24] It would also be the second worst day for Cork soldiers in the war after Aubers Ridge in May 1915.

The Germans had advanced up to 8 miles and had gained as much ground in one day as the Allies had in 140 days at the Somme. Ludendorff realised the success of the army in the sector which was partially fronted by the 16th Division and poured in more troops to capitalise. The next day, 22 March, the 1st Munsters and 2nd Leinster Regiment were 'cut to pieces in bitter fighting'.[25] The 16th Division were again pushed back as was the whole Fifth Army under General Gough at this point. French civilian refugees became evident again on the roads. Further north in Flanders, the BEF were also in retreat but not to the same extent. Sapper Timothy Kelly of the Tunnelling Corps was killed in action on 23 March while working for the 33rd Division in Flanders. By 25 March the 16th Division were at the Somme, holding some crossing points, when they were transferred to the Third Army under General Byng. It was with XIX Corps that they made they made their last major action as a fighting force at Rosières on 27–28 March. In fierce fighting the 16th Division managed to hold up the German advance for four and a half hours before they crossed the Somme on 28 March to Hamel. The remnant of the 16th, with a composite group of other personnel including US army engineers and training school staff, made a brief stand on 31 March and 1 April before retreating again. What was left of the division was finally relieved on 3–4 April after twelve days of fighting in which 7,149 were killed, wounded or counted as missing. One of the missing was Fr Duggan from Farranferris College in Cork: he remained behind to tend to the wounded and dying and was taken prisoner by the Germans.[26]

On 4–5 April Ludendorff halted the attack and prepared for the German army's next hammer blow. The Germans had succeeded in coming within 5 miles of the strategically important town of Amiens, taking 90,000 prisoners, 1,300 guns and inflicting 212,000 casualties on the Allies. But in turn, though Gough's Fifth Army had been severely mauled, it had not broken and the Germans had accrued casualties of 239,000 capturing a relatively unimportant area.[27] One of the reasons the BEF line remained intact was the ability of the French to send reinforcements to the British in time. To facilitate greater cooperation General Foch was made supreme commander of the Allied forces on the Western Front.

The next German offensive was called 'Georgette' aimed along the River Lys in Flanders. It started on 9–10 April along a much shorter front but also with fewer divisions (twenty, compared with the forty-seven used for 'Michael') on 21 March. Within two days all the gains made by the Allies at the Third Battle of Ypres (August to November 1917) were gone and the Germans were at the gates of Ypres itself. The 2nd Battalion of the Irish Guards were involved in the fighting that blocked the German advance on Hazebrouck and lost 250 men.[28] Ypres never fell and though fierce fighting continued for another two weeks the Germans failed to gain important military objectives. When the second offensive was called off on 29 April

Fr Duggan of Farrenferris College, chaplain to the Dublin Fusiliers (photo taken after the war). (Tower Books)

there were massive casualties: 146,000 on the Allies' side and 109,000 on the Germans'.[29]

Such losses on the German army were having an effect and the Germans' next military strike was longer in preparation but also timed with a new Austrian campaign against the Italians on their front in northern Italy. 'Blucher' was launched on 27 May in the Champagne region of France and initially this seemed to be the decisive blow. The German army here managed to push the French and British forces back 30 miles within a few days. On 29 May the Germans were on the Marne again, their first time since September 1914, and on 3 June were within 39 miles of Paris. One million Parisians fled the city. The British government in cabinet discussed the evacuation of the BEF from France on 5 June. General Foch eventually garnered reinforcements from Flanders and for the first time the American army gave considerable assistance to help stabilise the front. Fighting would continue in this region until July but by mid-June the Germans had reached the greatest extent of their advance, following their fourth hammer blow, 'Gneisenau', launched on 9–11 June and which directly threatened Paris. But significantly, the French were prepared and eventually successfully counter-attacked on 15 June, echoing their stand at the Marne nearly four years previously. This not only halted the advance but marked a turning point in the war.[30]

There are a number of interlocking reasons for this change in fortune, the most significant of which must be the collapsing morale of the German army itself. By the end of June it was clear to the

German soldiers that despite these huge military strikes against the Allies, the war was far from over. They had suffered nearly 1 million casualties and had no means of replacing them. The Allies, who had suffered just as much, had over 200,000 American troops arriving in France per month. The American army was a million strong by 20 July. By November it reached 1,872,000. The Royal Navy's trade blockade of Germany was also having an effect in reducing German civilian morale, and, in turn, their supplies and comforts to their soldiers at the front.[31] The advancing German soldiers in 1918 were generally very surprised at how well stocked and supplied they found the overrun Allied trenches. Once the advance was stalled, morale in the German army could only plummet at the prospect of months more of trench warfare. Thereafter, German soldiers surrendered more readily.

This is not to underestimate the fighting abilities of the Allied armies who were increasingly able to master the new offensive techniques of the German army and counter them. Ludendorff launched an attack in July at the Marne but this time it was more easily repulsed and the counter-attack by the French and American troops managed to capture 30,000 prisoners by 4 August. By this time the BEF were ready to take the offensive and began the Battle of Amiens on 8 August with the aid of 552 tanks. The interaction between artillery, tank, plane and advancing infantry made the attack a brilliant success, advancing up to 9 miles within a few hours though slowing down thereafter. Once Australian and Canadian troops encountered difficulties the attack was halted, which saved lives. The Battle of Amiens broke up six German divisions, inflicted 25,000 casualties and the BEF took 50,000 prisoners. Ludendorff called 8 August 'a black day' for the German army.[32] They were beginning to realise that not only did their offensive tactics no longer work but neither did their defensive ploys.

The Battle of Amiens started an Allied advance that would not stop till the end of the war in November, the so-called 'Hundred Days'. Advances up to mid-September were piecemeal but by then the Allies had reversed all the gains made by the Germans since March. A key military factor in the BEF advance was the firepower they could muster to compensate for the casualties they suffered. At the Battle of Amiens each BEF battalion carried thirty Lewis machine guns instead of four as before, eight trench mortars instead of one or two, and sixteen grenade-throwing rifles.[33] More importantly, in a war where 70 per cent of casualties were due to artillery shelling, the Allies could now not only seriously outgun the Germans, their shells were better and more accurate. The artillery, in both the French and British armies, expanded greatly as the war progressed. The French artillery consisted of 18 per cent of their army in May 1915 but by the end of the war it represented 32 per cent. The Royal Field Artillery had half a million men in 1918, which constituted a quarter of the BEF. By 1918 Germany could not produce the guns needed but, even more pressingly, they could not provide the men and horses to operate them. While the Germans matched the Allies in artillery strength at the start of 1918, by November the German had artillery capability that equalled only the British.[34]

The increasing preponderance of the artillery gun in the war was reflected in the casualties suffered by the soldiers from Blackpool. The five artillery and one machine gunner from Blackpool who died were killed in the last sixteen months of the war. John Lee, from Madden's Buildings, was a driver with the 79th Brigade of the Royal Field Artillery who were with the 17th Division. He arrived in France in June 1915 and took part in the Somme offensive in 1916 and the Arras offensive in the spring of 1917. On 5 July 1917 his brigade was still operating along the River Scarpe in the Arras region of France when, at 4 a.m. the 79th Brigade spotted about forty of the enemy near Hausa Wood, which prompted Battery A[35] to engage them. However, later that day, from 9.40 p.m. until 10.15 p.m., the roles were reversed as 'enemy shelled battery positions heavily with 10.5cm Hows. [Howitzers] from BIACHE' which hit directly C Battery's signal pit and killed John Lee along with two others, according to the brigade's war diary. One other was killed in the shelling and two wounded as they were transferring ammunition from 160 Brigade RFA to B Battery. The war diary also noted that three horses and a mule were killed and some more

Driver John Lee, Royal Field Artillery, from Madden's Buildings. (*Cork Examiner*)

wounded. The brigade retaliated with some heavy shelling of their own and the Germans only responded thereafter 'intermittently' during the night. This intermittent shelling pattern occurred the next day as well. The casualties inflicted on the 79th Brigade on 5 July were the only ones suffered for the whole of that month.[36]

On 30 November 1917 Patrick McNamara, from Slattery's Avenue in Blackpool, a gunner with the RFA, was killed in action at the Ypres Salient. Another gunner, John Dunlea from Hatton's Alley, this time with 13th Heavy Battery of the Royal Garrison Artillery, died in Salonika, Greece, on 29 July 1918. Two days before the Battle of Amiens, Joseph Corrigan from the Commons Road, died in England on 6 August 1918 and was buried at St Finbarr's Cemetery in Cork. He was part of the 5th Battalion of the Guards Machine Gun Regiment.

As the BEF advanced during the last hundred days of the war, half of the shells its artillery fired were gas shells. The BEF used mustard gas for the first time during this period. Gas shelling was very effective in counter-battery operations as precision in shelling was not necessary to neutralise the enemy's guns. The use of gas as a military weapon reached its maximum during the First World War and it was during 1918 that it was most heavily employed. In 1915 3,870 tons of gas were dispelled onto the battlefields. This rose to 38,635 tons by 1917 but in 1918 it reached 65,100 tons. From 1915 to 1917 gas caused 129,000 military casualties and in 1918 alone it resulted in 367,000 casualties of which 8,000 to 9,000 were fatalities.[37] One of these fatalities was Denis O'Callaghan from the Watercourse Road in Blackpool, a gunner with the 65th Siege

Battalion, Royal Garrison Artillery, who died on 13 September 1918. His brother, Thomas O'Callaghan of the 2nd Battalion Royal Munster Fusiliers, had been killed in action in March 1915. This was the third time a family from Blackpool would hear of a second son who had fallen in the war. There would be two more before the war was over.

The last artillery casualty from Blackpool actually survived the war but was suffering from wounds in hospital: Bombardier Patrick Walsh of the 45th Brigade RFA. He had been in France since November 1914 and his 8th Division had been at the Somme, Third Ypres and were active during the last hundred days. Patrick came from 66 Madden's Buildings in Blackpool which was around the corner from John Lee's family house. Patrick Walsh died of wounds in France on 23 November 1918.[38]

The Allies' dominance in artillery may have been the decisive factor in the winning of the war but it was the infantry who still had to win it. The 10th Irish Division was disbanded and reconstituted primarily as an English Division by the autumn. Its Irish troops helped to train the incoming American soldiers but they were also allocated to the fourteen other Irish infantry regiments still in France in the summer of 1918 (excluding the Irish Guards). In June 1918 the 2nd Munster Fusiliers regained fighting strength when they absorbed the 6th Battalion of the Munsters after their disbandment.[39] Jeremiah McCarthy, from Great Britain St/Great William O'Brien St, died on 20 June while with the 2nd Munsters. While the cause is unknown it was a fact that malaria was rampant among the newly absorbed 6th Munsters from Palestine, which weakened the physical constitution of the soldiers who had it, making them susceptible to more dangerous illnesses. The German army at this time suffered heavily from flu, or 'Spanish Flu' as it would at times be called, which spread to cause worldwide devastation after killing thousands of soldiers on the Western Front.[40]

By late September the Central Powers and Turkey were clearly losing the war. The Italians had repulsed the Austrians in June and the Austrian army thereafter began to disintegrate. The EEF in Palestine were pushing back the Turks throughout September. A renewed offensive in the Balkans prompted the Bulgarians to sue for peace in late September which finally forced the German High Command to seek an armistice. Germany had effectively been a military dictatorship under Generals Ludendorff and Hindenburg (the heroes of Tannenberg, the battle that had made them famous) for quite some time and they remained insistent on some gains for Germany in the event of a cessation of hostility. A major aim was to keep Belgium as some kind of vassal state to Germany as protection against Britain and France. The independence of Belgium was an issue at the start of the war and remained so at the end. Germany first started to explore the conditions for an armistice on 4 October and it would take over a month of diplomatic consultations for the warring parties to finally reach an agreement. For the German leaders it was imperative for the German army to be as tenacious and resolute as ever in opposing the Allied advance, to gain more leverage at the armistice negotiations. The protracted nature of these negotiations meant 500,000 soldiers were either killed or wounded before the war came to an end. Of course, there were Blackpool soldiers amongst the casualties.[41]

On 28 September the 1st Battalion Dublin Fusiliers and the 2nd Battalion Leinster Regiment were with the 29th Division of the Fifth Army in the Fifth Battle of Ypres which advanced towards Hooge, which was the site of a village and chateau, both of which were completely destroyed during the course of the war, having changed hands repeatedly. The 1st Munsters were with the Third Army in the second battle of Cambrai and helped take Lock 5 and Proville. Their advances were slowed, however, which meant both these armies were unable to assist the main thrust of the BEF offensive led by Fourth Army.[42] Fourth Army was tasked with breaking a line of defences called the 'Beaurevoir Line' in the neighbourhood of Le Catelet. But a number of military objectives had to be achieved before a proper assault on the line could begin which included taking Prospect Hill and the villages of Le Catelet itself and Gauy. The 50th Division of Fourth Army, which included the 2nd Munsters, 2nd Dublin Fusiliers, 5th Royal Irish and the 6th Inniskillings Regiment were given these objectives. The 50th Division attacked on 3 October with the 6th Inniskillings prominent but after initial successes in forcing the Germans back, the Germans counter-attacked and regained Le Catelet and Gauy. On 4 October at 2 a.m. the Munsters received orders to take Le Catelet and La Pannerie South, an area a mile further on from the village, in conjunction with the 3rd Royal Fusiliers on the left. According to their war diary, it was 'a very difficult operation' considering the ground had 'not been reconnoitred or seen by daylight'.[43]

The creeping barrage began at 6.10 a.m. but the Munsters were already ten minutes out of the trench to get as close as possible. 'The Battalion suffered very heavy casualties from machine gun nests in the village, but managed to force its way through and gain the rising ground immediately to N[orth].' By this time A Company had been forced to the slopes of Prospect Hill to the right and C Company pinned by trench mortar and machine-gun fire but D Company came through the village until held up by two machine-gun nests further on. Eventually sufficient cohesion for an attack on these positions was mustered, aided by the hunting horn of Lieutenant Colonel Tonson-Rye and after a short but bitter fight the positions were taken. The Munsters then took Le Catelet Trench by 9.45 a.m. at La Pannerie South.[44]

As the 1st Wiltshire Regiment were advancing on Prospect Hill to the extreme right, the Munsters' HQ received orders to fill the gap between them and the Wiltshires. Back in Le Catelet, C Company made its way into the right gap to reconnect with the Munsters at La Pannerie South but only a platoon managed to do so; the remainder were forced back. This group then followed the reconstructed B Company who went around Gauy to the east and then successfully rejoined the Munsters at La Pannerie South. The Munsters had suffered casualties during the assault due, amongst other factors, to the heavy shelling but, despite this, further attacks at dusk secured the gains made. During the day Private John Douglas Banks was killed. He was in his early twenties and was the same age as his elder brother, Patrick Banks, when he was killed at the battle of Aubers in May 1915. They both had been labourers in the Flax Factory before the war and lived next to it at Millfield

Cottages. The 2nd Munsters were relieved the following morning by the South Wales Borderers.[45]

On 6 October the 2nd Munsters were not as successful near Guisan in breaking the Beaurevoir Line and were relieved by the 2nd Dublin Fusiliers. However, 1st Munsters took part in the taking of Cambrai on 9 October with Third Army. It was probably here that Private David O'Connell from Spring Lane in Blackpool sustained a gunshot wound to his foot which invalided him out of the war. He was brother to James O'Connell, a prisoner of war in Germany since August 1914, and to Michael and Denis O'Connell who both died during the war. The 1st Munsters were themselves taken out of the line and became part of the force that reoccupied the city of Lille where they would form part of the guard of honour for the President of the French Republic, Raymond Poincaré, when he entered the liberated city.[46] Third Army had also been involved in an attack on another section of the Hindenburg Line on 8 October with the 8th Inniskillings and the 6th Dublin Fusiliers involved. The 5th Connaught Rangers attacked Serain with the 9th Manchesters and captured the village. Private John Mason, an old Roche's Guards Band man from Walshe's Avenue, was with the Rangers.

The Rangers were also prominent at the battle of the Selle, a river that the German army were told to defend at any cost to aid their negotiations for a ceasefire. Le Cateau was an important town on the Selle and it was captured by 17 October by the Rangers and the 6th Dublin Fusiliers, amongst others.[47] The next day the 2nd Munsters were in action again and took a further ridge behind that town and even advanced beyond their objective. In Flanders the Second Army were attacking along the River Lys, which proved successful. After the attack the 36th Ulster Division were relieved from the front line on 26–27 October and ended their active role in the war. Fourth Army was still thrusting forward and its last operation of the war was the crossing of the Sambre–Oise Canal after securing the formidable military obstacle of Forêt de Mormal, where the Germans had amassed a large number of machine guns. It was here that the 2nd Munster Fusiliers were to attack in a supporting role to the 2nd Northumberland Fusiliers and the 7th Wiltshire Regiment.[48]

Zero hour was 6.15 a.m. on 4 November and as the Northumberlands and the Wiltshires advanced into the Forêt de Mormal, the 2nd Munsters 'mopped up' the remaining enemy machine-gun nests with the aid of tanks. Sections of the Munsters ended up cooperating with the neighbouring 18th Division in taking the village of Preux-au-Bois and forced the enemy eastwards. All objectives were attained with the loss of seven men and sixty-one wounded amongst the Munsters.[49] Once more, sad news would affect Millfield Cottages exactly a month after the death of John Banks. This time Private Denis Jones had fallen and again another family would lose two sons in the war as his brother, James Jones, had died in Gallipoli in August 1915. Denis Jones was the last soldier from Blackpool to be killed in action in the Great War. Soon after, the Munsters were able to cross the Sambre and continued the advance with the 50th Division. They would continue to suffer casualties but they ended up in the village of Sars-Poteries on 9 November whistling the 'Marseillaise' to the delight of the villagers. Since 3 October the Munsters had advanced over 40 miles and in doing so helped to defeat sixteen divisions, captured 8,300 prisoners and 250 guns.[50]

Two days later – at the eleventh hour of the eleventh day of the eleventh month – the guns ceased and the war was over. Germany had finally signed the armistice. The sinking of the SS *Leinster* on 10 October on the Irish Sea had stiffened President Wilson's resolve in demanding tougher conditions on Germany for a final cessation.[51] Turkey had ended its war involvement on 28 October. In all, 10 million soldiers had died in what was at the time the most violent and bloodiest event in human history. What made that capitulation inevitable was the constant advance of the Allied armies against German opposition. The BEF played a prominent role in defeating one of the most formidable military forces ever. The British army had expanded over the four years from a small force to an army of millions capable of combining all the technical improvements of artillery, tanks, planes, grenades and machine guns, and defeating a resolute enemy in defensive positions. Mistakes were made but for the most part they were learnt quickly and corrected as much as possible. Massive casualties are inevitable when industrial nations pour all their resources into trying to annihilate each other. The Irishmen who fought with the BEF, and who were prepared to make the ultimate sacrifice, did so in the belief that they were defeating a militarised empire which sought to dominate Europe, or as Quartermaster Sheehan of Blackpool stated, 'to Prussianise the world'. The values they fought for are operating in Europe today, the freedom of free nation states to interact peacefully with one another.

For the Irish soldier at the front on 11 November, the reaction to the armistice was largely subdued. Maybe they were just thankful that some kind of fate had helped them to survive the then greatest war in history and maybe cognisant, also, of their comrades who had fallen while shoulder to shoulder with them.

The home fronts were more jubilant and Cork city on a rainy Monday on 11 November was no different. Expectations had been building and first news of the armistice signing was relayed through the military forces in Cork. The city centre was well populated throughout the day where 'an air of the utmost good humour pervaded everywhere';[52] Union Jacks and French flags flew from many buildings, soldiers and sailors mixed with the crowds, many festooned with Union Jacks themselves, in good-natured banter.

The *Cork Constitution* recorded:

> In the thickly populated parts of the city [the working-class districts] there were naturally the greatest rejoicings; for it was these districts contributed most liberally where recruits were called for, and continued to supply men to the Army. How welcome the news to them could be easily seen. They are seldom free from worry, but yesterday their faces beamed with good humour. All anxiety had been banished by the announcement that the war was over, and they saw no reason why they should refrain from indulging in a lusty cheer.[53]

This description certainly applied to Blackpool where around 350 men fought in the war. The *Cork Examiner* editorial praised the Allied soldiers as follows:

It was a war to prevent future wars, and to refute the doctrine that Might is Right, and if the peace now reached serves these results – one of them has already been achieved [namely the defeat of the German army] – the sacrifices that have been made are not in vain, and posterity will honour the memory of those who took up arms to dash the god of war from his pedestal and to place in its stead the Goddess of Peace.[54]

Of course, history did not fulfil this hope and within a few months of the Armistice and before the formation and signing of the Treaty of Versailles in June 1919, the Nazi Party in Germany was established.

Most of the soldiers in the army would not be demobbed until March 1919, by which time quite a number of them had experienced soldiering as an occupying force in Germany. The Irish Guards marched into Germany in early December to the sound of the pipes and drums playing such airs as 'Brian Boru' and later a Guardsman would remember that 'we were all wet most of the time and fighting with the mud in our boots. It was Jerry's own weather the minute we set our foot in his country, and none of us felt like conquerors. We were just dripping Micks [nickname given to the Irish Guards].'[55] Guardsman Paddy Foley, from Dublin St in Blackpool, was not with them as he had been assigned duties at the Guards base in London after developing synovitis in the right knee in April 1918. This was caused by a gunshot wound directly above his knee the previous January. My own grandfather Gus Birmingham's 6th Division ended up near Cologne and his division's history recorded that 'the Germans were very orderly and little trouble was given' but 'as the Germans did not play football there was a general lack of football grounds which had to be made'; maybe the start of something that many football nations rue today. They entertained themselves, and the locals, through a concert room where theatricals and even opera would be performed.[56]

Of course, when the war ended the prisoners of war were released and returned home from ther prison camps in Germany. The known prisoners of war who hailed from Blackpool were mostly from the 2nd Battalion Royal Munster Fusiliers captured

Guardsman Paddy Foley *(back row, second from left)* was the first soldier from Blackpool to arrive in France. He was wounded twice during the war. (Tom Foley)

at Étreux in August 1914, like William Foley of Narrow Lane, J. Donnelly, James O'Connell from Spring Lane, John Connors (Roche's Guards member) and Cornelius Murphy from the Commons Road who spent the four and a quarter years as prisoners in Germany. Patrick Kelleher, of the Royal Warickshire Regiment and previously of the Roche's Guards Band, had been a prisoner of war from at least 1915. Fr Duggan from Farranferris and chaplain to the Dublin Fusiliers, spent nine months imprisoned after being captured during the March Offensive in 1918. Conditions, seemingly, were not too bad for the first portion of the war but, as the Royal Naval blockade began to have an effect, conditions for the prisoners began to deteriorate seriously. Quite embittered letters from captured Irish soldiers were printed in the *Cork Examiner* in 1918 complaining of the hellish conditions, especially in relation to food and work demands, that they experienced in Germany and thanking those people who sent food parcels as, seemingly, they saved solidiers' lives.[57] Fr Duggan used to recount a story after the war to his students at Farranferris about how 'he himself and a Jewish prisoner celebrated Christmas 1918. [Jewish prisoner was probably a soldier.] They got two potatoes for dinner. The potatoes were boiled in the Jew's shirt ... but one of the potatoes had gone, neither of them knew how or where. The only explanation was that in their hunger, someone had increasingly swallowed them without realising what had happened.'[58]

Though the war was over, the spinning vortex of death it set in motion had not stopped. As mentioned previously, Patrick Walsh of the 45th Brigade Royal Field Artillery died in hospital from wounds on 23 November 1918 and was buried at St Roch Communal Cemetery, Valenciennes, France. The war was an incubator for the Spanish Flu that killed millions around the world in later 1918 and 1919. It has been estimated that 20,000 died in Ireland as a direct result.[59] Soldiers were particularly susceptible to the flu due to the physical demands of war on the body itself and the general conditions in which they lived. One soldier who succumbed was Private John Mason of the 5th Battalion Connaught Rangers on 16 February 1919 in Belgium. He was with the Rangers when they took La Cateau in mid-October 1918 as part of the Battle of the Selle. Like his next-door neighbour, Patrick Doyle of the 1st Munsters, John Mason was from Walshe's Avenue and a Roche's Guards Bandsman. His cousin Timothy Crowley had been killed on the HMS *Indefatigible* at the Battle of Jutland in May 1916. Four Roche's Bandsmen had died in the war out of the thirty-six pictured in the *Cork Examiner* in February 1916.

Private John Mason, Connaught Rangers (previously Leinster Regiment 10th Division and Spring Lane Band member). (*Cork Examiner*)

The war injured and wounded millions and, if military historians' estimates of the ratio between those who died and those wounded of 1 to 2 is correct, then over 100 men from Blackpool may have been wounded in some way during the war. At home their injuries might have been attended to at the North Infirmary or at Shanakiel Hospital, Sunday's Well. William Mehigan, 8th Battalion Royal Munster Fusiliers, received a war injury pension and ended up living in Delaney Park, Dublin Hill. In all, three-quarters of a million soldiers got some kind of financial compensation for being injured after the war was over. Thirty-eight per cent of those were due to wounds, a further 5 per cent due to amputation, 9 per cent due to mental illness and there were other categories related to health issues like malaria and TB, etc. It is hard, if not impossible, to truly empathise with the mental state of soldiers, especially those soldiers who were civilians before the war, to get an understanding of the effect such a singularly traumatic experience had on them. Coming from places like Blackpool might have helped them adjust, as life back then was a long day and week's work and, with disease more prevalent, life was more precarious in these 'thickly populated areas'.

Despite this, enduring the hellish experience of war for so long must have hardened a person's spirit to withstand such sights, but the emotional scars must have lingered to the grave to varying degrees. The only image of the war that has been passed down within my family from my grandfather, Gus Birmingham, a driver with the 2nd Brigade Royal Field Artillery, was that he 'ate and slept with the dead'. Thereafter it is silence. William Mehigan would

Private William Mehigan, Royal Munster Fusiliers, 16th Irish Division, wounded at the Battle of the Somme. (Mary Mehigan and family)

consistently for years after recall the horrific scenes in the taking of Guillemont at the Battle of the Somme (where he was injured) in what could be described as some kind of therapeutic exercise. Nowadays people are familiar with the term Post Traumatic Stress Disorder and no doubt thousands, even hundreds of thousands would have suffered in a similar manner after the Great War from what was known then as 'shell shock'. It probably affected every soldier who experienced the front line to some degree but this, of course, can only be speculation. But people are adaptable and there may have been aids to recovery that might not exist in the same way today. Traditional gender roles might have helped soldiers readapt to civilian life. Religion and the Church were also a great succour, I imagine, and of course the comradeship of ex-soldiers, that band of brothers, united forever by their searing experience.

James Lee of the 3rd Battalion Canterbury Regiment was shot on 20 December 1917 while his battalion was holding trenches at Polderhoek on the Ypres Salient. As his gunshot wound severely damaged his pelvis from behind, which suggested that James was injured while outside the trench, and the fact that nobody was killed in action from his battalion on that day, then it seems likely that he received the wound during a reconnaissance patrol or maybe a small raid. He survived but remained very ill even after being transferred to Brockenhurst Hospital in London, a hospital for New Zealand soldiers. Nearly a year to the day of his wounding he was transferred to Southampton and then on to the ship *Manama*, which brought him back to New Zealand after 2½ years away. He entered Christchurch Orthopaedic Hospital on 30 January 1919. He never recovered his health and died there on 3 July 1919. He was buried in Ashburton Cemetery on the South Island, near his residence of Tinwald where his aunt, Mollie Lee, also lived. His medals would be sent home to his mother, Annie Lee, at 9 Commons Road, Blackpool. James Lee was the last soldier from Blackpool to die because of the war.[60]

In all, fifty-three soldiers directly linked to or from Blackpool died in the war. Six Royal Navy sailors also lost their lives. Ten merchant seamen died doing their job and maintaining the home front during the war.

9

Integration and Remembrance in a New Ireland

NEXT OF KIN WERE NOTIFIED of the death of a loved one by letter, or if he was an officer, by telegram. In the case of Ellen Williams of Dublin Hill in Blackpool, news of the death of her husband, Thomas, in Gallipoli in August 1915 was broken to her by her brother-in-law, John Williams from Grattan St, Cork city, who had been notified by telegram from army headquarters in Australia. Mrs Kieley of York St/Thomas Davis St was initially informed that her son Patrick was missing. This painful uncertainty lasted for a few months before confirmation could be given that Patrick had died on 25 April 1915. A family story has passed down the generations that the news of his death was prefigured by a vision of Paddy appearing to his mother one night, and in ANZAC uniform (a uniform unknown to Mrs Kieley). Such communications with the dead, seemingly, were a common phenomenon in Britain during this time and spiritualism and 'mediators' with the dead had a spike in popularity.[1]

There was a committee set up and a fund in tandem to help widows and orphans of those who had fallen in the Great War. Ellen Williams and her daughter, Hannah, got a pension from the Australian government worth £70 per annum for Ellen and £13 per annum for Hannah, but Mrs Kieley did not, as being a shopkeeper made her ineligible. Hannah Williams and her sister would eventually end up working in the Flax Factory at Millfield. The factory became known popularly in Cork as Sunbeam and Woolsey. Catherine Twomey, daughter of Munster Fusilier Michael

Twomey from Great Britain St/Great William O'Brien St, worked in Harrington's paint factory after the war and would eventually emigrate to England. So would Bridget Kelly from Spangle Hill, wife of Sapper Timothy Kelly, when she married a visiting merchant seaman and moved to Liverpool. Support for grieving families obviously came from within the family circle. It was the family that also provided most of the care for the wounded, both in Ireland and in Britain.[2] Those families who had lost a member in the war also had the support of each other and there were over sixty such families in Blackpool to share their burden. These wives, mothers, fathers, sisters and brothers of the fallen were often working side by side in the factories of Blackpool.

Such a network of support may have been aided by organisations, like the Widow and Orphan Fund and by the National Federation of Discharged and Demobilised Sailors and Soldiers (NFDDSS), a British organisation that was formed in Cork in December 1917.[3] Its task was to look after the interests of ex-servicemen in relation to government pensions and general employment. Through such organisations the widow's pension for the wives of those who had fallen became established as a right and not a privilege and helped to develop the welfare state for future generations.[4]

From consolation and support to the families of the fallen there is a short step to public commemoration. This had begun in Britain and other countries even before the war ended. The first anniversary of the beginning of the Somme offensive was commemorated on 1 July 1917 in Belfast. The anniversary of the landing at Gallipoli, 25 April (ANZAC Day), became a day of commemoration in Australia before the war was over. In memory of the soldiers who died, memorial plaques were erected in a public park in Brisbane; one such plaque is dedicated to Thomas Williams. His wife, Ellen, had previously written from Dublin Hill on 18 August 1917 to the Australian army in relation to her husband's posthumous elevation in rank from Sergeant Major to Warrant Officer II Class:

> In my loneliness it will always be to me a source of pleasure and
> consolation to know that he has performed his duty in such a manner

as earned for him the commendation and recommendation of his superiors and that the spirit with which he had tried to serve his King and country had been recognised in the proper quarter.[5]

Whether Ellen Williams would have expressed these views in public, especially after 1917, is another matter in an Ireland that had changed radically from the time when popular MP Augustine Roche could publicly praise some newly recruited Irish Guards at Cork's train station in 1914 as fighting for Ireland and the Empire. Commemoration in Britain at this time has been described as a recognition of shared grief, of a 'nation in mourning' where all made the sacrifice. There was also an attempt to give it meaning and ease that grief.[6] It could be seen as a war that secured the independence of Belgium, Serbia, Poland and other countries but also a 'war for civilisation' and a 'war to end all wars'. John Redmond and Tom Kettle of the Irish Party had also embraced this vision and saw those values embodied in the new Home Rule Ireland coming at the end of the war. The southern Irish soldiers who died in the war would have been the martyrs of Home Rule Ireland, cast in the same light as Sarsfield and the Wild Geese who fought with the French in the seventeenth and eighteenth centuries. Every new state needs its myths, and in time life moves on, people marry and remarry and their children grow up, but the Irish soldiers of the Great War would have remained in the collective memory if their sacrifice had secured Irish Freedom.

If the war had ended in 1916 or early 1917 even, some kind of Home Rule might have been instituted with Redmond hailed by the people as Prime Minister. The cauldron of the war, however, cracked the Irish constitutional edifice and through the fissure of the 1916 Rising flowed hitherto unseen forces of cultural and religious nationalism that swept Sinn Féin to electoral victory in December 1918. The Irish Party's two candidates, who were ex-servicemen, were rejected in Cork city, as they were nationally in that election which was the first that was universal (with some age qualifications). This was the first time in modern Irish history where the majority of Irish people supported a policy of complete separation and rejection of the British connection. Disenchantment with the war was a vital backdrop for the rise of Sinn Féin and the alternative vision of a Gaelic Ireland: a vision that would have seen Ireland economically stronger after perceived British mismanagement and culturally pure, unsullied by anglicised influences. It also produced a decidedly antagonistic British government which viewed Sinn Féin as German collaborationists who tried to 'stab Britain in the back' in 1916. Anti-Irish sentiment had increased in Britain since 1916.[7] This dynamic framed the British government's relationship with Sinn Féin, and also the relationship between the British army, the Black and Tans and the Auxilliaries with the Irish Republican Army in the War of Independence.

It was a dynamic that would deny commemoration of the Irish fallen in the Great War as an act of 'the nation in mourning' and confine that mourning as the years went by to a select few. This widespread endorsement of Sinn Féin's absolutist position, however, was not as dramatic or surprising as it seemed. Irish constitutional nationalism had been a broad political church and the rhetoric of nationalism, of an independent Ireland, shared the same language as Sinn Féin. Indicative of the amorphous nature of Irish nationalism was a report by the *Cork Constitution* on 12 November 1917 about some 'Angry Munsters':

> Before the departure of the Munsters from _____, a remarkable scene was witnessed, a number of soldiers of the rank and file holding an informal meeting in a large square, and declaring that they were as good Irishmen and Nationalists as any Sinn Féiners. Though they fought for England against the Huns, and would continue to fight till the war was won, their interest in their own country was just as 'Sinn Féin' as that of anyone else. A day would come, declared the speaker, when they would return from the trenches and take their part in the life of the country, and they would have some scores to pay off with those men who tried to belittle them and hit them in the back when they were fighting the common foe. The soldiers were loudly applauded by a number of people who had gathered in the vicinity.

Another example was the commemoration of the Manchester Martyrs, who were Fenians, which was perfectly acceptable to those in the Home Rule Movement. Conversely, support for the Empire was never unqualified and ultimately never profound.

The war and the example of the 1916 Rising further polarised Irish politics. From a British perspective the subsequent rise of Sinn Féin coupled with the ongoing war prevented any kind of experiment with Home Rule, which in turn undermined the Irish Parliamentary Party even further. The bridge between the supporters of the Irish Party and Sinn Féin proved not to be a wide one or, to put it another way, most Irish Catholic Home Rulers would not actively oppose a nationalist movement for the sake of retaining the King as head of state. They acquiesced to this new nationalist zeitgeist and were eventually absorbed. But it was not a painless absorption for the ex-servicemen, the families of those who fought and even for those committed supporters of the Irish Party. They might have expected to be welcomed home as heroes and collectively feted as such, which might have acted as a lever on government to create an Irish society fit for these heroes as was Lloyd George's promise in Britain. However, they might have experienced what Fr J. Scannell (chaplain to the Irish Guards and Military Medal recipient) did as he visited his old, and future, school Farranferris to see the Bishop in December 1918, being booed by a student as he was still wearing his British military uniform.[8]

There were cases nationally of the NFDDSS, and its rival, the more government-funded organisation the Comrades of the War Association, being attacked with one such occurrence in August 1919 at Washington St in Cork.[9] As Sinn Féin gained power, first through local government, ex-servicemen were often discriminated against with regard to employment, admissions to technical colleges, and hospital and asylum placements.[10] With regard to the War of Independence and the indelible impression which it left of the British army as oppressors of the Irish people, it was from one perspective a self-fulfilling prophecy by those militant republicans who started the war in January 1919. It had been thirty or forty years since the British authorities were perceived to be acting unjustly and in a heavy-handed manner and that was during the land agitation of the 1880/90s. Sinn Féin's electoral victory in December 1918 gave democratic legitimacy to a complete separation for Ireland from Britain and hence the subsequent war waged by the IRA on the British authorities in Ireland but it was a war that was started locally, developed incrementally, and never had a clear mandate from the electorate.

The British reaction was also a factor in its development and the perception of the IRA and Sinn Féin as German collaborationists coloured the view of both the British government and the British authorities on the ground, be they soldier, Black and Tan or Auxiliary, on the whole political framework that was emerging in this new Ireland.[11] It was undoubtedly a factor in the number of atrocities that British forces committed during the War of Independence which only alienated further southern Catholic opinion. One of the most famous examples of this was the murder of Tomás MacCurtain, Lord Mayor of Cork at the time, at his home on Thomas Davis St in March 1920. The coroner's jury on the death condemned the government and Prime Minister Lloyd George as abetting murder. Coincidently, on that jury was Joseph Kieley, a neighbour of Tomás MacCurtain and father of Patrick Kieley who died on 25 April 1915 at Anzac Cove.

In the escalating violence Irish ex-servicemen would become suspect in the eyes of the IRA and between 1919 and 1924, including anti-treatyites, 120 civilian ex-servicemen were killed as spies and informers.[12] Many of those killings happened in Cork. Families were divided by their Great War participation. The Foley family on Dublin St is an example: Paddy Foley had gone to war with the Irish Guards and was the first Blackpool man to land in France, in August 1914. He was wounded twice, one being a gunshot through the thigh. His younger brother became involved in the IRA and was active during the War of Independence. Some families became estranged from one another but a lot did not and accepted the new roads charted by current events. One can imagine how families helped ease the tensions and frictions that were inherent in the emergence of a new society from the old. There is evidence that a Cork section of the ex-servicemen began to support the separatist movement of Sinn Féin. The Cork Branch of the

NFDDSS (and not the Comrades of the War who were strong in the towns of County Cork) played a prominent part in the funeral of Tomás MacCurtain. His widow later thanked them for their public condemnation of the murder and wrote, 'Men who know how to fight in a noble cause are the first to denounce treachery and cowardly assassination.'[13]

However, a dramatic incident occurred in Cork city on 18 July 1920 when a British army patrol killed James Bourke, a former 2nd Royal Munster Fusilier, as they were arresting a group of rowdy ex-servicemen at the North Gate Bridge. During the next day anger in the streets rose, fomented by ex-servicemen, which resulted in an attack on British soldiers who were chased back to Victoria Barracks. The army responded by sending patrol vehicles onto the streets which dispersed the crowds by machine gun, killing two people and injuring twenty-four. One of those killed was William McGrath, an ex-soldier of the Leinster Regiment and the other was IRA volunteer John O'Brien, who had dashed to help an old lady who had fallen in the street.[14] John was a younger brother of Tim O'Brien from Green Lane in Blackpool who had been saved from the sinking of the SS *Kenmare* (see Chapter 6). Over 5,000 ex-servicemen attended and officiated at the funeral of James Bourke. Tom Barry was one of the Bandon delegates. Lord Mayor MacSwiney appealed to the NFDDSS to quell the anger amongst its members in fear of provoking the army again which they did, and even joined local IRA 'peace patrols' to disperse any angry crowd. Such cooperation was only temporary and the organisations remained separate. The NFDDSS did, however, support Terence MacSwiney during his hunger strike in autumn 1920, calling for him to be released. They also participated at his funeral.[15]

From that point onwards they remained aloof from political events. In the summer of 1921 they amalgamated with the Comrades of the War to form the British Legion branch in Cork.[16] Such aloofness did not deter individual ex-servicemen from joining the IRA, the most famous being Tom Barry. For most who participated in the War of Independence, and the Civil War, it became one of the most defining periods in their lives. It is said that a week is a long time in politics but two years of guerrilla warfare followed by a year of bitter civil war was a lifetime for most. John Redmond's Home Rule party and, it could be argued, the Great War itself, became remote, even foreign. For most parts of Ireland, and Cork included, memory of the Great War would have been refracted through the actions of that war's veterans who, in the shape of the Black and Tans and the Auxiliaries, killed Irish people and burned their homes. It must be said that some of the Black and Tans and the Auxiliaries were Irish ex-servicemen. France, Flanders and Anzac Cove, Gallipoli were all distant places now and the exploits of Irish soldiers might be better forgotten in such bitter times.

It would seem probable that a significant proportion of the support for the Treaty in the election of 1922 came from ex-servicemen and their families. When the Free State came into being, half of the 55,000 Free State soldiers were ex-servicemen, like William Foley of Narrow Lane, Blackpool, formerly with the 2nd Battalion Royal Munster Fusiliers, who was taken prisoner at Étreux in August 1914. The officer camp of the new Irish Defence Forces between 1922 and 1924 included 600 veterans of the war.[17] The attainment of independence by Sinn Féin and the IRA embodied a political perspective and historical narrative that gave reflexive endorsement to a binary vision of Irish history in which the British army were the colonising oppressors of the Irish people. The memory of those men who fought in the British army during the Great War was eclipsed, so much so that few in Blackpool would remember that from these very same streets nearly seventy men died in one of the most momentous events in modern history.

This was aided by the Catholic Church's tradition of not erecting memorials within their churches to those who died. The contrast with Protestant churches and cathedrals is striking; they are a kind of cocoon of British history with tablets dedicated to the dead of Waterloo, the Crimea and of course the First World War. At St Anne's at Shandon, the name of Frederick W. Oakley from York St/Thomas Davis St can be seen amongst others. He was nineteen at the time of his death and the heartache for his family must have been eased, however slightly, by such recognition of their family's

St Anne's Memorial to the Fallen, Shandon St. (Author's collection)

sacrifice by the local Protestant community of which they were a part. For the vast majority of Irish Catholic soldiers who died in the war, their graves and memorials are in foreign countries, making it very difficult to visit especially for family members from poor communities like Blackpool.

Paddy Foley of the Irish Guards left the army and re-entered his old job at Goulding's Chemical Factory at Spring Lane. He tried to get a pension from the British government for 'neuraesthenia', which in modern parlance is Post Traumatic Stress Disorder, but was refused as such conditions were not given due recognition as they are now. Patrick died at a relatively young age and it is probable that his wartime wounds and experience were contributory factors, as they would be for other ex-servicemen. Fr Charles O'Connor was gassed during the war and suffered from its side effects thereafter in peacetime. He never returned to Blackpool as a priest but ministered instead at Passage West, in County Cork. While there he also was chaplain to the Little Sisters of the Poor and dedicated a weekly column called the 'Little Flower' to those who suffered from psychiatric problems, probably borne out of his own experience and of those soldiers whom he met during and after the war. He died in 1952.

Fr Duggan became secretary to Bishop Colohan and acted as a peace go-between during the War of Independence and the Civil War. References to the war would infuse the talks of Fr Joe Scannell in Farranferris and at one Sunday morning Mass he spoke of the need for high ideals among students and referred to 'Big Bertha', the German 16-inch howitzer as 'to shell Liege in Belgium' it had to aim higher than its target. 'So too, must students aim higher than they think necessary to achieve their goal in life.' He became the first chaplain at Collins Barracks in the Free State and the third President at Farranferris in 1923.[18]

Time moves on and during the 1920s life settled down after the tumultuous years from 1912 to 1923. The 1916 Rising and the War of Independence became the state's guiding compass. Ex-servicemen sometimes married into families with strong IRA connections. For ex-servicemen, silence about the war even among family members seemingly was common. What they and their families thought of the war became largely forgotten. For the immediate family of those who had fallen in the war, private mementos would be kept often in a public place in the house but sometimes not. Initially 11 November might have become a time for the recognition of public grief but later an act of remembrance. The memorial in Cork on the South Mall was opened in 1925, with the help of contributions like that from Murphy's Brewery. It was self-consciously dedicated to those 3,800 Cork people who died 'Fighting for the Freedom of Small Nations'. A national monument was built in the 1930s but was not officially opened until 1988. Remembrance Sunday was faithfully attended by the ex-servicemen and their families and the families of the fallen, till one by one they began to die and now is attended by only a select few.

Conclusion

THE FIRST WORLD WAR was the first human experience of 'total war' that necessitated mass participation of men as soldiers and the wider civilian population in sustaining the war effort. Ireland was an integral part of that event which swept across Europe and these isles. Irish men and women made the greatest military (and naval) contribution to a war in the history of this island. This study of a local Irish urban community like Blackpool indicates the depth of that involvement. The war was not a distant event. Its painful, and invariably horrific, twists and turns had direct consequences for places like Blackpool. A decision by British or German generals to launch a military campaign or attack led to Blackpool soldiers being killed or wounded. This sacrifice was continuous for the four years of the war, from the 'race to the sea' in October 1914 when Private Timothy O'Leary from Dublin Hill fell to 'the last hundred days' when Private Denis Jones from Millfield Cottages was killed in action in November 1918 as the Fourth Army pushed the Kaiser's army back to Germany.

Blackpool as an industrial hub also gives a glimpse of what 'total war' meant for the more industrialised countries like Britain, France and Germany. The supportive and collaborative effort of Blackpool industry towards the war was probably indicative of a more widespread Irish industrial endorsement of the war. The facilitation and even encouragement of employees to enlist, the financial support by both management and workers, separately and together, to aid primarily those most affected by the war through death or injury, but also directly to the war itself, show how 'total war' entwined itself around the day-to-day lives of people from

Blackpool. Murphy's Brewery and the Cork Spinning and Weaving Company (Goulding Ltd more indirectly but probably more self-consciously under its chairman Sir William Goulding) had direct commercial contact with the British war effort. The Flax Factory at Millfield supplied linen to wrap around British fighter and observational planes, which were flown by Cork pilots.[1] For the workers of Blackpool, not only did their fellow workers die in the war, but their fathers, sons, brothers and friends also.

It makes the political rise and eventual hegemonic dominance of Sinn Féin such a momentous and, apparently, unexpected event. It is surprising, knowing the overwhelming support given to Redmond from the Irish Volunteers near the start of the war in September 1914 and that in communities like Blackpool over 350 men would participate in the war and 69 would die. Such a transformation to a total rejection of the Irish involvement in the war can only be explained by the war itself and the grim, unrelenting toll it exacted from the people through the financial burdens it placed on them, the material curtailments it entailed and also emotionally in the war's embrace of death and destruction. It needed the example of the Easter Rising of 1916 led by Pearse and Connelly to give such growing discontent a political, even spiritual, framework and vision of an Ireland reborn from the ashes of a Europe mired in an unholy abyss. It must also be remembered that by 1916 the war had taken on a mode and shape that made the prospect of a German invasion seem remote and improbable, a prospect not altogether unlikely in the confusing early period of the war which was new to everybody concerned. This security was largely thanks to the British navy.

The success of Sinn Féin at the December 1918 election and its subsequent dominance of southern Ireland meant that the Irish nationalist, and particularly Irish Catholic, contribution to the Great War would be overridden by a meta-narrative of Irish history that would see the IRA of the War of Independence as the culmination of 750 years of Irish opposition to foreign, be it Norman, English or British, rule. It blew away Redmond's vision of a Home Rule Ireland where the victorious returning Irish soldiers with British uniforms would have been seen not only as saviours of European civilisation and its liberty, but also as the heroes and founders of the new Home Rule state. Years later, no doubt, revisionist historians would have written of the economic motivations that would have induced soldiers to join the British army from poor areas like Blackpool and punctured the patriotic myths that might have helped build the fledgling Home Rule state. Instead, Sinn Féin began this revisionism back in 1918 and for large parts of the twentieth century nearly revised these Irish soldiers out of Irish history.

There are consequences in every political choice and in rejecting Irish constitutional nationalism as the foundation stone of the new Irish State, it could be argued that physical-force nationalism had unmoored itself from a long-standing political tradition that might have been a secular counterweight to the fledgling state's embrace of a Catholic ethos. Home Rule-ism had sought a return to 'Grattan's Parliament' but that parliament had been firmly buttressed within the English constitutional tradition that encompassed the 'Glorious Revolution' of 1690, the Norman parliaments and right back to Magna Carta in the early thirteenth century. Acknowledged or not, it was this tradition that helped steer the new Irish state through the choppy political waters of the twentieth century. If it had been acknowledged and embraced, as a Home Rule Ireland would have done, then Irish Catholic conservatives might have had a secular alternative and language upon which to build their future. Instead, Irish republicanism never had the deep-seated anti-clericalism that inspired their European counterparts, and its mercurial origins in violent agitation made it prone to seeking the safe harbour of Catholic social thought once the state was established. It also provided a continuing framework and reference point for the many dissident republican groups from 1922 to the present day.

It was precisely the acknowledgement of 'the principle of consent' (a central phrase in the William O'Brienite pre-war movement) amongst both loyalists and nationalists in Northern Ireland by the modern-day 'dissident' republican movement that has opened up the peace process which in turn has allowed a greater acknowledgement of Irish nationalist soldiers' massive participation in the First World War. It has created a greater civic space in which to explore more fully the plurality of our past. This has been aided by a more liberal, individualistic, you could say consumerist, Irish society that might not need the binds of a set, shared past as it once did. We are more tolerant of diverse views in a globalised Internet age. This book has been written with the hope firstly, to recognise more the plurality of our past, its more fluid nature and thus, maybe, enhance the need for empathy and tolerance and more importantly to acknowledge the sacrifice made by the men of Blackpool in a war that was seen by them as a fight for freedom and civilisation.

> They shall not grow old,
> As we who are left grow old:
> Age shall not weary them,
> Nor the years condemn.
> At the going down of the sun,
> And in the morning
> We will remember them.

Laurence Binyon from *For the Fallen*, 1914

Acknowledgments

I WOULD LIKE TO THANK especially the relatives of the people mentioned in the book whom I have met: to Margaret McGrath and her husband Anthony for their kind hospitality and the discussions we had about Mrs McGrath's grandfather Thomas Williams; to Tom Foley who gave me books and other items related to his uncle Paddy Foley; to Eileen Jones and our conversation about her two uncles, James and Denis Jones, and her father Patrick; to Fr Basil O'Sullivan and Paul French who communicated to me about Fr O'Sullivan's uncle Patrick Kieley; to Ken Daly and his lengthy investigation into the O'Connell family from Spring Lane and more particularly for information about his great-grandfather David O'Connell and great-grand uncles Michael and Denis O'Connell. David O'Connell married one of the O'Flynn girls of Spring Lane and another would marry my grandfather Gus Birmingham. I found out from Michael, Margaret and Paul O'Reilly about Timothy O'Flynn (their brother) from Spring Lane who participated in the war with the Royal Irish Regiment; to William Kelly, a Liverpudlian who has returned to family roots and resides in Cork, concerning his grandfather Timothy F. Kelly; to Ann Griffiths from England who kindly donated pictures of her great-grandfather Michael Twomey and grand-uncle Christopher Twomey and cousin William Kelly; to Breda Sheehan and her relative Robert Spillane; to Pat and Maureen Goggin concerning William Higgins and James and Daniel Donovan; to Adrian Foley who gave me details on the military career of his great-grandfather William Foley; to Trish Harrington, whose relative was Michael Coleman of the SS *Kenmare*, who very obligingly allowed me to use her office facilities at the Blackpool Community Centre for this project; to Kathleen Evans of Seminary Road who talked to me about her family's experience of the war; to the committee members of the Blackpool Historical Society, especially Tom Foley and Rita Coughlan; to the Rev. Brian O'Rourke, rector of St Anne's, Shandon; to the Cork branch of the Western Front Association under the chairmanship of Gerry White; to the staff of the Blackpool and Grand Parade Libraries, most especially to the librarians in the Local Studies section for their always courteous help; to the archivists at Cork City Archives and Boole Library University College Cork; to Gabriel Doherty, Department of History, University College Cork; to the staff at the National Archives, Kew, London; to my publishers, The Collins Press. Finally, I would like to thank members of my own family whose discussions have aided my research, particularly Angela French and Diarmuid Cronin; to uncle John Cronin, who has always been the most accommodating host every time I have visited London; to Cllr Brian Bermingham who urged me to start this book in the first place, a book whose idea emanated from previous projects initiated by Jerry Conroy.

Endnotes

ABBREVIATIONS USED

AIF   Australian Infantry Force
RIR   Royal Irish Regiment
RMF   Royal Munster Fusiliers

INTRODUCTION

1. Adrian Gregory, *The Last Great War: British Society and the First World War.*
   (Cambridge, 2008), Jay Winter, *Sites of Memory, Sites of Mourning: The Great
   War in European Cultural History* (Cambridge, 1995) and John Horne (ed.),
   Our War: Ireland and the Great War (Dublin, 2008).
2. Florence O'Donoghue, *Tomás MacCurtain: Soldier and Patriot* (Tralee,
   1971); Francis J. Costello, *Enduring the Most: The Life and Death of Terence
   MacSwiney* (Dingle, County Kerry, 1996).
3. O'Donoghue, *op. cit.*
4. *Cork Constitution,* 11 October 1915.

1. THE STORY OF BLACKPOOL AND THE LEAD-UP TO THE GREAT WAR

1. Breda Sheehan, 'Blackpool Village: An Industrial and Social History from
   1800 to 1900' (unpublished MA, Local History UCC, 2008).
2. Maura Cronin, 'Blackpool People' in M. F. Hurley, G. Johnson, and C. Brett,
   Old Blackpool: An Historic Suburb (Cork 2006), p. 40; Sheehan, *op. cit.*
3. Patrick Beirne, *Reminiscences of Blackpool and District in the Year 1912* (Self-
   published: Blackpool Library), p. 13.
4. Andy Bielenberg, *Cork's Industrial Revolution 1780–1880: Development or
   Decline?* (Cork 1991), p. 20.
5. Sheehan, *op. cit.*, p. 38.
6. Colin Rynn, 'Industrial Blackpool, *c.*1750–1930', in Hurley, *op. cit.*, p. 60.
7. *Ibid.*, p 59.

8. Sheehan, *op. cit.*, p. 31.

9. Philip Orr, '200,000 volunteer soldiers', in John Horne (ed.), *Our War: Ireland and the Great War* (Dublin, 2008), p. 65.

10. Jérôme aan de Wiel, *The Catholic Church in Ireland 1914–1918: War and Politics* (Dublin, 2003), p. 8.

11. Jonathan Githens-Mazer, *Myths and Memories of the Easter Rising: Cultural and Political Nationalism in Ireland* (Dublin, 2006), pp. 29–30.

12. Florence O'Donoghue, *Tomás MacCurtain: Soldier and Patriot* (Tralee, 1971), pp. 18 and 23.

13. Diarmuid O'Donovan, 'Beaten and Bloodied ...' in *Holly Bough* (Cork, Christmas 2012), pp. 154–55.

14. Cronin, *op. cit.*, p. 41; Jean Prendergast, 'Cork Bands in the Great War' in Gerry White and Brendan O'Shea (eds.), *A Great Sacrifice: Cork Servicemen who Died in the Great War* (Cork, 2010), pp. 157–160.

15. O'Donoghue, *op. cit.*, p. 22.

16. *Ibid.*, pp. 46 and 66.

17. Niall Ferguson, *Empire: How Britain Made the Modern World* (London, 2004).

18. Michael MacDonagh, *The Life of William O'Brien the Irish Nationalist* (London, 1928), p. 31.

19. O'Donoghue, *op. cit.*, pp. 30 and 46 for the dominance of Home Rule movement before the war.

20. Francis J. Costello, *Enduring the Most: The Life and Death of Terence MacSwiney* (Dingle, County Kerry, 1996), p. 20.

21. *Ibid.*, p. 23.

22. Beirne, *op. cit.*, p. 22.

23. Sean O'Faolain, *Vive Moi!: An Autobiography* (1965), p. 27.

24. Diarmaid Ferriter, *The Transformation of Ireland, 1900–2000* (Dublin, 2004), p. 173; Paddy McCarthy, *Cork During the Years of the Great War 1914–1918: Years That Shaped the Future* (Midleton, County Cork, 2009), p. 33.

25. O'Faolain, *op. cit.*, pp. 9 and 52.

26. Gerry White and Brendan O'Shea, *'Baptised in Blood': The Formation of the Cork Brigade of the Irish Volunteers 1913–1916* (Cork, 2005), p. 24; Cork City and County Archives, List of Irish Volunteers Cork Corps (online) www.corkarchives.ie.

27. *Ibid.*, pp. 27, 39 and 44.

28. John C. G. Rohl, *The Kaiser and his Court: Wilhelm II and the Government of Germany* (Cambridge, 1994); Richard F. Hamilton, and Holger H. Herwig, *Decisions for War, 1914–1917* (Cambridge, 2004).

29. Hamilton and Herwig, *op. cit.*, pp. 34, 83 and 84.

30. Orr in Horne (ed.), *op. cit.*, p. 65.

31. White and O'Shea, 'Baptised in Blood', p. 47.

32. *Cork Examiner*, 12 January 1915; *Cork Constitution*, 14 September 1914.

33. *Cork Constitution*, 3 September 1914.

34. *Ibid.*

35. *Cork Examiner*, 29 January 1915, report on a speech by Joe Devlin, Irish Party MP for Belfast, given at Enniskillen reiterates some of these points.

36. *Cork Constitution*, 21 December 1914.

37. Mazer, *op. cit.*

38. Senia Paseta, *Before the Revolution: Nationalism, Social Change and Ireland's Catholic Elite, 1879–1922* (Cork, 1999), pp. 137–8; Mazer, *ibid.*

39. Donal Nevin, *James Connolly 'A Full Life'* (Dublin, 2006), pp. 483–84 and 514.

40. White and O'Shea, 'Baptised in Blood', p. 53.

41. *Ibid.*, while Terence Denman cites 22,000 as the figure for National Volunteers who enlisted in the British army.

42. Murphy Brewery Papers, UCC Archives.

43. Diarmuid Ó Drisceoil, and Donal Ó Drisceoil, *The Murphy's Story: The History of the Lady's Well Brewery* (Cork, 1997), p. 74; Murphy Brewery Papers, UCC Archives.

44. Ó Drisceoil, *op. cit.*, pp. 73–74; *Cork Constitution* 11 August 1915.

2. 'Blackpool to the Front!' The Beginning of the War on the Western Front

1. Tom Johnstone, *Orange, Green & Khaki: The Story of the Irish Regiments in the Great War, 1914–1918* (Dublin, 1992), p. 6; Peter Verney, *The Micks: The Story of the Irish Guards* (London, 1970), p. 17.

2. David Stevenson, *1914–1918: The History of the First World War* (London, 2005), p. 52.

3. Johnstone, *op. cit.*, p. 19. For a very good description of the Royal Irish Rifles' role during the battle see the excellent *There's a Devil in the Drum* by John F. Lucy (Uckfield, East Sussex, 1992 edition).

4. *Cork Examiner* 12 February 1916.

5. H. S. Jervis, *The 2nd Munsters in France* (Sussex, England), p. 6.

6. Stevenson, *op. cit.*, pp. 58–60 and 75.

7. Johnstone, *op. cit.*, p. 38.

8. *Ibid.*, pp. 40 and 53.

9. *Cork Examiner*, 4 January 1915.

10. Johnstone, *op. cit.*, p. 41.

11. War Diary of the 2nd Battalion Royal Irish Regiment (National Archives, London).

12. Johnstone, *op. cit.*, p. 43.

13. *Ibid.*, p. 44, and War Diary 2nd Battalion RIR.

14. Jervis, *op. cit.*, p. 8.

15. Johnstone, *op. cit.*, pp. 53 and 54; Verney, *op. cit.*, pp. 29 and 30.

16. War Diary of 2nd Battalion Royal Munster Fusiliers (National Archives, London).

17. Johnstone, *op. cit.*, p. 56, quoting from the *History of Royal Munster Fusiliers*.
18. Jervis, *op. cit.*, pp. 10 and 11; War Diary of 2nd Battalion RMF.
19. Stevenson, *op. cit.*, p. 76.
20. Johnstone, *op. cit.*, p. 59.
21. *Cork Examiner,* 14 December 1914.
22. Gordon Corrigan, *Mud, Blood and Poppycock: Britain and the First World War* (London, 2003), p. 63.
23. *Ibid.*, p. 48; Stevenson, *op. cit.*, pp. 179 and 180–82.
24. Richard van Emden, *The Trench: Experiencing Life on the Front Line, 1916* (London, 2002).
25. *Ibid.*, p. 39.
26. Verney, *op. cit.*, p. 21.
27. Alan Clark, *The Donkeys* (London, 2006).
28. *Cork Examiner,* 21 April 1915.
29. Van Emden, *op. cit.*, p. 167.
30. Corrigan, *op. cit.*, p. 116.
31. *Cork Examiner*, 10 June 1915.
32. War Diary of the 1st Battalion Royal Leinster Regiment (National Archives, London)
33. *Cork Examiner,* 16 March 1915.
34. War Diary, 2nd Battalion RMF; Jervis, *op. cit.*, p. 16.
35. Stevenson, *op. cit.*, pp. 158 and 157.
36. Clark, *op. cit.*, p. 47.
37. Stevenson, *op. cit.*, p. 154.
38. Johnstone, *op. cit.*, p. 80; Clark *op. cit.*, p. 107.
39. *Cork Examiner*, 27 January 1916.
40. *Ibid.*
41. *Ibid.*, 1 March 1916.
42. *Ibid.*, 18 March 1916.
43. Clark, *op. cit.*, p. 112.
44. *Ibid.*, p. 126.
45. *Ibid.*, p. 106.
46. Verney, *op. cit.*, p. 36; Stevenson, *op. cit.*, p. 59.

3. THE BLACKPOOL HOME FRONT AND THE SUPPORT FOR THE WAR

1. *Cork Constitution*, 16 December 1914.
2. *Cork Examiner*, 16 March 1915.
3. *Cork Constitution* 4 April 1915.
4. Jérôme aan de Wiel, *The Catholic Church in Ireland 1914–1918: War and Politics* (Dublin, 2003), pp. 26–27; Jane Leonard, 'The Catholic Chaplaincy' in David Fitzpatrick (ed.), *Ireland and the First World War* (Dublin, 1986), p. 5.
5. *Cork Examiner,* 12 August 1915.

6. Henri Bodart was born at Ledberg, Belgium on 14 April 1888 and began schooling at the age of eleven to become a soldier. He became a corporal in 1904 and a sergeant in 1907. He left the service in 1909 but was recalled to arms on 30 July 1914 when he joined the 5th Battalion of the 9th Fortress Regiment of the line. He was injured on 18/19 September 1914 and returned to the front line with the field ambulance a month later. He seemingly did not return to front-line duty after his tour of Ireland. He was discharged from the Belgian army in August 1922 and died in Lambert, Belgium in 1951. Thanks to Commander Dirk Doms, Chief of Belgian Military Archives.

7. *Cork Constitution,* 19 August 1915.

8. aan de Wiel, *op. cit.*, p. 138, quoting Keith Jeffrey, *Ireland and the Great War.*

9. James Christopher Flynn (1852–1922) was elected MP for Cork North in the 1885 general election and was returned unopposed at each of the five subsequent elections until he retired in January 1910. He took the anti-Parnellite side in the 1890s and also served as secretary to the Cork Evicted Tenants' Association. (Timothy Cadogan and Jeremiah Falvey (eds.), *A Biographical Dictionary of Cork* (Dublin, 2006)).

10. *Cork Examiner,* 17 September 1915.

11. *Cork Constitution* 11 August 1915.

12. Diarmuid Ó Drisceoil, and Donal Ó Drisceoil, *The Murphy's Story: The History of the Lady's Well Brewery* (Cork, 1997), p. 74 and 73.

13. *Ibid.*, p. 75.

14. *Cork Constitution* 11 August 1915, 24 January 1916 and 25 September 1917.

15. Cork City and County Archives, Cork Spinning & Weaving Company Ltd. Ref. IECCCA B530/2/8.

16. *Ibid.*, and *Cork Constitution,* 25 July 1917.

17. Gerry White and Brendan O'Shea, *'Baptised in Blood': The Formation of the Cork Brigade of the Irish Volunteers 1913–1916,* (Cork, 2005), p. 61.

18. Florence O'Donoghue, *Tomás MacCurtain: Soldier and Patriot* (Tralee, 1971), p. 56.

19. Fionnuala MacCurtain, *Remember ... It's for Ireland: A Family Memoir of Tomas MacCurtain* (Cork, 2006), p. 52.

20. Donal Nevin, *James Connolly 'A Full Life'* (Dublin, 2006), p. 608.

4. Gallipoli and Loos: Defeat and the Long War

1. David Stevenson, *1914–1918: The History of the First World War* (Penguin Books, London, 2005), pp. 114–18.

2. L. A. Carlyon, *Gallipoli* (London, 2003), p. 146.

3. War Diary 11th Battalion Australian Infantry Force (AIF) and War Diary 15th Battalion AIF (National Archives, London).

4. Tom Johnstone, *Orange, Green & Khaki: The Story of the Irish Regiments in the Great War, 1914–1918* (Dublin, 1992), p. 101.

5. Carlyon, *op. cit.* (London, 2003), p. 190.
6. Johnstone, *op. cit.*, p. 102.
7. War Diary 1ˢᵗ Battalion Royal Munster Fusiliers (National Archives, London), 4310.
8. Carylon, *op. cit.*, p. 203; War Diary 11ᵗʰ Battalion AIF.
9. War Diary 11ᵗʰ Battalion AIF; Austrialian War Memorial, www.awm.gov.au, ref. Patrick Kieley 11ᵗʰ Battalion AIF.
10. War Diary 1ˢᵗ 11ᵗʰ Battalion RMF.
11. Johnstone *op. cit.*, pp. 106–07.
12. *Ibid.*, pp. 108–09.
13. *Cork Examiner,* 14 June 1915.
14. Stevenson, *op. cit.*, p. 119.
15. Johnstone, *op. cit.*, p. 114; Carlyon, *op. cit.*, p. 421.
16. Carlyon, *op. cit.*, pp. 461 and 464.
17. Johnstone, *op. cit.*, p. 125.
18. War Diary 15ᵗʰ Battalion AIF; Carlyon *op. cit.*, pp. 523–24.
19. Australian War Memorial, www.awm.gov.au, ref. Thomas Williams 15ᵗʰ Battalion AIF.
20. Johnstone *op. cit.*, pp. 129–130.
21. *Ibid.*, pp. 136–38.
22. *Ibid.*, pp. 144–37 and War Diary 5ᵗʰ Battalion Connaught Rangers (National Archives, London).
23. Carylon, *op. cit.*, p. 585.
24. Stevenson, *op. cit.*, p. 117.
25. War Diary 2ⁿᵈ Battalion Royal Leinster Regiment (National Archives, London).
26. Stevenson, *op. cit.*, pp. 159–160; Clark, *op. cit.*, pp. 140 and 143.
27. Clark, *op. cit.*, pp. 145 and 148.
28. Johnstone, *op. cit.*, p. 157.
29. Clark, *op. cit.*, p. 173.
30. Johnstone, *op. cit.*, pp. 158–9.
31. War Diary 2ⁿᵈ Battalion RMF (National Archives, London).
32. Johnstone, *op. cit.*, p.159.
33. War Diary 2ⁿᵈ Battalion Irish Guards (National Archives, London).
34. www.1914-1918.net
35. *Cork Examiner,* 24 November 1915.
36. *Ibid.*, 25 November 1915.

5. Easter Week 1916 on the Western Front and the Somme

1. *Cork Constitution,* 22 January 1916.
2. *Cork Examiner,* 12 December 1914.
3. *Cork Constitution* 22 September and 30 December 1915.

4. *Cork Examiner,* 25 February 1916.

5. Billy Good, 'The Chaplaincy Service' in Gerry White and Brendan O'Shea (eds.), *The Great Sacrifice: Cork Servicemen Who Died in the Great War* (Cork, 2010), p. 149.

6. *Ibid.,* between 19 January and 2 February 1917; *Cork Constitution* 23 November 1916.

7. *Ibid.,* 27 December 1916.

8. Caitriona Clear, 'Fewer ladies, more women' in John Horne (ed.), *Our War: Ireland and the Great War* (Dublin, 2008), p. 162; Paddy McCarthy, *Cork During the Years of the Great War 1914–1918: Years That Shaped the Future* (Midleton, County Cork, 2009), p. 43.

9. David Stevenson, *1914–1918: The History of the First World War* (London, 2005), p. 104.

10. Diarmuid Ó Drisceoil, and Donal Ó Drisceoil, *The Murphy's Story: The History of the Lady's Well Brewery* (Cork, 1997), p. 82.

11. Stevenson, *op. cit.*, p. 349.

12. *Cork Constitution,* 11 November 1915.

13. *Ibid.,* 7 December 1915.

14. Gerry White and Brendan O'Shea, *'Baptised in Blood': The Formation of the Cork Brigade of the Irish Volunteers 1913–1916* (Cork, 2005), pp. 77–79 and 89.

15. Florence O'Donoghue, *Tomás MacCurtain: Soldier and Patriot* (Tralee, 1971), p. 65.

16. White and O'Shea, 'Baptised in Blood', pp. 104–09.

17. *Ibid.,* pp. 115–6.

18. *Cork Examiner,* 1 May 1916.

19. War Diary 9th Battalion Royal Munster Fusiliers (National Archives, London).

20. War Diary 8th Battalion Loyal North Lancashire Regiment (National Archives, London).

21. www.naval.net and www.U-boat.net ref. UB–18

22. Tom Johnstone, *Orange, Green & Khaki: The Story of the Irish Regiments in the Great War, 1914–1918* (Dublin, 1992), p 210.

23. Terence Denman, *Ireland's Unknown Soldiers: The 16th (Irish) Division in the Great War* (Dublin, 2008), p. 62.

24. Born near Listowel, County Kerry, Field Marshal Horatio Herbert Kitchener was British Agent and Consul-General in Egypt before the war and was appointed War Minister in the British government after the war commenced. One of his tasks was to raise and develop a mass army through the training of newly enlisted recruits. His face became famous through recruitment posters which declared that 'Your Country Needs You!'

25. Stevenson, *op. cit.*, p. 169.

26. *Ibid.,* pp. 169 and 170.

27. War Diary 2nd Battalion Royal Leinster Regiment (National Archives, London).

28. *Ibid.*

29. Major Gen. T. O. Marden, *A Short History of the 6ᵗʰ Division* (Naval and Military Press: Uckfield, East Sussex, England), p. 15.
30. Denman, *op. cit.*, pp. 80–81 and 82.
31. *Cork Examiner,* 19 September 1916.
32. War Diary 1ˢᵗ RMF (National Archives, London); Denman, *op. cit.*, p. 85.
33. Denman, *op. cit.*, pp. 95–96; Johnstone, *op. cit.*, p. 251.
34. Johnstone, *op. cit.*, pp. 2 and 251.
35. *Ibid.*, p. 252.
36. *Cork Examiner,* 24 October 1916.
37. Johnstone, *op. cit.*, p. 254.
38. Peter Verney, *The Micks: The Story of the Irish Guards* (London, 1970), p, 48.
39. Colonel G. W. L. Nicholson, *Canadian Expeditionary Force 1914–1919: The Official History of the Canadian Army in the First World War* (1962), p. 168.
40. *Ibid.*, p. 170; Corrigan, *op. cit.*, p. 292.
41. Nicholson, *op. cit.,* p. 171.
42. War Diary 2ⁿᵈ Irish Guards (National Archives, London).
43. Verney, *op. cit.*, p. 53.
44. Stevenson, *op. cit.*, pp. 168, 170 and 171.
45. Thomas P. Dooley, *Irishmen or English Soldiers? The Times and World of a Southern Irish Man (1876–1916)* (Liverpool, 1995), p. 200.
46. *Cork Constitution*, 1 January 1917.

6. The Naval War and Blackpool

1. David Stevenson, *1914–1918: The History of the First World War* (London, 2005), p. 86.
2. Geoffrey Bennett, *The Battle of Jutland* (1972), pp. 36 and 40–42; Stevenson, *op. cit.*, pp. 86–87; John de Courcy Ireland, *Ireland and the Irish in Maritime History* (1986), p. 327.
3. Bernard Ireland, *War at Sea 1914–1945* (2002), p. 79 and Stevenson, *op. cit.*, pp. 86–87.
4. De Courcy Ireland, *op. cit.*, p. 328.
5. *Cork Constitution*, 19 December 1914.
6. Ireland, *op. cit.*, pp. 40–1 and 44; Oliver Warner, *Great Sea Battles* (1968), pp. 56–57, de Courcy Ireland, *op. cit.*, p. 327.
7. Stevenson, *op. cit.*, p. 90.
8. Ireland, *op. cit.*, p. 55, Bennett, *op. cit.*, p. 47 and Stevenson, *op. cit.*, p. 91.
9. Bennett, *op. cit.*, pp. 55–56, 63, 69–70 and 78; Stevenson, *op. cit.,* pp. 252–53.
10. Bennett, *op. cit.*, p. 78.
11. *Cork Constitution*, 6 June 1916. Note the use of the term 'hydroplane' in the report, (later called aircraft carriers). This was the first battle in which such ships were used and showed how the necessity of war produced military and naval innovation.

12. *Cork Examiner*, 3 June 1916.
13. Stevenson, *op. cit.*, pp. 254–5 and 259–262.
14. *Ibid.*, pp. 247 and 321–42; de Courcy Ireland, *op. cit.*, p. 329; G. Barnett: 'How successfully did Britain respond to German Unrestricted U-Boat Warfare in 1917 and 1918' at www.gwpda.org/naval/brgerm.htm: 1999.
15. Stevenson, *op. cit.,* pp. 321–4; Ireland, *op. cit.*, p. 75.
16. Gerry White and Brendan O'Shea (eds.), *The Great Sacrifice: Cork Servicemen Who Died in the Great War* (Cork, 2010).
17. *Cork Examiner*, 23 April 1917.
18. www. wreck site.eu reference SS *Bellucia*.
19. *Cork Examiner*, 7 March 1918.
20. Bennett, *op. cit.*, quoting Cyril Falls, pp. 173–74.
21. Stevenson, *op. cit.,* p. 244.

7. BRAVERY OF BLACKPOOL SOLDIERS

1. *Cork Examiner*, 20 May 1915. The writer was Private Pat McCarthy of the 2nd Royal Munster Fusiliers.
2. *Cork Examiner*, 25 February 1916.
3. *Ibid.*, 14 April 1916.
4. *Ibid.*, 13 February 1918 and 12 March 1918.
5. *Ibid.*, 9 August 1916; H. S. Jervis, *The 2nd Munsters in France* (Naval and Military Press: Sussex, England)., p. 25.
6. Jervis, *op. cit.*, p. 26; War Diary 2nd Battalion Royal Munster Fusiliers (National Archives, London).
7. *Ibid.*, p. 28.
8. War Diary 2nd Battalion RMF.
9. War Diary 1st Battalion Royal Dublin Fusiliers; *Cork Examiner*, 24 March 1917.
10. David Stevenson, *1914–1918: The History of the First World War* (London, 2005), p. 176.
11. Colonel G. W. L. Nicholson, *Canadian Expeditionary Force 1914–1919: The Official History of the Canadian Army in the First World War* (1962), pp. 280 and 281.
12. War Diary 50th Infantry Battalion Canadian Army (National Archives, London).
13. Terence Denman, *Ireland's Unknown Soldiers: The 16th (Irish) Division in the Great War* (Dublin, 2008), pp. 114 and 115.
14. Stevenson, *op. cit.*, pp. 331–32.
15. *Ibid.*, pp. 333–34.
16. Denman, *op. cit.*, p. 116.
17. *Ibid.*, p. 117; War Diary 6th Battalion Connaught Rangers (National Archives, London).

18. Tom Johnstone, *Orange, Green & Khaki: The Story of the Irish Regiments in the Great War, 1914–1918* (Dublin, 1992), p. 294.

19. Stevenson, *op. cit.*, p. 335.

20. War Diary 3rd/10th Battalion Middlesex Regiment (National Archives, London).

21. Stevenson, *op. cit.*, pp. 332–33.

22. War Diary 2nd Royal Marine Battalion (National Archives, London).

23. Jervis, *op. cit.*, p. 38; War Diary 2nd Battalion RMF.

24. Jervis, *op. cit.*, pp. 39–40.

25. *Ibid.*, pp. 38–41; War Diary of 2nd Battalion RMF.

26. Stevenson, *op. cit.*, p. 336.

27. New Zealand Archives, www.archway.archives.govt.nz; Captain David Ferguson, *History of the Canterbury Regiment NZEF 1914–1919* (Auckland, 1921) pp. 209–213.

8. Blackpool and the Last Year of the War 1918: Ireland sheds its old political skin

1. Adrian Gregory, *The Last Great War: British Society and the First World War* (Cambridge, 2008), p. 187.

2. *Ibid.*, p. 245.

3. John Borgonovo, *The Dynamics of War and Revolution, Cork City, 1916–1918*, (Cork, 2013), pp. 38, 80, 164, 170–3, 180–4 and 186–7; Ben Novick, *Conceiving Revolution: Irish Nationalist Propaganda During the First World War* (Dublin, 2001), p. 25.

4. *Cork Constitution,* 11 May 1917.

5. Novick, *op. cit.*, pp. 63–65 68, 96.

6. Jonathan Githens-Mazer, *Myths and Memories of the Easter Rising: Cultural and Political Nationalism in Ireland* (Dublin, 2006), presents a very persuasive argument on this point in relation to how the 1916 Rising became interpreted within a religious framework, which formed the backdrop to the rise of Sinn Féin in popularity from late 1916 onwards. To give a sense of how the Rising was perceived and how a religious understanding could form part of that interpretation, see a letter penned in May 1916 from Tralee by John Moynihan to his brother Michael, who was actually in the British army at the time. Michael Moynihan was killed on 3 June 1918 at the Western Front. His political views, and the changes they underwent, from flirting with the imperially minded Conservatives in 1909 to outright separatism by 1918 even though he was in the British army, indicate how fluid political beliefs and identities were at the time, a fluidity no doubt due in large part to the Great War. Deirdre McMahon (ed.), *The Moynihan Brothers in Peace and War, 1908–1918: Their New Ireland by John and Michael Moynihan* (Dublin, 2004), pp. 123–126.

7. *Cork Examiner,* 10 December 1917.

8. *Ibid.*

9. *Ibid.*

10. *Ibid.*

11. *Ibid.*

12. Gregory, *op. cit.*, p. 216.

13. Tom Johnstone, *Orange, Green & Khaki: The Story of the Irish Regiments in the Great War, 1914–1918* (Dublin, 1992), p. 322.

14. *Ibid.*, p. 326; War Diary 6th Battalion Leinster Regiment (National Archves, London).

15. Johnstone, *op.cit.*, pp. 328, 330 and 332.

16. *Ibid.*, p. 336.

17. David Stevenson, *1914–1918: The History of the First World War* (London, 2005), pp. 402–3.

18. *Ibid.*, pp. 399 and 400–1.

19. Terence Denman, *Ireland's Unknown Soldiers: The 16th (Irish) Division in the Great War* (Dublin, 2008), p 156.

20. *Ibid.*, pp. 154 and 156.

21. *Ibid.*, pp. 159 and 161.

22. *Ibid.*, p. 166; War Diary 7th Royal Irish Regiment (National Archives, London).

23. Denman, *op. cit.*, p. 166.

24. *Ibid.*, pp. 166–167.

25. *Ibid.*, p. 168; Stevenson, *op. cit.*, p. 409.

26. Johnstone, *op. cit.*, pp. 382–83; Denman, *op. cit.*, p. 168.

27. Stevenson, *op. cit.*, p. 412.

28. Peter Verney, *The Micks: The Story of the Irish Guards* (Peter Davies, London, 1970), pp. 63 and 65.

29. Stevenson, *op. cit.*, pp. 412–13.

30. *Ibid.*, pp. 416, 418 and 419.

31. *Ibid.*, p. 419; David Welch, *German Propaganda and Total War 1914–1918*, pp. 253–54.

32. *Ibid.*, pp. 423 and 426–27.

33. *Ibid.*, p. 426.

34. Hew Strachan, *The First World War* (London, 2006 ed.), pp. 308–09.

35. A Royal Field Artillery brigade consisted of four batteries, A, B, C and D, with each battery containing an 18-pounder artillery gun; the attendant gunners and ammunition suppliers numbered ten in all, with six operating the gun in action and the other four in reserve.

36. War Diary 79th Brigade of the Royal Field Artillery (National Archives, London).

37. Stevenson, *op. cit.*, pp. 446–47.

38. War Diary 45th Brigade of the Royal Field Artillery (National Archives, London).

39. H. S. Jervis, *The 2ⁿᵈ Munsters in France* (Naval and Military Press: Sussex, England), p. 50.
40. Stevenson, *op. cit.*, p. 498.
41. *Ibid.*, pp. 486 and 481.
42. Johnstone, *op. cit.*, p. 413.
43. Jervis, *op. cit.*, p. 51; War Diary 2ⁿᵈ Battalion RMF.
44. *Ibid.*, p. 52.
45. War Diary 2ⁿᵈ Battalion RMF.
46. Johnstone, *op. cit.*, p. 416.
47. *Ibid.*, p. 419.
48. *Ibid.*, pp. 422–23 and Jervis, *op. cit.*, p. 59.
49. Johnstone, *op. cit.,* pp. 423–24 and Jervis, *op. cit.*, p. 60.
50. Jervis, *op. cit.*, p. 63.
51. Stevenson, *op. cit.*, p. 473.
52. *Cork Examiner,* 12 November 1918.
53. *Cork Constitution* 12 November 1918.
54. *Cork Examiner,* 12 November 1918.
55. Verney, *op. cit.*, p. 68.
56. Major Gen. T. O. Marden, *A Short History of the 6ᵗʰ Division* (England, 1920), p. 79.
57. *Cork Examiner,* 23 January 1918 and 12 April 1918.
58. J. C. Walsh, *Farranferris: The Heritage of St Finbarr 1887–1987* (Cork, 1987), p. 70.
59. Ferriter, *op. cit.*, p. 185; Paddy McCarthy, *Cork During the Years of the Great War 1914–1918: Years That Shaped the Future* (Midleton, County Cork, 2009), p. 120; Stevenson, *op. cit.*, p. 498.
60. New Zealand Archives, www.archway.archives.govt.nz/James Lee

9. The Soldiers Return to a Different Ireland: Integration and Remembrance

1. Jay Winter, *Sites of Memory, Sites of Mourning: The Great War in European Cultural History* (Cambridge, 1995), pp. 31 and 57–58.
2. Gregory, Adrian, *The Last Great War: British Society and the First World War* (Cambridge University Press, Cambridge, 2008), p. 266.
3. John Borgonovo, '"Justice We Will Have" The Cork Branch of the NFDDSS' in White and O'Shea (eds.), *Great Sacrifice*, p. 577.
4. Jay Winter, *Sites of Memory, Sites of Mourning: The Great War in European Cultural History* (Cambridge, 1995), p. 47.
5. Australian War Memorial, www.awm.gov.au, Archives Reference Thomas Williams 15ᵗʰ Battalion AIF.
6. Winter, *op. cit.*, pp. 2, 29, 30 and 80; Gregory, *op. cit.*, pp. 250 and 255.
7. Gregory, *op. cit.*, pp. 242–43.

8. J. C. Walsh, *Farranferris: The Heritage of St. Finbarr 1887–1987* (Cork, 1987), p. 72.

9. Borgonovo, *op. cit.*, p. 579.

10. Jane Leonard, 'Survivors', in John Horne (ed.), *Our War: Ireland and the Great War* (Royal Irish Academy, Dublin, 2008), p. 215.

11. MacDonagh, Michael, *The Life of William O'Brien the Irish Nationalist* (London, 1928), for reference to Lloyd George's correspondence to William O'Brien and Lloyd George's perception of Sinn Féin as German collaborators during the war and his refusal to deal with them on that count. P. 239.

12. Leonard, 'Survivors', in Horne (ed.), *op. cit.*, p. 218.

13. Borgonovo, *op. cit.*, p. 580.

14. *Ibid.*, p. 581.

15. *Ibid.*, p. 582.

16. *Ibid.*, p. 582.

17. Leonard, 'Survivors', in Horne (ed.), *op. cit.*, p. 219.

18. Walsh, *op. cit.*, p. 66.

CONCLUSION

1. Gerry White and Brendan O'Shea (eds.) *The Great Sacrifice: Cork Servicemen Who Died in the Great War* (Cork, 2010).

Bibliography

aan de Wiel, Jérôme, *The Catholic Church in Ireland 1914–1918: War and Politics* (Irish Academic Press, Dublin, 2003)

Barry, Denis, *The Unknown Commandant: The Life and Times of Denis Barry 1883–1923* (The Collins Press, Cork, 2010)

Beirne, Patrick, *Reminiscences of Blackpool and District in the year 1912* (Self-published, Blackpool Library)

Bennett, Geoffrey, *The Battle of Jutland* (David and Charles, 1972)

Bielenberg, Andy, *Cork's Industrial Revolution 1780–1880: Development or Decline?* (Cork University Press, Cork, 1991)

Birmingham, Cathy, *The Cork Butter Exchange Band* (Upper Case Ltd, Cork, 1996)

Borgonovo, John, *The Dynamics of War and Revolution, Cork City, 1916–1918* (Cork University Press, 2013)

Brown, Malcolm, *The Imperial War Museum Book of the Western Front* (Pan Macmillan, London, 2003)

Cadogan, Timothy and Falvey, Jeremiah (eds.), *A Biographical Dictionary of Cork* (Four Courts Press, Dublin, 2006

Carlyon, L. A., *Gallipoli*, (Bantam Books, London, 2003)

Chavasse, Noirin, *Terence MacSwiney*, (Clonmore and Reynolds Ltd, Dublin, 1961)

Clark, Alan, *The Donkeys*, (Pimlico, London, 2006 edition, 1961 first published)

Corrigan, Gordon, *Mud, Blood and Poppycock: Britain and the First World War*, (Cassell, London, 2003)

Costello, Francis J., *Enduring the Most: The Life and Death of Terence MacSwiney*, (Brandon: Dingle, County Kerry, 1996)

Cullen, Clara (ed.), *The World Upturning: Elsie Henry's Irish Wartime Diaries, 1913–1919* (Merrion: County Kildare/Oregon USA, 2013)

de Courcy Ireland, John, *Ireland and the Irish in Maritime History* (Glendale, 1986)

Denman, Terence, *Ireland's Unknown Soldiers: The 16th (Irish) Division in the Great War* (Irish Academic Press, Dublin, 2008 edition, originally published 1992)

Dooley, Thomas P., *Irishmen or English Soldiers? The Times and World of a Southern Irish Man (1876–1916): Enlisting in the British Army During the First World War* (Liverpool University Press, 1995)

Ferguson, Captain David, *The History of the Canterbury Regiment NZEF 1914–1919* (Whihanke and Tombs Ltd, Auckland, 1921)

Ferguson, Niall, *Empire: How Britain Made the Modern World* (Penguin Books, London, 2004)

Ferriter, Diarmaid, *The Transformation of Ireland, 1900–2000* (Profile, 2004)

Fitzpatrick, David (ed.), *Ireland and the First World War* (Trinity History Workshop, Dublin, 1986)

Githens-Mazer, Jonathan, *Myths and Memories of the Easter Rising: Cultural and Political Nationalism in Ireland* (Irish Academic Press, Dublin, 2006)

Gregory, Adrian, *The Last Great War: British Society and the First World War* (Cambridge University Press, Cambridge, 2008)

Hamilton, Richard. F. and Herwig, Holger. H., *Decisions for War, 1914–1917* (Cambridge University Press, Cambridge, 2004)

Harris, Henry, *The Irish Regiments in the First World War* (Mercier Press, Cork, 1968)

Horne, John (ed.), *Our War: Ireland and the Great War* (Royal Irish Academy, Dublin, 2008)

Hurley, M. F., Johnson, G., and Brett, C., *Old Blackpool: An Historic Suburb* (Cork City Council, Cork, 2006)

Ireland, Bernard: *War at Sea 1914–1945* (Cassell Military, 2002)

Jervis, H. S., *The 2nd Munsters in France* (Naval and Military Press: Sussex, England)

Johnston, Kevin, *Home and Away: The Great War and the Irish Rebellion* (Gill & Macmillan, Dublin, 2010)

Johnstone, Tom, *Orange, Green & Khaki: The Story of the Irish Regiments in the Great War, 1914–1918* (Gill & Macmillan, Dublin, 1992)

Kenneally, Ian, *The Paper Wall: Newspapers and Propaganda in Ireland 1919–1921* (The Collins Press, Cork, 2008)

MacBride, Ian (ed.), *History and Memory in Modern Ireland* (Cambridge University Press, Cambridge, 2001)

McBride, Lawrence W. (ed.), *Images, Icons and the Irish Nationalist Imagination* (Four Courts Press, Dublin, 1999)

McCarthy, Paddy, *Cork During the Years of the Great War 1914–1918: Years that Shaped the Future* (Litho Press, Midleton, County Cork, 2009)

MacCurtain, Fionnuala, *Remember ... It's for Ireland: A Family Memoir of Tomas MacCurtain* (Mercier Press, Cork, 2006)

MacDonagh, Michael, *The Life of William O'Brien the Irish Nationalist* (Ernest Benn, London, 1928)

McMahon, Deirdre (ed.), *The Moynihan Brothers in Peace and War, 1908–1918: Their New Ireland* (Irish Academic Press, Dublin, 2004)

Marden, Major Gen. T. O., *A Short History of the 6th Division* (Naval and Military Press, Uckfield, East Sussex, England, 1920)

Nevin, Donal, *James Connolly 'A Full Life'* (Gill & Macmillan, Dublin, 2006 edition)

Nicholson, Colonel G. W. L., *Canadian Expeditionary Force 1914–1919: The Official History of the Canadian Army in the First World War* (1962)

Novick, Ben, *Conceiving Revolution: Irish Nationalist Propaganda During the First World War* (Four Courts Press, Dublin, 2001)

Ó Conchubhair, Brian, (ed.), *Rebel Cork's Fighting Story 1916–21: Told by the Men Who Made it* (Mercier Press, Cork, 2009)

O'Donoghue, Florence, *Tomás MacCurtain: Soldier and Patriot* (Anvil Books, Tralee, 1971 edition)

Ó Drisceoil, Diarmuid and Ó Drisceoil, Donal, *The Murphy's Story: The History of the Lady's Well Brewery* (Murphy's Brewery Ltd, Cork, 1997)

O'Faolain, Sean, *Vive Moi!: An Autobiography* (Rupert Hart-Davis, 1965)

Paseta, Senia, *Before the Revolution: Nationalism, Social Change and Ireland's Catholic Elite, 1879–1922* (Cork University Press, Cork, 1999)

Rohl, John C. G., *The Kaiser and his Court: Wilhelm II and the Government of Germany* (Cambridge University Press, Cambridge, 1994 edition, originally published 1987)

Sheehan, Breda, 'Blackpool Village: An Industrial and Social History from 1800–1900' (unpublished MA Local History UCC, 2008)

Stevenson, David, *1914–1918: The History of the First World War* (Penguin Books, London, 2005)

Strachan, Hew, *The First World War* (Simon and Schuster, London, 2006)

van Emden, Richard, *The Trench: Experiencing Life on the Front Line, 1916* (Bantam Press, London, 2002)

Walsh, J. C., *Farranferris: The Heritage of St. Finbarr 1887–1987* (Tower Books, Cork, 1987)

Welch, David, *German Propaganda and Total War 1914–1918* (Rutgers University Press, New Jersey, 2000)

White, Gerry and O'Shea, Brendan, *'Baptised in Blood': The Formation of the Cork Brigade of the Irish Volunteers 1913–1916* (Mercier Press, Cork, 2005)

White, Gerry and O'Shea, Brendan (eds.), *The Great Sacrifice: Cork Servicemen Who Died in the Great War* (Cork Evening Echo Publications, Cork, 2010)

Verney, Peter, *The Micks: The Story of the Irish Guards* (Peter Davies, London, 1970)

Warner, Oliver, *Great Sea Battles* (Spring Books/Hamlyn, 1968)

Winter, Jay, *Sites of Memory, Sites of Mourning: The Great War in European Cultural History* (Cambridge University Press, Cambridge, 1995)

OTHER SOURCES

London Gazette
Cork Examiner
Cork Constitution
Cork City and County Archives (Cork Spinning & Weaving Company Ltd)

Cork City and County Archives Website: Irish Volunteers
UCC Archives (Murphy's Brewery Papers)
National Archives, Kew, London (War Diaries)
1911 Census
NavalHistory.net
www.U-boat.net
www.wreck site.eu
www.archway.archives.govt.nz
www.awm.gov.au

Index

Note: numbers in *italics* refer to photographs.